SCIENTIFIC DISCOURSE
IN SOCIOHISTORICAL CONTEXT

The Philosophical Transactions
of the Royal Society of London,
1675–1975

RHETORIC, KNOWLEDGE, AND SOCIETY
A Series of Monographs Edited by
Charles Bazerman

SCIENTIFIC DISCOURSE
IN SOCIOHISTORICAL CONTEXT
The Philosophical Transactions
of the Royal Society of London,
1675–1975

Dwight Atkinson
University of Alabama

LEA LAWRENCE ERLBAUM ASSOCIATES, PUBLISHERS
1999 Mahwah, New Jersey   London

Lawrence Erlbaum Associates, Inc., Publishers
10 Industrial Avenue
Mahwah, NJ 07430

Cover design by Kathryn Houghtaling Lacey

Parts of this text have appeared in different form in "The Philosophical Transactions of the Royal Society of London, 1675–1975: A Sociohistorical Discourse Analysis," by Dwight Atkinson, in Language and Society, vol. 25, pp. 333–371, copyright © 1996, and are reprinted here with permission of Cambridge University Press.

Table 3.1 on page 66 of this volume, adapted from Variation Across Speech and Writing by Douglas Biber, copyright © 1988, is used with permission of Cambridge University Press.

Library of Congress Cataloging-in-Publication Data

Atkinson, Dwight.
Scientific discourse in sociohistorical context: The Philosophical Transactions of the Royal Society of London, 1675-1975 / Dwight Atkinson.
    p.   cm.
    Includes bibliographical references and indexes.
    ISBN 0-8058-2085-X (alk. paper). — ISBN 0-8058-2086-8 (pbk. : alk. paper)
    1. Royal Society (Great Britain)—History. 2. Science—Great Britain—History. 3. Science—Social aspects—Great Britain—History. 4. Historiography—Great Britain—History. I. Royal Society (Great Britain) II. Title.
    Q41.A76 1999
    506'.041—dc21   98-25130
                                                                 CIP

Books published by Lawrence Erlbaum Associates are printed on acid-free paper, and their bindings are chosen for strength and durability.

Printed in the United States of America
10 9 8 7 6 5 4 3 2 1

Contents

Editor's Introduction

Charles Bazerman, Series Editor
University of California, Santa Barbara

The Royal Society of London and the journal that early became affiliated with it, *The Philosophical Transactions*, have long been of interest to science historians, rhetoricians, literary critics, and linguists. These two institutions have been seen as influential in the formation of modern science, the development of scientific language and indeed all modern writing style, and the emergence of the periodical with its corresponding creation of an intellectual and literary public sphere. The Royal Society and the *Philosophical Transactions* are associated with deep changes in where social and intellectual authority resides, the means by which authoritative knowledge emerges and is asserted, and intellectual authority's relationship to the state, church, and other centers of authority and power. However, the story that has emerged through these multiple arenas of inquiry is not simple or simply progressive. The society and journal have turned out to be the site of many historical contingencies, contradictory and particular interests and dynamics, ideologies and beliefs, and individual careers, each having their own shape. What we now call science only emerged and promoted itself within and as part of the great, teeming social, cultural, representational, symbolic, material, economic, and political world.

Dwight Atkinson's study *Scientific Discourse in Sociohistorical Context:* The Philosophical Transactions of the Royal Society of London, 1675–1975 makes several major contributions to our understanding of how these two interrelated institutions have come to shape the world of knowledge and authority in which we now live.

First, this book provides the most complete and particular institutional account of a scientific journal, in this case, a journal that stands as an icon of scientific publication. Important material recounted here appears nowhere else in the historical literature, including details about the operation of the journal and its relation to the society. In literary studies it is well understood that the founders and editors of journals are important actors in opening up, defining, and maintaining a cultural space that encourages particular kinds of productions, but beyond the exemplary work done on Oldenburg by the Halls, little work has been done on scientific editors. Atkinson's work is especially important because it embeds the history of the journal and its editors within the history of the Royal Society and within other developments in science and society.

Even more originally, Atkinson applies a powerful multidimensional linguistic analysis to the contents of the journal to show the larger trends of changing linguistic practice. Atkinson then interprets these corpus-based findings in relation to a detailed rhetorical analysis to reveal the changing position of the author, object, and narrative in the texts, and even more important, to locate tensions within the discourse. These tensions, when considered within the history of science, suggest the struggles between the personal gentlemanly forms of authority and trust on which the Royal Society was founded and object-oriented, distanced discourses of distrust that developed within scientific disagreement.

Atkinson's synthesis of historical, linguistic, rhetorical, and cultural analysis combines the several lines of inquiry into the society and journal and shows how these different lines of inquiry can mutually lend support to each other's project. These multiple perspectives make visible and intelligible complex communicative dynamics that could be seen from no single vantage point. Atkinson also reminds us how such deep historical examinations of linguistic and rhetorical practices as carried out by particular individuals within particular historical circumstances have direct bearing on how and what we read and write now, and thereby need to inform our current teaching of language, so as to provide access to those who have come to be excluded in the historical emergence of our current practices. We live and communicate within the social consequences of our history, and only by developing a sociohistoric understanding of where we are can we direct ourselves to a more satisfying place. For those of us who study and teach language, the social history we necessarily focus on is the sociohistory of language practices.

Acknowledgments

It is more than purely conventional, I believe, that acknowledgments come often at the ends of academic articles, but always at the beginnings of books. I have benefitted from so much direct help, good counsel, intellectual and emotional support, and exceptional kindness in bringing this work to fruition that those involved cannot but be thanked "right up front."

This work would not exist without the unstinting aid and encouragement of Douglas Biber. He was present at the beginning, and has been there continuously throughout. No matter how busy, Doug has always somehow found time to give generously of his wide knowledge, critical acumen, and technical expertise—all, amazingly enough, accompanied by seemingly infinite patience. I wish there were a more adequate way to thank Doug for all he has done.

Equally important has been the role of my mentor, Robert B. Kaplan. It was through Bob's work that I first became interested in written discourse, and it was Bob who introduced me to the study of scientific writing. His good advice, bluff criticism, unfailing support, and geniality have largely sustained me in the years since then.

Edward Finegan has also played an important, although perhaps less direct, part in this work. As critic, boss, and friend, Ed has influenced and enriched my understanding of both linguistics and life in many ways. In a sense, working and studying with him also constituted my academic apprenticeship—what I now know about "doing academics" I have learned substantially from Ed.

Ellen Valle has been my close (if mostly virtual) compatriot in the study of the historical discourse practices of the Royal Society, and has provided much stimulating dialectic and debate on their nature. Ellen has also generously provided valuable information about the history of the Royal Society, based on her own research. As she is fond of pointing out, we have in a sense constituted a two-person discourse community since meeting each other in 1993.

John Swales and Ulla Connor have benefitted me in so many ways that I do not know exactly how or for what to thank them. I hope that this book will at least repay, in some small part, their support of my work.

James Paul Gee and Elinor Ochs (most likely unbeknowst to the latter) have provided ways of looking at language-in-the-world which have influenced and inspired me deeply. Jim has also been a continuing source of intellectual provocation and friendship.

Stimulating and useful comments on earlier versions of this or related work have come from Michael Stubbs, Charles Bazerman, Carol Berkenkotter, Bryce Allen, Greg Myers, Susan Peck MacDonald, Suzanne Romaine, Tony Dudley-Evans, Suresh Canagarajah, Shirley Ostler, Vikram Ramanathan, Patricia Carrell, and Diane Belcher. I would like to thank them all for their interest and efforts.

Ellen Barton and Gail Stygall, John Battalio, William Grabe, Rosamund Mitchell and Craig Chaudron, Douglas Biber, and William Bright have given me the opportunity to work out various aspects of the arguments presented here in publications they have edited; I thank them for this opportunity as well as for their thoughtful editorial contributions.

I would like to acknowledge Adrian Johns, Michael Hunter, Michael Barefoot, Roy Porter, David Philip Miller, Peter Dear, and Peter Jones for reading and commenting on this or related work as historians of British science and medicine. Their flexibility in considering a different approach to historical studies of science has greatly impressed me.

I would also like to thank Douglas Biber, Adrian Johns, Ellen Valle, and Suresh Canagarajah for reading and commenting on individual chapters of the present volume as it was being completed.

Librarians at various institutions have helped me immensely. Mary Sampson, Archivist at the Royal Society, deserves special thanks for willingly sharing with me her deep knowledge of the Society's records, as did also librarians Glynnis Knowles and Sandra Cumming. Librarians at the Huntington Library in San Marino, CA, the Clark Library in Los Angeles, and the Hancock

Library of Biological Science at the University of Southern California also provided critical archival support.

Support from the National Science Foundation (grant # BSN-9010893) enabled me to collect the data on which this study is based, and to work closely with Doug Biber and Ed Finegan on a related project. Two summer grants from Auburn University supported archival work at the Royal Society, and a small grant from the University of Southern California linguistics department covered some copying expenses. I have also benefitted from the support of the Auburn University English department, especially its head, Dennis Rygiel, and Norman Hubbard, whose guidance in producing the figures was invaluable.

Lisa Spalding, Timothy Clark of the British Museum, and Seamus Curran generously housed, fed, and looked after me while I was in London. I am indebted to them for their kindness and support.

The editors involved in this project, Charles Bazerman, Dorothy Gribbin, Hollis Heimbouch, Kathleen O'Malley, and Linda Bathgate, allowed me both the time and intellectual space needed to undertake this project; their involvement is most gratefully acknowledged.

I would also like to thank my friends and family for their patience and support in this extended endeavor: Michelle Burnham and Chip Hebert; Lisa Spalding; Les Bowman, JoAnn Fujikawa, and their energetic triplets; Nick Watson and Jerry Cassel; Bruce Kikuyama; Paul Bruthiaux; Diane Colvin; John Hedgcock; Marybone Loquvam and Robert Peskowitz; Joe Abbott, Vaidehi Ramanathan, and their little Aasha; Edward C. and Laetitia Atkinson; Will and Sharnette Atkinson and their boys; and, last but not least, Yumiko Kiguchi. I am quite sure that at various points each one of them had good reasons to disown me, and I can only love them the more for not doing so.

Finally, I would like to acknowledge the special role of two dear friends who, sadly, are not alive to accept my gratitude, and one who (quite happily of course!) is. Ann Daubney-Davis and Frank Diffley were the best of supporters and companions from the start of this project, and I was continually inspired by the strength and determination both displayed in living their lives joyfully and well, even in the face of death. Although Ann and Frank can never be replaced, the sorrow of losing them has been balanced by the new and enriching presence of Vai Ramanathan. This book is dedicated to these three wonderful people.

—*Dwight Atkinson*

If all the books in the world, except the Philosophical Transactions, were destroyed, it is safe to say that the foundations of physical science would remain unshaken, and that the vast intellectual progress of the last two centuries would be largely, though incompletely, recorded.

—Huxley, 1866/1968, p. 23

No one successfully investigates the nature of a thing in the thing itself; the inquiry must be enlarged....

—Bacon, 1620/1900

One should approach the study of genres with a Darwinian rather than a Platonic perspective.

—Jamieson, 1974, p. 168

Introduction:
Overview and Motivations

Empirical science is generally considered to represent the dominant knowledge system in the industrialized world today. For many years, the hegemony of the sciences went unquestioned in this world—as a form of knowledge which was self-evident, self-regulating, and beyond the reach of human subjectivity. Only in the last 40 years have these assumptions begun to be critically examined.

Once one begins to probe the epistemological basis of the empirical sciences, their historical foundations and development take on an importance they lacked when the sciences were simply received knowledge. That is, one wants to know *how* the seamless edifice that the sciences have presented to the public was constructed—how scientists developed their claim to unique understanding of the natural world. In the terms adopted by Latour (1987), we want to know the story of "science in the making" rather than of "all-made [or *already-made*] science."

One way to study science in the making is to examine the developing symbolic means used by scientists to express themselves scientifically—or, more accurately, to examine *the evolution of these forms of meaning as an integral part of the changing scientific form of life*. Written language in the service of reporting original research has been a major form of symbolic expression in science, so it stands to reason that a focus on the development of such language across time will tell us much about the dynamics of science in the making.

In the present study, I seek to describe the written language and rhetoric of a highly influential group of scientists, the Royal Society of London and its associates, from the 17th-century birth of modern empirical science to the present day. To do so adequately, I adopt two independent approaches to the analysis of written discourse—from the fields of linguistics and rhetoric/composition, respectively—and attempt to integrate and interpret the resulting findings in light of the history of the Royal Society and British science. This study therefore represents the intersection of knowledge and method from three distinct disciplines: linguistics, rhetoric/composition, and history.

This study is by no means the first to look at scientific research writing from a cross-historical perspective. Ground-breaking work by Bazerman (e.g., 1984; 1988), Dear (1985), Halliday (1988), and Berkenkotter and Huckin (1995) has contributed much to our knowledge of this evolving prose form. The present study, however, differs from past research in several respects. First, it represents a new direction in that it attempts to combine independent analytical methodologies in the description of scientific writing across time. Particularly important here is the addition of a powerful form of linguistic analysis to the repertoire of analytical tools heretofore available to scientific writing researchers. Based on the computer-aided analysis of large, representative collections of texts, this approach to linguistic analysis brings a quantitative and macroscopic dimension to an area of study that to this point has relied almost exclusively on qualitative, microscopic methods.

Second, the present study provides a *longue durée* view (Braudel, 1980) of the evolution of scientific research writing—that is, across substantially its full modern history. Examining such writing at 50-year intervals from 1675 to 1975, this study therefore provides a "wide-angle" perspective that complements past work, the latter having treated the evolving scientific prose form across more limited time periods. Thus, the present study provides a portrait of textual evolution-in-context broad enough to encompass massive practical and epistemological change in science, change that is evidenced at the linguistic and rhetorical levels in profound ways. The historical *scope* of the present study is therefore one of its special features, complementing the depth of other historical research on the development of scientific writing.

Third, in contrast to most past work, this study treats scientific research writing across a broad range of modern sciences including astronomy, biology, physics, chemistry, physiology, and geology. As complex as it may make the cross-time analysis of science, the sciences were substantially unified into the first part of the 19th century. To be sure, divisions were sometimes drawn between natural philosophy and natural history (as, for example, by Newton and his followers), or between experimental philosophy and nonexperimental alternatives. But these distinctions do not diminish the fact that the evolution of discrete scientific disciplines is a *result* or *achievement* of modern science—and a relatively recent one at that—rather than a preexisting condition influencing its development. I therefore adopt a basically holistic view of modern science ab initio, and depend significantly on the texts themselves to reveal the development and gradual separation of the disciplines. As is well known, this was an especially slow and painful process in Great Britain.[1]

Finally, this study differs from much past work in that it does not focus exclusively on *experimental* research writing. Understandably but regrettably, historical investigators of scientific writing have tended to focus on reports of experiment, leaving us with an unbalanced view of the range of activity that actually obtained in different periods. For example, Bazerman (1988, chap. 3) found that experimental reports represented a definite minority of articles in the Royal Society's *Philosophical Transactions* up to the 19th century, and other researchers (e.g., Katzen, 1980; Sorrenson, 1996) have corroborated this assessment. Thus, although I do describe the evolution of experimental reports in this study, I do not focus exclusively on this form of discourse. As a result, a more fully representative range of research writing becomes available for treatment.

OVERVIEW OF RESEARCH METHODS

As mentioned previously, this study relies on two independent methods of discourse analysis, one issuing from linguistics, the other from rhetoric/composition, to reveal textual development across time in a collection of scientific research articles.[2] Because part of my aim is to show that independent approaches to discourse analysis can work together, and in combination can tell us more about texts, and ultimately contexts, than when used alone, in the following paragraphs I describe the methods of analysis in summary form.

Rhetorical analysis, the approach most commonly taken to this point by students of scientific writing, is a primarily qualitative research methodology. It examines what rhetorical activity is/was going on within a social group at a particular time, and its organic place and functionality within that group.[3] Greg Myers' (1985) classic study of two biologists' efforts to get problematic research papers published can be taken as an exemplar. By closely analyzing the changes reviewers asked for in the biologists' draft submissions, Myers found that the main point of contention was the status of knowledge claims each author made. By the time the papers were finally accepted for publication, they had become thoroughly conventional products of their disciplinary communities in both form and content. As part of his analysis, Myers interviewed the two biologists—and solicited information from other scientists as well—in order to get a better grounded perspective on the situated activity he was studying. This latter step reveals a crucial element of rhetorical analysis: The need to have an articulated sense of the rhetorical situation (or *context*, as linguists might call it) surrounding texts.

Rhetorical analysis as I use it here has at least five identifying characteristics. First, it is *eclectic*, in that it borrows concepts and techniques from a broad range of fields. Second, it is *highly contextual*, because in order to apply it successfully, its users must have articulated knowledge of the text-producing communities and their specific social contexts, as well as broad exposure to the textual genres under examination. Third, rhetorical analysis is *interpretive*, assuming that the researcher can "read off" important aspects of the surrounding context from the text itself. Fourth, it is a *bottom–up*, or inductive, type of analysis, in which analytical categories or foci are emergent. That is, analytical categories grow out of engagement with the individual texts themselves, rather than strictly preceding the analysis. Fifth and finally, rhetorical analysis operates, theoretically speaking, at the level of *genre*.

The form of linguistic analysis used in the present study is known as *Multidimensional Analysis* (Biber, 1988), or MD analysis for short. MD analysis is a complex form of quantitative discourse analysis based on: (a) the concept of *linguistic register*, i.e., that certain characteristic "styles" or forms of language depend on recurrent clusterings, or *co-occurrence* patterns, of various linguistic features for their identity and function; (b) the use of the multivariate statistical procedure known as factor analysis to detect such patterns; and (c) the computer's unique capacity to analyze large, systematically constructed corpora of human language. MD procedures themselves can be broken down into two categories or stages, which I will call the baseline analysis and the target analysis.

The baseline analysis was performed by Biber (1988), but as the foundation of the whole approach it requires description here. In step 1 of the baseline analysis, Biber (1988) wrote a computer program that identified and counted 67 linguistic features in texts. These were features of English which had been described in past research in terms of their textual and sociolinguistic functionality. In step 2, Biber used this program to analyze a roughly one million-word computerized corpus of English covering a wide range of modern-day texts from 23 spoken and written genres. In step 3, Biber performed factor analysis on the frequency counts of features resulting from step 2. The output of the factor analysis was five main *factors*—five basic patterns underlying the apparent randomness of the full data set—which in this case were five sets of linguistic features with a high probability of co-occurrence across the full corpus. In step 4, these factors were interpreted and labeled (following standard factor-analytic procedure) in terms of the common, or shared, linguistic/communicative functionality of the features making up each factor, as indicated in the functional linguistics literature on English (e.g., Chafe, 1982, 1985; S. Thompson, 1987; Weiner & Labov, 1983).

In step 5 of the baseline analysis, scores on each factor were computed for each of the 481 texts in the corpus under study. These scores were arrived at by making frequency counts of each feature on each factor for each text, which were then: (a) normalized to a text length of 1,000 words; (b) standardized in order to make feature counts comparable, because some linguistic features, such as present tense verbs, occur much more frequently in general than others, such as conditional subordination; and (c) added together with all other counts of the features comprising that same factor for each individual text, thereby yielding individual factor scores for each text on each of the five factors. In step 6, the factor scores for all texts in each of the 23 genre categories were averaged one with another, yielding a single mean factor score for each genre. Finally, in step 7, the 23 genres were scaled relative to one another on each factor on the basis of their relative mean factor scores. For this purpose the factors were treated as continua, or dimensions, of functional linguistic variation whereby different genres could be shown to vary in regard to how much or little a particular shared linguistic/communicative function was represented in that genre's texts.

In the second, or target-analysis stage of MD analysis, the particular texts used in this study—70 texts chosen from the *Philosophical Transactions of the Royal Society of London* for seven 50-year intervals from 1675 to 1975—were input and analyzed as in step 2 of the baseline analysis. The resulting frequency counts for each feature in each text were then normalized, standardized, and added together with the other feature counts making up each factor, as in step 5. In the next step, however, instead of averaging together the factor scores from individual texts in particular genre categories to arrive at a mean factor score for each genre, scores were averaged together for each of the seven time periods in the study, producing a set of five mean factor scores for each of the seven time periods. By so doing, texts from different time periods could be compared according to relatively how much they participated as a group in the particular factors. In other words, although comparisons were made *among different genres from the same time period* in Biber's original (1988) study, comparisions were made *within the same putative genre, the scientific research article, sampled at seven different time periods* in the present study. This comparison was ultimately accomplished in the final step, by arraying together mean factor scores for each of the seven time periods on the dimensions or scales of variation set up in step 7 of the baseline MD analysis. This procedure allowed these scores to be compared relative to one another in order to show linguistic change or stability in the scientific research article across historical time.

OVERVIEW OF HISTORICAL CONTEXT

Widely considered one of the preeminent institutions of modernity, the Royal Society of London has a history well-known in broad outline; recent research, however, has revised some of its more important historical particulars. Begun in 1660 as a largely Baconian and dominantly genteel organization devoted to the "new science," the Royal Society provided the first stable and continuing international forum for the practice and development of that science through its formal meetings, the informal networks it fostered, and its sponsorship of the *Philosophical Transactions of the Royal Society of London* (hereafter *PTRS*), my main subject in the present volume.

After an auspicious start, the Royal Society suffered a decline in the last 20 years of the 17th century, only to be rejuvenated when Isaac Newton assumed its presidency in 1704. From that point until Newton's death in 1727, the Society was a center of Newtonian research, a refuge for professional researchers, and a lightning rod for dispute with non-Newtonians. Newton's successors reestablished control over the Society (if it had ever been seriously threatened) by genteel amateurs, the dominant figure among whom was Sir Joseph Banks, president from 1778 to his death in 1820. Perhaps unsurprisingly, genteel leadership inspired genteel science, or at least science based substantially on genteel norms of social conduct; the well-known "troubles" that wracked the Society in the years following Banks' death were substantially reactions to the nonprofessional, antispecializing science that had long been favored there.

Although the upheavals of the 1820s and 1830s led to no immediate radical change, by the second half of the 19th century the Royal Society was a rather different organization than it had been earlier. Scientific standing and activity had begun to emerge as the main criterion for membership, with publication of scientific papers being an important indicator of such activity. Likewise, relations between the Society and the British government became more fully institutionalized in this period, as the Society took on the job of administering state support for science. Finally, the leadership of the Society itself changed to the extent that by century's end, it was being run basically by professional scientists, whereas 100 years previously it had been firmly in the hands of the genteel elites and their operatives.

With enormous growth in the first half of the 20th century in both numbers of professional scientists and the internationalization of science, the Royal Society became Britain's national scientific academy. In this role, its duties included supporting and administrating scientific research within the United Kingdom, and officially representing the nation in international bodies and large-scale research colloborations abroad. At present, the Society administers approximately £21 million in government grants a year, funds large numbers of research fellowships and scientific exchanges, actively promotes the public understanding of science in Britain, and is instrumental in setting national and international science policy. Equally importantly, it continues to be a major forum for the development of all aspects of science in its meetings, special seminars, and the national and international conferences and collaborations it supports.

OVERVIEW OF FINDINGS

At the rhetorical level of analysis, three major aspects of cross-time textual development are described in this study: (a) change regarding the author's "place" in the text; (b) change in the genre forms favored for reporting research; and (c) changing orientations to "discourse community"—the community or communities of contemporary text-users as represented in the texts themselves.

Generally speaking, a strong authorial persona is evidenced in *PTRS* articles from the 17th and 18th centuries. Authors typically present themselves as at the center of events described in their texts, referring to themselves in the first person and freely describing their actions, thought processes, and feelings. Much the same holds, as well, into the early 19th century, although detailed descriptions of scientific methods, instruments, and, in a sense, the objects of investigation themselves also begin to be foregrounded at this time. This "object-centered" approach then comes to the fore in the course of the 19th century; by century's end, it has largely replaced the earlier "author-centered" norm.

Conventional genre forms for reporting research evince similar levels of change across the 300-year period of study. In the 17th- and 18th-century *PTRS*, research was most commonly reported in the form of "polite letters." These letters typically began "Sir/s" or "Dear Sir/s," had introductions and sometimes closings honoring their addressee/s, and tended to be short and miscellaneous in content and organization. Over the course of the 18th century, however, reports in letter form came to more closely approximate their nonepistolary counterparts. By the early 19th century, polite letters were being used less commonly as vehicles for reporting research, dropping out of the generic repertoire altogether by the second half of the century.

Although sometimes appearing in letter form in the early *PTRS*, reports of experimental research also demonstrated their own patterns of generic development. In the 17th and 18th centuries, accounts of experiments were comparatively rare, and tended to be unelaborated, miscellaneously organized, and relatively narrative in character. By 1775, however, experimental methods were beginning to be described in more detail in these reports, and results were starting to receive interpretive discussion. Methods descriptions then underwent dramatic growth in the 19th century, and an overall *theory* → *experiment* → *discussion* organization was evidenced commonly for the first time.

By the latter 19th century, experimental reports in the *PTRS* had increased greatly in length, numbers of experiments reported, and attention given to reviewing past literature, as they developed into exhaustive treatments of their objects of study. Additionally, top-level discourse structure was for the first time clearly marked by section titles and headings, and methods descriptions continued to expand.

By the 20th century, experiments were being reported in the majority of articles. At the same time, they were deemphasized as the only or primary means of investigation, becoming increasingly supplemented with observational or mathematical/theoretical accounts. Experimental narratives were presented in much-reduced form, results were commonly displayed visually, and methodological information was foregrounded in only a minority of reports. Instead, the rhetorical focus was increasingly placed on theoretical discussions. Virtually all reports show explicit top-level discourse structures by this period, and conventionalization within specific report sections on the present-day model (cf. Swales, 1990) was rapidly underway.

Finally at the rhetorical level of analysis, articles in the *PTRS* show radical change over the 300-year period of study in their orientation to discourse community. Articles from the 17th and 18th centuries can best be described as "dialogic": They were frequently addressed to personally known parties, and tended to foreground overt cooperative purposes. This approach was dominant into the early 19th century, when a revolutionary new dynamic emerged. At that point, research problem-statements and primitive literature reviews began to appear, which, along with innovations like the precise description of research methods mentioned previously, indicate that specialist approaches to research "problems" were actively under development. By the second half of the 19th century, these innovations reached their fullest form in what I described previously as an exhaustive approach to carrying out and reporting research.

By the mid-20th century, *PTRS* articles display much less concern for self-embedding in discourse communities by exhaustively reviewing past literature and describing research methods. Instead, they tend to focus on quite tightly defined research problems for which literature is selectively cited. Articles in some areas—for example, theoretical physics—cite little if any previous research; instead, they concentrate immediately on the problem at hand.

Turning now to the linguistic level of analysis, articles in the *PTRS* exhibit both gradual development and overall dramatic change on the five dimensions of MD variation described previously. On Dimension 1, *involved versus informational production*, texts show exceptionless linear development between 1675 and 1975, from norms marked by low levels of "involved production" (i.e., language of the sort typically produced "online" in casual and interactive contexts) to those marked by notably high levels of "informational production" (informationally dense language produced in conditions allowing deliberate planning and revision). A detailed examination of this dimension's specific linguistic features in individual texts reveals the major locus of change: Early texts are relatively "verbal," featuring short noun phrases connected by a range of fully functioning verbs, while later texts are highly "nominal," featuring "markedly long noun phrases" (Vande Kopple, 1994) encompassing much of the text's content.

A similar overall pattern of change is seen on Dimension 2, *narrative versus nonnarrative concerns*. Texts start in 1675 at a low level of "nonnarrativity," and increase gradually but without exception in the "nonnarrative" direction. By the latter 20th century, they are comparable to the most "nonnarrative" modern-day genres found by Biber (1988). At the level of individual texts, there is substantial variability in earlier periods regarding the degree to which "narrative" features are represented in them, while in later periods such features occur for the most part rarely across texts. Interestingly, the most dramatic and systematic decline over time of a single linguistic feature on this dimension is for third person personal pronouns, suggesting that the increasing "nonnarrativity" of texts also relates to their progressive depersonalization.

Dimension 3, *situation-dependent versus explicit reference*, concerns the different referential strategies dominant in texts. Features referring to the extratextual environment (e.g., adverbial *now* in a soccer announcer's "And now the ball comes out just below us") are considered "situation-dependent," while features contributing to the specification and precision of in-text references (e.g., relative clauses introduced by WH-relative pronouns such as *which* and *who*) are considered "explicit." *PTRS* articles start in 1675 at a moderate level of "explicit reference" and move generally farther in that direction over time; there are notable exceptions to this pattern, however, in both 1825 and 1925. Further analysis of specific features in individual texts on this dimension shows that the scores from these two periods can be partly accounted for by the interaction of just two linguistic features: WH-relative clauses and nominalizations.

Dimension 4, *overt expression of persuasion*, characterizes variation in the degree to which texts evidence explicit persuasive purposes. Suasive verbs (i.e., verbs intended to bring about changes in thought or action such as *suggest* and *propose*) and two types of modal verbs are major features making up this dimension. There is substantial evolution over time in the *PTRS* on Dimension 4 toward a "nonpersuasive" norm: The variation shown by texts over the 300 years studied is nearly half the total found among the 23 modern-day spoken and written genres analyzed by Biber (1988). But there are also two exceptions to clear linear development.

Finally, Dimension 5, *abstract versus nonabstract information*—where "abstract information" is roughly synonymous with "passivized style"—reveals a profound shift in the use of passives and associated features in scientific research writing over the last 300 years. Texts in the 17th- and 18th-century *PTRS* cluster at a moderately "abstract" level, while their 19th- and 20th-century counterparts are as "abstract," or passivized, as any of the 23 modern-day genres analyzed by Biber (1988). This clustering at two varying levels of "abstractness" represents a quite different pattern than that seen on the other four dimensions, suggesting dramatic developments in the linguistic history of scientific research writing between 1775 and 1825 (for which see next section).

SYNTHESIS AND INTERPRETATION OF FINDINGS

The rhetorical and linguistic findings described previously can be synthesized and interpreted as follows. The profound shift from comparatively "involved" and "verbal" discourse to highly "informational" and "nominal" discourse on Dimension 1 appears to accord closely with the shift from an "author-centered" to an "object-centered" rhetoric. Although by no means neglecting natural phenomena as the ultimate objects of study, early scientific research writing emphasized human actors and their actions, an orientation that was expressed linguistically in more-or-less "involved" and "verbal" terms.

The relatively "involved," author-centered character of early modern scientific writing was part of a larger sociohistorically conditioned view of reality, one which might be termed *genteel discourse*. In this ideology, the British gentleman represented a moral and social ideal—the center around which British society revolved, and from which power flowed. As made clear in recent historical research, early modern scientists traded on this conventional image of the gentleman for rhetorical purposes, using it to gain for themselves its special claims to authority, disinterestedness, and moral rectitude. This borrowing was all the more natural since many scientists were in fact gentlemen. When early modern scientific authors placed themselves in the midst of their texts, they therefore brought to bear a whole social system that powerfully warranted the truth of what they were reporting.

Additional markers of genteel discourse are also evident in the 17th- and 18th-century texts analyzed in this study. Commonly used linguistic features such as "stance markers" (e.g., *may, seems*), for example, marked the modesty and humility that were the special province of the British gentleman, and the polite letter, the genre form in which articles most commonly appeared in the *PTRS* of this period, was a central emblem of genteel culture. Along with these features, the "dialogic" norms of interaction within the early modern scientific discourse community were modeled on the social norms of face-to-face civic conduct and established personal acquaintanceship that held specifically among gentlemen at this time.

As seen in both this study and the recent work of historians of science, early modern European science thus depended crucially on a rhetorical *technology of trust and proximity* (Daston, 1991a). "Trust" here represents the credibility conventionally accorded free and independent gentlemen, and "proximity" describes the personal ties and face-to-face contact that were both the normative means of social contact and the primary basis of genteel trust. Being a gentleman, or being able to position oneself within genteel norms of discourse, was therefore generally the best way to validate one's science.

By the beginning of the 19th century, however, an alternative scientific discourse—one which at first augmented but eventually replaced its predecessor—was actively under development. In this new discursive approach, the rhetorical focus was on detailed accounts of scientific technologies, whether elaborated sets of methods and procedures or minute descriptions of sophisticated instruments. Linguistically, there is a sudden jump in scores on the "abstract"/passivized dimension (Dimension 5) in this period, and continued steady increases in "informational production" (Dimension 1) and "nonnarrativity" (Dimension 2). All these developments mark the growth of an "object-centered" textual norm, one in which scientific "objects," rather than scientific people, assume increasing centrality and importance.

This 19th-century discursive shift ramifies with a period of profound change in the sociocognitive organization of science wherein a substantially undifferentiated science began to fragment into semiautonomous disciplines. In this reorganization, the nascent disciplines developed their identities largely on the basis of distinct investigative methodologies and instrumentation, and (partly as a result) research began to be viewed in terms of specialized and deperson-alized scientific problems. Historians of science have recently begun to concep-tualize these changes in terms of an interplay of scientific and nonscientific forces. On the nonscientific side was the increasingly felt need of bureaucrats to centralize political power and of capitalists to rationalize economic systems, while on the scientific side there was enhanced interest in quantitative meas-urement systems as a means of methodological systematization and control. In both cases, there was an impulse for rational, impersonal means of measure-ment-at-a-distance—measurement that did not depend on the particular char-acter of a social actor, or particular relations of trust or proximity. The eventual, laboriously established outcome of these impulses were, in the terms of Porter (1995), technologies of distrust and distance—represented in the present study in terms of the growth of object-centeredness in scientific research writing in the course of the 19th century.

The object-centered turn in scientific discourse, first clearly evident in and increasingly represented throughout the 19th century, also marks a textual norm in the 20th. Texts, in fact, grow ever more "informational" and "nonnarrative" linguistically, and more impersonal or effaced rhetorically. At the same time, elaborate methods and instrument descriptions become increasingly circum-scribed in the 20th century, their rhetorical place appearing to be taken by theoretical descriptions and discussions. This finding is corroborated by other studies that examine the evolution of scientific research writing in the 20th century.

MOTIVATIONS UNDERLYING THE RESEARCH

An account of what brings one to write on a particular subject usually enhances understanding of what has been written.[4] I entered graduate school planning to take a degree in applied linguistics, thereby improving my job prospects as a university English as a Second Language teacher in Japan, where I had worked the previous 6 years and where I planned to return. But a set of fortuitous (if initially unpromising) circumstances led me to study medical and scientific research writing. First, citing an unusually heavy work schedule, a professor (Robert B. Kaplan) proceeded to read a just-finished manuscript verbatim in a first-year class I was taking, thereby opening my eyes to the work of Bazerman, Latour, Myers, and Shapin (while closing the eyes of nearly everyone else in the class). Second, a diagnosis of cancer, caught, luckily, in its early stages, led me in the summer following my first year to devour substantial quantities of medical research writing. And third, a PhD-program admission requirement to write a "publication-quality" paper in my second year of graduate school compelled me to reach for a topic I already had at least a practical background in by that point: medical research writing. The result of these converging circumstances was a "PhD screening paper" on the discourse conventions of present-day medical research writing.

My next step followed a lifelong pattern of proceeding backward—or from the immediate and concrete to the distant and abstract. Having read Bazerman's (1988) research on the *PTRS*, and having found work in the meantime on a linguistics research project constructing and analyzing a large cross-historical corpus of English texts, I wrote a "PhD qualifying paper" on discourse development in a historical medical journal, the *Edinburgh Medical Journal*, over a period of 250 years. This paper represented my first attempt to marry linguistic analysis to rhetorical analysis, and to place their synthesis in some sort of historical context. I received encouragement in this work from one professor (Douglas Biber) in particular, who was struck by the largely hermetic approaches to scientific writing taken at that time by applied linguists, historians, and rhetoricians. But by far the most enjoyable part of the research in my own mind was reading medical history while working with old texts. Put academically, I was (and continue to be) more interested in knowing about the social context, and particularly in finding out what the language variety being studied could tell us about that context, than I was in knowing the converse. As might be expected in a linguistics department at a large U.S. university, this was in sharp contrast to the interests of most of my fellow students and professors.

By the dissertation writing stage the project had mutated into a study of the *PTRS*, because I had begun to realize that, for all its immediacy and fascination, writing in medicine was addressing a somewhat particular set of rhetorical situations—ones that did not necessarily generalize to other domains of scientific activity. The present study is therefore based on my dissertation, completed in 1993. Both during and since that time I have read as much as possible of the history of the Royal Society and British science, topics on which there is naturally an enormous amount written. In my understanding of these topics, I have been especially influenced by the work of historians who take a "social" approach—Shapin, Daston, Dear, D. P. Miller, Morrell, R. Porter, T. Porter, Rudwick, and Thackray are just a few of the students of British and European science who eschew the boundary between "internal" and "external" studies, and who themselves (although variably) have been influenced by the sociology of scientific knowledge.

My other direct influences are perhaps more obvious, as they may be better known to most readers of this book. Patent to those in the area of rhetoric and composition will be my reliance on researchers taking a "sociorhetorical" stance—most notably Bazerman, Myers, and Berkenkotter and Huckin. In particular, the present work operates in a dialogic relationship with the historical research of Bazerman, attempting to consider many of the same questions that have engaged him while employing a somewhat different methodological toolkit. If I can shed complementary light on what *PTRS* articles across history have been "doing [by] looking at the worlds in which these texts served as significant activity" (Bazerman, 1988, p. 4), and reciprocally come to a better understanding of the text-using communities themselves, I will have accomplished much of what I set out to do in this book.

A different set of direct influences on this work derives from sociolinguistics and applied linguistics, the latter my disciplinary home. One possibly all-too-apparent influence from these sources may be found in an inductive "data conquers all" approach to argumentation. Most linguists consider themselves scientists, and although I am less committed to this view than some, I am neither able nor willing to place myself totally beyond its grasp, even at the risk of being nonreflexive. At a different level, I have been heavily influenced by the main tradition of linguistics that studies professional language use—register analysis—as practiced both by American sociolinguists (e.g., Biber & Finegan, 1994a) and linguists worldwide (e.g., Halliday, 1988; Swales, 1990). Since it was first pointed out to me several years ago, I have become much more conscious of the unproductive gap between this research domain and the area of rhetoric/composition that studies much the same thing, and often for similar purposes. Part of the goal of the present work—and the main motivation behind my choice of research methods—is to attempt to integrate these two traditions of research. I do not mean to suggest, by any means, than I am the only one engaged in this task; I do hope, however, to be able to highlight both the problem and one possible approach to a solution here.

In closing, I should also note a *difference* between myself and some other applied linguists—and perhaps some rhetoric/composition researchers as well. Applied linguistics has traditionally taken as its main task the improvement (through the more-or-less immediate application of linguistic concepts) of language teaching practices and domain-specific language use. Although I have sometimes worked in this mold, I prefer to adopt a more political view of applied linguistics here. That is, I would like to define applied linguistics for present purposes as *the study and explication of situated linguistic practices that exclude individuals and groups from participation in particular spheres of human activity* (cf. Gee, 1990; Kress, 1991; and Pennycook, 1994, for related definitions of applied linguistics and discourse analysis). It has been argued that potentially *all* language varieties have this basic function (cf. D. Atkinson, 1991), but most would agree, I believe, that scientific language has powers of exclusivity matched by few other uses of language in the present day. My goal in advocating such a task for applied linguistics is hardly to tear down the institutions that sponsor such language practices—in truth, I do not believe that scientists *could* conduct their work without the specialized language they have developed over the past 300 years. Rather, I am trying to help make these practices as explicit and nonexclusive as possible, and by so doing to enable a better understanding of the scientific form of life so as to employ that form of life to humankind's best and fullest advantage. In other words (and certainly not mine alone), science is far too important to be left merely to scientists. This is the overall purpose motivating the present work.[5]

ENDNOTES

[1]The eminent historian of science M.P. Crosland (1978) gives an additional rationale for the historical study of science generally rather than as a set of discrete disciplines:

> Unfortunately the separate study of the history of individual sciences precludes the appreciation of general patterns. There are more similiarities between problems of quite different sciences than one would at first imagine. I shall be referring in the course of this paper to the general question of agreement on a common language. (p. 114)

[2]A third type of discourse analysis—analysis at the level of (not necessarily linguistic) social practice (Fairclough, 1992; Gee, 1990)—is also partly undertaken in this book, as explained in chapter 1.

[3]There are, of course, versions of rhetorical analysis that differ substantially from the one presented here (e.g., Fahnestock & Secor, 1988; Gross, 1990).

[4]A different but largely complementary version of this story is told in the acknowledgments at the beginning of this volume.

[5]Although democratizing science may sound like a hopelessly utopian project in this age of high specialization and technical expertise, various initiatives are currently underway in this regard. In Denmark, for example, citizens' panels are being consulted on scientific decisions having the potential for broad social and ecological impact, and clinical trials of various AIDS drugs were undertaken in the United States largely on the basis of popular political demand. Sclove (1995) and Sarewitz (1997) describe the "science-for-everyone" movement in Denmark, the United States, and other countries.

1

Conceptual Framework

*If "discourse" is nothing less than language itself, and "discourse analysis"
attempts to admit a broad range of research to the analysis of language,
then it is by nature interdisciplinary.*

—Tannen, 1990, p. 10

*Discourse is a difficult concept, largely because there are so many con-
flicting and overlapping definitions formulated from various theoretical
and disciplinary standpoints.*

—Fairclough, 1992, p. 3

Discourse is language-in-the-world, and discourse analysis is thus the study
of language in all its located complexity and glory. Although discourse and
discourse analysis have been variously conceptualized, these are the definitions I will adopt here.

Given these broad definitions, studies in rhetoric/composition of how
people use language to operate in and on their worldly environments are
located squarely within the field of discourse analysis. At the same time,
rhetorical studies at least has maintained an existence, historically speaking,
somewhat apart from the more linguistically oriented traditions of discourse
analysis. It has therefore developed theoretical assumptions and methods
that do not always comport comfortably with—and which in some cases may
even oppose—their counterparts in the linguistics-influenced traditions. To
give but one general example: The former's emphasis on rhetorical *effectiveness* seems epistemologically opposed to the latter's relativist stance that
all language is by nature equally suited to its contexts of use and culture.[1]

As an interdisciplinary endeavor, discourse analysis will always contain within it the potential for internal discoherence and fragmentation based on such differences in "professional vision" (Goodwin, 1994)—this is not a unique feature of the relationship between rhetorical and linguistic discourse analysis. It does suggest, however, that the introduction of concepts central to a study such as this one, which attempts to bring the two traditions closer together, may be a necessary place to begin. In order therefore to establish grounds for clear communication and understanding in this complex, "pluralistic" endeavor (Kirsch, 1992), this chapter is devoted to defining major theoretical concepts, or "conventions for construing reality" (Bizzell, 1982), underlying the research on which this book is based. As will be seen, the definitions themselves often aim to integrate theory in rhetoric/composition and linguistics, or to use earlier attempts at integration as points of departure. Similar but less involved integrative efforts are also made in chapter 3 in regard to the research methodologies used in this study, and in chapter 6 at the level of empirical results. Both of the latter two attempts, however—as well as much of the rest of the book—are predicated on the concepts established first in this chapter.

DISCOURSE AND DISCOURSE ANALYSIS

Having defined discourse broadly as language-in-the-world, and discourse analysis as its study, I will now specify these concepts more closely. Given the complex worldliness of discourse, however, discourse analysis will be treated not as a discrete science with precise definitions and a rational internal structure, but as a process of "entering something messy with messy tools—probably the only way of doing it" (Galtung, 1988, cited in Phillipson, 1992, p. 3).

Fairclough (1992) distinguishes among three levels of discourse and its analysis:

> Any discursive "event" . . . is seen as being simultaneously a piece of text, an instance of discursive practice, and an instance of social practice. The "text" dimension attends to language analysis of texts. The "discursive practice" dimension . . . specifies the nature of the processes of text production and interpretation. . . . The "social practice" dimension attends to issues of concern in social analysis such as the institutional and organizational circumstances of the discursive event and how that shapes the nature of the discursive practice, and the constitutive/constructive effects of discourse. (p. 4)

This conceptualization provides a useful heuristic for moving toward an integrative definition of discourse for analytical purposes. Fairclough's level of "text"—of discourse as more-or-less pure language—is what has historically been studied by linguists: Such definitions of discourse as "language above the level of the sentence," although less popular than formerly, are even now current in linguistically oriented discourse analysis (Pennycook, 1994; Tannen, 1990). Fairclough's discourse as "discursive practice," on the other hand, is substantially congruent with the traditional concerns of rhetoric, perhaps even much of the "new rhetoric" into the 1980s. Bitzer's (1968) classic analysis of the rhetorical situation, for example, would seem to be located squarely in this tradition, as would—though perhaps less squarely—Miller's (1984) concept of genre as social action.

Fairclough's third category—discourse as social practice—is the one that has received special attention across academic fields over the past 15 years. Its root formulation is, of course, that of Foucault, although his ideas have been widely modified and adapted. When Jarratt (1994, p. 1) defines rhetoric as "a set of inquiries around the uses of language, the institutional and power structures creating and created by historically specific discourse worlds," I take her to be describing, in Fairclough's terms, the analysis of discourse as social practice.

Having used Fairclough's categorization to bootstrap us into the discussion, let me now complexify it. His categories are obviously mere analytical conveniences; there is no such thing, for example, as "pure language"—all language is language in context, so to speak. Likewise, Fairclough's intermediate level—the production and reception of language/texts—is predicated on their imminent, immediate, or trace material existence (Fairclough's "language/text" level) and their discursive social histories (Fairclough's "social practice" level), and nontrivially involves these phenomena at every turn. Similarly, although pioneers like Foucault were less than cognizant of the importance of microlevel linguistic detail in realizing and modifying macrolevel social action and organization, discourse as social practice presupposes dynamic activity at all levels of discourse, as later theorists have shown (e.g., Bazerman, 1994, chap. 12; Berkenkotter & Huckin, 1995, chap. 1; Fairclough, 1992; Gee, 1990; Giddens, 1984; Stubbs, 1996).

A theory of discourse that usefully complements and expands on Fairclough's is that of Gee.[2] For Gee (1990), *discourse* is always part of a specific form of life, or a "Discourse," which he defines as:

> a socially accepted association among ways of using language, of thinking, feeling, believing, valuing, and of acting that can be used to identify oneself as a member of a socially meaningful group or "social network," or to signal (that one is playing) a socially meaningful "role." (p. 143)[3]

Gee's definition is useful in that it clarifies the place of language in social life, wherein language enjoys equal status with a variety of other sociocognitive practices but is in no sense privileged over or to be studied apart from them. Rather, it functions as an organic part of a larger sociocognitive whole—a Discourse.

Together with those of Fairclough, Gee's ideas provide an "opportunity space" for the form of discourse analysis I try to develop in this study. Viewing all concrete instances of language as part of one or more larger "saying–writing–doing–being–valuing–believing" combinations (Gee, 1990, p. 142)—combinations that are furthermore always historically constituted (p. 145)—licenses the use of non-language focused historical resources and knowledge as an integral part of a discourse/analytic framework. Thus, the study of discourse can—indeed must—be undertaken by studying social practices (including historical ones) that may have little to do with language per se.

With rare exceptions,[4] linguistically oriented discourse analysts have avoided granting *any* status to historical concerns in their research, perhaps due to Saussure's foundational separation of synchronic and diachronic perspectives on language, and his subsequent banishment of the latter (D. Atkinson, 1994, 1995).[5] Even studies in composition/rhetoric have tended to treat history more as a variably powerful contextual *explanans* than as an integral part of the object under analysis (Bazerman, 1988, chap. 1, note 1). Gee's decentering of language from a privileged position, however—a move made less explicitly also by Fairclough—allows history in as a more equal partner.

My own version of discourse analysis, described in more detail in chapter 3, attempts to capture activity at all three of the levels described by Fairclough (1992), and to treat them integratively. It does so gradually, however—historical social practice, rhetoric, and language are first treated more or less independently (in chapters 2, 4, and 5, respectively), and only afterwards do I attempt to bring them together (in chapter 6). This is partly for analytical convenience, and partly because my understanding of the relationships between these different aspects of discourse—and the very fact that they can be encompassed in a larger integrated conception of discourse/Discourse at all—evolved substantially in the course of writing this book. Such an approach makes for a less-than-homogeneous presentation of material—and no doubt for some internal inconsistencies—but is, I believe, a more accurate record of the thinking that has gone into this volume.[6]

The four main concepts described in the remainder of this chapter—discourse community, discourse conventions, genre, and register—serve further to undergird the integrative model of discourse analysis I have introduced here.

DISCOURSE COMMUNITY

Gee's Discourses represent complex combinations of cognitive but intersubjective knowledge and activity with external, socially purposive activity and practice.[7] The much-discussed concept of "discourse community," on the other hand, has focused largely on the outward manifestations and consequences of the intersubjective knowledge systems accounted for partly in Discourses.

Since the discourse community concept has been widely discussed and debated (e.g., Bizzell, 1982, 1992; Cooper, 1989; Freed & Broadhead, 1987; J. Harris, 1989; Killingsworth, 1992; C. R. Miller, 1993; J. Porter, 1986; Rafoth, 1988, 1990; Swales, 1990, 1993), I will limit my discussion here to two or three major points focusing on the single most widely cited definition of "discourse community"—that of Swales (1990, chap. 2). This definition has been criticized for emphasizing the foundational, consensual, and realist nature of discourse communities. In my own view, Swales' six definitional criteria are useful as identifying features of mature discourse communities, but they have an after-the-fact status as mostly the public *results* or *consequences* of the strong social and communal motivations and mechanisms that lead, in the first place, to the constitution and maintenance of such groups.

A first point to make regarding Swales' definition is that the weakness mentioned just above is partly addressed by Gee's notion of Discourses, because, fully developed, the latter foregrounds the underlying motivations for and socialization/apprenticeship practices by which people are actually inducted into sociocultural groups. An additional element of Gee's notion not mentioned so far—that humans are normally participants in *multiple* such Discourses, some of which will be mutually inconsistent with or opposed to one another in terms of their inherent systems of values and practices—also suggests how dissonance, fragmentation, heterogeneity, and change can be natural attributes of discourse communities, and the individuals who make them up.[8]

Second, Swales (1993) himself has backed away from some of the more realist implications of his earlier definition, preferring what he calls a "virtual existence" for discourse communities of the sort theorized by Giddens (e.g., 1979; cf. Berkenkotter & Huckin, 1995, chap. 1; Stubbs, 1996, chap. 3) for social structures and systems in general. As is widely recognized, Giddens' structuration theory is important here because it suggests a mechanism by which ongoing social change can operate in conjunction with relatively stable (or *meta*stable) social systems and structures. Bakhtin's (1981) "centripedal versus centrifugal" tendencies in language use and development, Foucault's (1972) juxtaposition of "inclination versus institution" in discourse, and Bourdieu's (1977) social fields versus individual habitus in social life are other dialectical conceptualizations of the relationship between microlevel social practices and macrolevel social structures.

An alternative way of conceptualizing expert communities—as "communities of practice" with their multiple, historically evolved "activity systems"—has been proposed by students of Vygotskian psychology and situated cognition (e.g., Brown, Collins, & Duguid, 1989; Chaiklin & Lave, 1993;

Lave & Wenger, 1991; Rogoff, 1990; cf. Berkenkotter & Huckin, 1995, chap. 1). Such concepts would seem to capture some of the multiplex variety of interwoven human actions and activities that characterize disciplinary networks. That is, rather than seeing such communities as necessarily organized around texts per se, we can profitably view texts as part of larger, integrated systems around which sociodisciplinary activity is organized and through which it is accomplished. As with Gee's notion of "Discourse(s)," language/text is thereby decentered and thus able to be viewed in a holistic ecological relationship with other social practices.[9]

At a different conceptual level, the pragmatic notion of *discourse conventions* also helps to explain the dynamics underlying the establishment, survival, and change inherent in discourse communities.

DISCOURSE CONVENTIONS

In Lewis (1969), a convention is defined as *an institutionalized solution to a recurring coordination problem.* A coordination problem, in turn, is a class of interpersonal situations in which a mutually beneficial activity, in order to be performed, demands the coordinated efforts of those involved. The idea here, then, is that where social action of any type will bring greater benefit to individuals than they could achieve acting separately, *and* where conditions for such action recur, this coordinated action will tend to become regularized, or conventionalized. Such conventions can be found in virtually all domains of human social activity—*written discourse conventions* are simply conventionalized solutions to recurring coordination problems that are addressed through written communication (D. Atkinson, 1991).

Written discourse conventions, from this perspective, exist for the primary purpose of ensuring smooth and efficent communication among discourse community members. Although linguists commonly view all language as conventional in this sense, some of the most concrete examples of conventions beyond the basic units of language are certain collocationally restricted grammatical features, formulaic phrases, and technical vocabulary that are highly discourse-community specific. Legal formulas, for example, such as *in good faith* or *by or on behalf of,* or technical medical expressions like *human blood group B* and *acute myocardial infarction,* can be seen as providing the tools necessary to communicate about events either particular to, or viewed from the particular standpoints of, the communities that use them (Goodwin, 1994). At a more abstract level, principles of textual organization such as the conventionalized three-part "rhetorical move" sequence of experimental research article introductions (Swales, 1981, 1990)— or the highly conventionalized Introduction—Methods—Results—Discussion (IMRD) experimental research-report format (e.g., Bazerman, 1985)—have been shown to provide templates by means of which both scientific reading and writing can be performed with maximal efficiency.

At the most abstract level of discourse conventions are what Bizzell (1982) has called "conventions for construing reality." These are basically the socially normative folk theories that Gee (1990, 1992) has characterized as partly making up Discourses, and which likewise in part constitute the communal knowledge bases of discourse communities. For example, a dominant shared assumption in the scientific community is that of "scientific objectivity" (e.g., Daston, 1992); that is, that by following a certain prescribed set of methods in the study of nature, enough analytical rigor can be attained to effectively neutralize fallible human judgments. Although such guiding conventions are substantially nonlinguistic, they have significant rhetorical-linguistic parallels; thus, such features as the "scientific passive" (Ding, in press; Halliday & Martin, 1993, chap. 3), and heavily sanctioned restrictions like those on lexical self-reference (i.e., the use of "I" or "we"), are powerful linguistic indexes of the convention of scientific objectivity.

But perhaps the most significant aspect of discourse conventions is that they "look both ways," or are *multifunctional.* That is, although they are often directly represented in language and rhetoric, discourse conventions serve larger social and cognitive functions as well. Cognitively, they represent the input to and output of the schematic patterns or mental models that are believed to organize thought and memory (e.g., Adams & Collins, 1979; Holland & Quinn, 1987). Socially, besides serving as tools for efficient in-group communication, they provide means by which group solidarity and internal control are fostered. Again socially, but this time from the outsider's point of view, such conventions also provide barriers to group entrance. Thus, technical vocabulary, while it allows community members (e.g., doctors or lawyers) to communicate efficiently among themselves, also excludes would-be members from becoming active partners to such communication.[10]

GENRE

The notion of genre has been widely discussed in some of the various disciplines involved in the study of discourse. Swales (1990) reviews the treatment of the notion across these disciplines, showing that each has its own unique and useful perspective, while Kamberelis (1995) provides an extended and valuable synthesis of current genre theory. Like Swales and Kamberelis, I will attempt to synthesize multiple disciplinary perspectives on genre into a coherent definition, although my own synthesis departs somewhat from theirs.

Goffman (1974/1986) describes "primary frameworks" for interpreting sense experience—such abstract frameworks provide answers to the fundamental human question, "What is going on here?" It will be assumed here that genres represent such primary frameworks for interpreting sense experience in the rhetorical–linguistic domain. More explicitly, genres constitute the external counterparts of intersubjective models or typifications for interpreting discourse, and it is only by applying such models that we can narrow down—and finally produce approximate agreement on—the apparently infinite number of possible interpretations that might be given any particular text.

As the preceding definition suggests, genres depend for their utility on the fact that they are conventionalized. More specifically, genres are comprised of *conventionalized associations of conventions*, such that the *co-occurrence* of conventionalized features will be what signals generic activity (P. Atkinson, 1992; Kamberelis, 1995).[11] Not all generic conventions, however, are created equal; some—for instance the *Dear Sir/Madam* heading of business letters, or the distinctive formatting of such letters themselves—may be more powerful than others, for example, the apparently conventionalized use of *we* and *us* in preference to *I* and *me* in such letters (cf. Jenkins & Hinds, 1987). The former type of generic feature may be thought of as having a role in *cueing* or *activating* the relevant cognitive "business letter" model, while the latter may serve merely to maintain the application of this model once it has been activated.[12]

Two characteristics of genres given prominence in the literature are: (a) that genres are goal- or purpose-oriented; and (b) that they are historical. Regarding the first point, C. R. Miller (1984; cf. Biber, 1988; Swales, 1990) has argued that genres should be categorized according to the purposes they are used to accomplish in their social settings. Thus, formal criteria alone are never sufficient to distinguish genres. Although this claim has a strong intuitive attraction, it is incomplete as it stands. Instead, it seems more accurate to claim that while purpose is an important defining feature of genre, such purpose is mediated in part through language conventions. That is, language conventions, as solutions to various types of communicative (coordination) problems, are themselves purpose-oriented. And genres, as associations of such conventions, are ultimately designed out of their component conventions to address complex communicative problems (or *rhetorical problems*). Thus, when genres are working properly, the question of "Why am I engaged in (this) generic activity?" rarely comes up. Instead, genres in use to some extent *have their purposes built in.*[13]

The second point mentioned just previously—that genres are historical— is of central and immediate import to the present research. Simply put, it seems clear that genres develop and change over time, in relation to changes in their sociocultural environments (e.g., Bazerman, 1984; Campbell & Jamieson, 1978; Ferguson, 1994; Yates & Orlikowski, 1992). The logical extension of this assumption is that genres will become extinct on occasion, and new ones arise. The correspondence, however, between environmental and generic change is not always direct; there are, for instance, genres which outlive their patent usefulness in a culture but still manage to survive for one reason or another[14]—but the connection can generally be established. Diachronic generic change is a relatively well-studied phenomenon for selected types of written discourse: The genre of the scientific research article, for example, has been studied in terms of its rhetorical evolution by, among others, Bazerman (1984, 1988), Berkenkotter and Huckin (1995), and Dear (1985). A primary goal of the present research is to test the claims of these researchers, and where such claims appear valid to give them a better empirical grounding.

Finally, it should be noted that genres are not simply iron-clad molds into which language or text is poured, so to speak, even at a single point in historical time. Rather, genres can be thought of as "opportunity spaces" or "meaning potentials" (Kamberelis, 1995)—abstract norms or prototype models that are always underspecified and therefore perpetually generative, and which can only be realized in messy, heterogeneous human practice (Bakhtin, 1986; Fowler, 1982; Kamberelis, 1995). For such reasons, as well, genres are constantly changing. However, different genres differ in regard to the amount of variation and "creativity" they allow at a particular moment in time: Neither the experimental research article (e.g., Bazerman, 1984) nor the Amish gazette (Galindo, 1995) appear to permit notably free play of written expression in the present, while, relatively speaking, less formally institutionalized genres like the personal letter and diary may. Bakhtin (1981), Foucault (1972), and Giddens (1979) all theorize profound tensions in social institutions (including, notably, texts) that, while they are worked out in particular instances—and instances that lead to changes in the institutions themselves—cannot, finally, be resolved.

REGISTER

Halliday (1988, p. 162) defines a register as "a cluster of associated [linguistic] features having a greater-than-random . . . tendency to co-occur." He then cites "scientific English" as an exemplar of the concept because "any speaker of English for whom it falls within the domain of experience knows it when he sees it or hears it" (p. 162). Other linguists, such as Biber (e.g., 1993, 1994; cf. Ferguson, 1983), view registers as varieties of language that occur in speech situations of varying contextual specificity. In the present study, I adopt a concept of register that closely approximates Halliday's, while attempting to relate it to the notions of genre and convention developed previously.

The relationship between the concepts of register and genre is in fact a complex and often confused one in the study of discourse. It may even be the case that the primary difference is merely one of disciplinary preference, and that the two words denote basically the same phenomenon. Thus, Swales (1990) points out that the discomfort recently caused in linguistics by the introduction of the concept of genre may be due to the fact that register is a longer-established notion in that field.

At least two perspectives on the relationship of genre and register can be found in discourse linguistics. Couture (1986) details one position:

> genres can only be realized in completed texts or texts that can be projected as complete, for a genre does more than specify kinds of codes [i.e., registers] extant in a group of related texts; it specifies conditions for beginning, continuing, and ending a text. (p. 82)

In contrast to genres, then, registers for Couture—as for Halliday (1988)— are groupings of linguistic features into certain functional communicative codes or styles (e.g., journalistic writing, "legalese"). Genres and registers are, in this view, theoretically *independent,* and can be combined in various (although not all possible) permutations.

Martin (1985) describes a fundamentally different genre–register relationship than the one proposed by Couture. For Martin, genre is manifested in register, and register is manifested in language. That is, genre is an abstract sociocultural system that underlies and determines the permissible combinations of registral components (these components being categorized within the systemic linguistic framework of field, tenor, and mode), in a way similar to that by which register constrains language.

Although Couture and Martin differ in regard to the relationships they posit between register and genre, they agree in clearly distinguishing the two concepts from one another, and in placing the latter on a more abstract plane. For the purposes of the present study, I will make a less absolute distinction between register and genre, while retaining the basic difference in level of abstraction; to a certain degree, my version of the relationship synthesizes the views of Couture and Martin. Thus, whereas genre represents the complex, conventionalized *rhetorical* form and content of whole texts, register primarily represents the patterns of co-occurring *linguistic* structures that comprise such texts. By "rhetorical," however, I do not intend to exclude such linguistic structures—properly speaking, the generic level of text will *include* the registral level, as register is centrally involved in solving the rhetorical problem(s) for which a genre is constituted. But register will *not* typically include many of the generic components of text, as the latter make sense only holistically. It is thus possible to describe a disembodied "strip" of language as, for example, legal register, while generic components would make little or no sense if similarly decontextualized. In this view, then, register is a (theoretically) detachable part of a larger organic concept—genre. In actual language use, however, register will rarely if ever occur in such a detached mode.

Bakhtin (1986) places genre and register (which he calls "functional style") in substantially the same relationship as I have:

> [Functional] [s]tyle is inseparably linked to particular thematic unities, and—what is especially important—to particular compositional unities: to particular types of construction of the whole, types of its completion, and types of relations between the speakers and other participants in speech communication. . . . Style enters as one element into the generic unity of the utterance. Of course, this does not mean that language style cannot be the subject of its own independent study. Such a study, that is, of language stylistics as an independent discipline, is both feasible and necessary. But this study will be correct and productive only if based on a constant awareness of the generic nature of language styles . . . (p. 64)

The idea that register is a component of genre motivates the analytical methodology employed in the present study. As described in chapter 3 of the present work, language-oriented discourse analysis is undertaken at two levels: the rhetorical (or generic), and the registral. But whereas genre subsumes register—and registral elements (inasmuch as they have rhetorical significance) are therefore considered at the former level of analysis—at the latter level, register is treated as primarily a self-contained phenomenon.

THE SOCIOHISTORICAL STUDY OF SCIENTIFIC DISCOURSE

In this chapter I have attempted to articulate the background assumptions and theoretical concepts on which the current work is based. It was necessary to do so at some length because of the interdisciplinary nature of this project, and the multidisciplinarity of my hoped-for readership. What must seem at this point like free-floating ideas and notions will be grounded in the following chapters in more concrete discussions of the sociohistorical context—including Discourses—of modern British science (chaps. 2 and 6), methodological apparatus (chap. 3), rhetorical and linguistic findings (chaps. 4 and 5), and the synthesis and interpretation of the findings (chap. 6). Taken together, I believe they provide a coherent approach to the variegated career of scientific discourse as seen in its rich, sociohistorical context.[15]

ENDNOTES

[1]There is also a version of applied linguistics, briefly referred to in the introduction to this volume, that attempts to improve field-specific language use (e.g., the way doctors talk to their patients). This movement in linguistics has not been squared, to my knowledge, with the larger relativist belief in the functional equality of language systems. See also Hymes (1972, 1996) for a sociolinguistic alternative to the relativist principle in linguistics.

[2]Gee's notion of "Discourse(s)" also owes an obvious debt to Foucault, although they differ in interesting ways.

[3]Gee further posits five corollaries to his definition: (a) Discourses are ideological—by participating in particular Discourses, one takes on the value systems inherent in them; (b) Discourses are largely insulated from internal criticism because "uttering viewpoints that seriously undermine them defines one as being outside them" (1990, p. 144); (c) Discourses are established and defined in opposition to other Discourses; (d) Discourses, in providing different views of "reality," dismiss or marginalize fundamental assumptions and values of other Discourses; and (e) Discourses are implicated in the distribution and exercise of power in society, with *dominant Discourses* being those that "lead to social goods in a society" (1990, p. 144).

[4]The rare exceptions to this generalization are: (a) critical discourse analysis (e.g., Kress, 1991), a relatively recent development that follows Foucault in seeing history as crucially influencing current language practices, although this principle seems to have been honored more in theory than in practice—Fairclough (1992) is part of this movement; (b) register and genre analysts, in particular Douglas Biber, Edward Finegan, M. A. K. Halliday, and John Swales, have done valuable theoretical and empirical work in this respect (e.g., Biber, 1995; Biber & Finegan, 1989, 1992; Halliday, 1988; cf. Atkinson & Biber, 1994); and (c) the 1990 volume of the *Annual Review of Applied Linguistics (ARAL)*, devoted to discourse analysis, which has several articles touching on historical issues. This latter has much to do, however, with the fact that *ARAL*'s Editor-in-Chief at the time, Robert B. Kaplan, had a longstanding interest in historical discourse analysis.

[5]In fact, discourse analysis developed substantially in opposition to another of Saussure's postulates; that is, Chomsky's modification of Saussure's *langue versus parole* distinction, whereby linguists were authorized to study language decontextualized from its settings in everyday life. What I am suggesting here, however, is that other somewhat less examined assumptions of modern linguistics were passed on quite unproblematically in the development of discourse analysis, which is a reasonable assumption if we take an "academic disciplines-as-forms-of-life" view of discourse analysis.

[6]In particular, chapter 2 was originally conceptualized and written as a description of the social "background" of the written language and rhetoric of the Royal Society—the sociohistorical context in which they were situated, as indicated in the title of this book. For this reason, chapter 2 of the present volume is more a standard history than a description focusing on the sociohistorical forms of life, or Discourses, that undergirded scientific activity in the Royal Society across its history, although I try at various points to indicate these. I do, however, present the most influential of these historical Discourses more directly in chapter 6. Obviously, much more work on the Discourse/social practice history of the Royal Society remains to be done.

[7]Gee develops the mind–society–Discourse relationship further in his 1992 *The Social Mind,* whose concluding chapter begins:

> Meaning and memory, believing and knowing, are social practices that vary as they are embedded within different Discourses within a society. Each Discourse apprentices its members and "disciplines" them so that their mental networks of associations and their folk theories converge towards a "norm" reflected in the social practices of a Discourse. These "ideal" norms, which are rarely directly statable, but only discoverable by close ethnographic study, are what constitute meaning, memory, believing, knowing, and so forth, from the perspective of each Discourse. The mental networks in our heads, as well as our general cognitive processing abilities, are tools that we each use to get in and stay in the social "games" our Discourses constitute. (p. 141)

[8]A primary tenet of poststructuralist theories, also evident in Gee's, is that individuals are made up of multiple and sometimes competing "subjectivities," rather than having unified, coherent personalities as posited in modernist thought (see Pennycook, 1996).

[9]An excellent example of one such complex activity system is given by Hutchins (1993, chap. 2; 1995). In a close ethnographic study, Hutchins describes the task of navigation on large military ships as an intricate and highly integrated combination of individual and social activities, including (and crucially) but by no means limited to the production and use of texts.

[10]The notion of discourse convention itself does not preclude acts of creativity whereby conventions are supervened and altered, although such activities presume the operations of other, related conventions, the development of new conventions, or new combinations of conventions. In other words, linguistic communication (and other cooperative social activity) cannot take place entirely without the operation of some conventions, or of activity that quickly becomes more or less conventionalized. (See D. Atkinson, 1991, for more on the institutionalization of discourse conventions).

[11]Kamberelis (1995), quoting Bakhtin (1986), makes this same basic point regarding texts:

> Texts . . . always embody sets of generic conventions. "Genres [and thus their conventions] correspond to typical situations of speech communication, typical themes, and, consequently, also to particular contacts between the meanings of words and the actual concrete reality under certain typical circumstances." (p. 122)

[12]Recent versions of cognitive processing theories such as connectionism would see the difference between such cognitive model-activating and cognitive model-maintaining cues/conventions as one of degree (usually expressed in terms of a stronger or more frequent neuronal "impulse" or "connection") rather than of kind (see Gee, 1992, chap. 2).

[13]Others have made similar points about the purposes of genres being built in. Goffman (1974/1986), for example, pointed out that when primary frames are working properly, their contribution to understanding the nature of the ongoing speech event does not generally enter the consciousness of the user. It is only when frame expectations are subverted that one usually becomes aware of the original frame. I also take Bahktin's (1986, p. 93) statement: "Each speech genre in each area of speech communication has its own typical conception of the addressee, and this defines it as a genre," as making a closely related point.

Regarding the identification of genres as associations of purpose-oriented conventions of varying scope, consider Brown and Fraser's (1979) discussion of social "purpose" in discourse:

> [P]urposes come in sets of different scope. That is, certain overarching purposes can continue to operate for considerable periods of time, but within such a purpose there are less sustained purposes, which in turn involve even more short-lived purposes. Whereas big fleas are held to have smaller fleas on their backs, which have smaller fleas on their backs . . . large purposes contain their smaller ones within them, as diverse means to overarching ends. (p. 39)

It is my claim that such purposes are mediated to some degree through language conventions of varying scope.

[14]The "hear ye hear ye"-prefaced proclamations of town criers—still a part of at least some people's generic knowledge in the 20th century though probably nonfunctional since at least the Renaissance—can be considered a case in point. It might be argued, however, that this genre still plays a kind of role (although a highly derivative one) in entertainment and literature.

[15]The unfortunate (but perhaps economically necessary) emphasis on "news value" in academic discourse (Berkenkotter & Huckin, 1995, chap. 2) prevents me from including a review of research on scientific discourse in the main body of this study. I can, however, provide a brief list of studies here, while also referring readers to articles which have as a major function the review of such works.

Reviews of work on scientific discourse include: Ashmore, Myers, and Potter (1995); D. Atkinson (1993; in press); Golinski (1990); Harris (1997, introduction); Kaplan and Grabe (1991); Myers (1996); Swales (1990, chap. 7); Taylor (1996, chap. 4); and van Naerssen and Kaplan (1987).

Single- or dual-authored volumes on scientific discourse include: Bazerman (1988); Gilbert and Mulkay (1984); Gross (1990); Halliday and Martin (1993); Locke (1992); Montgomery (1996); Myers (1990); and Prelli (1989).

Edited volumes in which many, if not all, chapters treat scientific discourse include: Battalio (to appear); Bazerman and Paradis (1991); Gross and Keith (1997); Harris (1997); and Martin (to appear).

Two journals that frequently contain work on scientific discourse are *English for Specific Purposes* (Pergamon/Elsevier) and *Written Communication* (Sage).

Articles or chapters on (nonhistorical) scientific discourse include: Berkenkotter and Huckin (1995, chaps. 3 & 4); Butler (1990); Crismore and Farnsworth (1990); Dubois (1982, 1987); Fahnestock (1986); Fahnestock and Secor (1988); Gosden (1993); Grabe and Kaplan (1997); Harré (1990); Harris (1991); Hunston (1993); Hyland (1996); Knorr-Cetina (1981, chap. 5); Latour (1987, chap. 1); Latour and Woolgar (1986, chap. 2); Master (1991); Medawar (1964); Myers (1989, 1992); Ochs, Gonzales, and Jacoby (1996); Rodman (1994); Rymer (1988); Salager, 1984; Tarone, Dwyer, Gillette, and Icke (1981); D. K. Thompson (1993); and Vande Kopple (1994).

Work on the history of scientific discourse includes: Allen, Qin, and Lancaster (1994); D. Atkinson (1992, 1996); Battalio (1996); Bazerman (1988, 1991, 1994, chap. 9; in press); Berkenkotter and Huckin (1995, chap. 2); Broman (1991); Campbell (e.g., 1986, 1987, 1990); Cantor (1989); Dear (1985, 1991); Ding (in press); Golinski (1987); Gross (1988; 1990, chaps. 4, 7, 8, 10, 11); Halliday and Martin (1993, chaps. 1, 3, & 5); Hannaway (1975); Harmon, (1989); Holmes (1987, 1991); Johns (1991; in press); Katzen (1980); Kronick (1976, 1978, 1988); Locke (1992, chaps. 3, 4, 5); Lyne and Howe (1986); Meadows (1974, chap. 3); Montgomery (1996, chaps. 2 & 4); Paradis (1987); Paul and Charney (1995); Shapin (1984); Shapin and Schaffer (1985, chap. 2); Valle (1993, 1997).

2

The Royal Society and Its
Philosophical Transactions:
A Brief Institutional History

THE FOUNDING OF THE ROYAL SOCIETY[1]

The birth of the Royal Society followed an extremely tumultuous period in British history. In the England of the preceding 25 years a civil war had been fought, a king had been beheaded, and extreme political and religious repression had been endured. For part of this period English society had been on the verge of anarchy. The revival of the monarchy in 1660 was therefore looked upon not so much as an attempt to reimpose the old social order, but as a last chance to restore *any* social order.

In November 1660, a group of gentlemen met in London to form what was initially envisioned as "a College [i.e., a collegial society] for the Promoting of Physico-Mathematical Learning." This group was heir to at least two earlier confabula devoted to the study of non-Aristotelian natural philosophy: an informal London discussion circle known as the "Invisible College"; and an offshoot of that group which met in Oxford. Both of these organizations—and the Royal Society to follow—were directly inspired by the approach to natural philosophy championed by Francis Bacon. Bacon had been the first to articulate fully a close, empirical approach to the study of nature; it was Bacon, as well, who proposed accomplishing such ends through cooperative public endeavor.

At its formation in 1660, the new group agreed to:

> meete together Weekly . . . to consult and debate concerning the promoting of Experimental Learning: And that each of us will allowe, one shilling weekely, towards the defraying of occasional charges. ("Royal Society Journal-Book," cited in Lyons, 1944, p. 23)

They also agreed on an elaborate organizational structure, consisting, at the top, of a revolving president, treasurer, and register-keeper. A gathering of 115 gentlemen and aristocrats, including such notables as Robert Boyle, Robert Hooke, John Wilkins, Christopher Wren, and John Evelyn, signed their names to the original founding document. It was Evelyn as well who, for reasons described below, first referred to the group as the "Royal Society," a name that was afterwards officially adopted. The full name used by the Society in this period became "The Royal Society of London for Improving Natural Knowledge."

In October 1661, the Society petitioned the new king for royal approval as a chartered corporation. That it did so less than a year after its founding—and that the petition was quickly granted—testifies to the political power of some of the Society's members. A second, revised charter was approved in 1663, and the Society thereafter enjoyed the special privileges granted to royally chartered organizations. These included the direct patronage of the king, permission to print without government censorship, and the right to correspond freely with citizens of other countries.

In several significant ways, the fledgling Royal Society was unique and even revolutionary for its time (Hunter, 1989, chap. 1). Thus, it represented the first *public institution for the pursuit of scientific research.* The fact that it was *public*—in the sense that, in principle, membership in the Society was available to all interested individuals[2] and attempts were made to disseminate society goings-on—distinguished it from a handful of patron-based scientific groupings located mostly on the Continent. The fact that its focus was *research* distinguished it from the universities, whose main purpose was naturally education, and from professional interest groups like the Royal College of Physicians. Furthermore, the type of research to which the Society claimed primary devotion was *experimental* research, only one of numerous (if poorly defined) approaches to natural philosophy current at the time.[3] Partly for these reasons, the Royal Society has constituted since its founding a prototype for organized scientific activity throughout the modern world, making it a major formative influence on the conduct of modern science.[4]

No less importantly, the Royal Society was also, as commonly described by contemporaries, "a society of gentlemen." In part, this meant that the Society acted as a gentleman's club, a place to socialize with one's own kind according to strict, if "polite," norms of social conduct. But being a British gentleman meant more than having a particular set of acquaintances or following particular rules of conduct; it meant being part of a distinctive "form of life," or Discourse (Gee, 1990)—one that conditioned potentially all aspects of the genteel individual's existence. As recent historical research (e.g., R. Porter, 1978; Shapin, 1988, 1994) has made clear, the career of British science became intertwined in this period with the Discourse of the British gentleman.

This linkage was mediated partly by the social category of the gentleman virtuoso, the financially worry-free individual who cultivated various socially approved pastimes as ways of occupying and improving himself, and sometimes improving his society, as well, in the eyes of his fellow men and Creator. The study of nature and technology was one such approved pastime, whether represented in collecting floral, faunal, or mineral specimens on one's ancestral property holdings, in discovering or improving upon agricultural or mining techniques, or in recording meteorological or astronomical observations to share with like-minded peers. Robert Boyle, in many ways the leading light of the Royal Society and Restoration science, was a highly public embodiment of the Christian virtuoso, who found his life's purpose in uncovering the "argument by design"—evidence of God's will in the intricate workings of nature. In sum, the Royal Society was a society of gentlemen in the fullest sense—run by gentlemen, for genteel purposes, via genteel standards of conduct and communication, as part and parcel of a genteel form of life.

THE BIRTH AND EARLY HISTORY
OF THE *PHILOSOPHICAL TRANSACTIONS,* 1665–1700

An integral part of the Royal Society from almost the beginning, and without a doubt its most durable achievement over its first 100 years of existence, was the publication of the *Philosophical Transactions* (hereafter *PTRS*). In much of Europe, the Royal Society was originally known *only* as the source of the *PTRS*, which reached a wide international audience in the 17th and 18th centuries, whether in its original form or its numerous vernacular and Latin translations. From 1665 through the end of the 18th century, the *PTRS* was consistently regarded as, if not *the* leading, then one of the two leading scientific journals of its time. The journal's preeminence was challenged in the 19th century with the rise of specialized scientific publications, but it still held a commanding position in European science in the last third of the century, as T. H. Huxley (1866/1968) made clear:

> If all the books in the world, except the Philosophical Transactions, were destroyed, it is safe to say that the foundations of physical science would remain unshaken, and the vast intellectual progress of the last two centuries would be largely, although incompletely, recorded. (p. 23)

Although Huxley's statement was an exaggeration, it still indicates the enormous significance of the journal to late 19th-century Western science. Even today, as only one of a very large number of scientific journals, the *PTRS* and its more modern offshoot, the *Proceedings,* maintain a strong reputation both as journals of general science and within specific scientific disciplines.[5]

As described previously, the Royal Society's identity as the first public forum for organized empirical science was based partly on its efforts to communicate its work to the learned community at large. Thus, great emphasis was placed from the very beginning on accurately recording events at the Society's weekly meetings, and on reviewing correspondence sent by scientifically minded individuals in Britain and abroad. These activities also represented an effort to carry out Bacon's program of natural philosophy, as presented in his *Novum Organum* (1620/1900) and *New Atlantis* (begun around 1624 but left unfinished). In these works, Bacon proposed the "description and delineation of a Natural and Experimental History such as may serve to build philosophy upon" (1620, cited in Vickers, 1987, p. 23), including the exhaustive cataloguing of both eyewitness and previously published accounts of natural/experimental phenomena by a widely distributed group of scientific reporters.

The Royal Society's concern for compiling and promulgating scientific information provided one important impetus for a more fully public version of such information, the *PTRS*. The earliest evidence of plans for the journal comes in a letter written by Robert Hooke, probably in 1663 or 1664:[6]

[The Royal Society] designe to print a Paper of advertisements once every week, or fortnight at furthest, wherein will be contained the heads or substance of the inquiries they are most solicitous about, together with the progress they have made and the information they have received from other hands, together with a short account of such other philosophicall matters as accidentally occur, and a brief discourse of what is new and considerable in their letters from all parts of the world, and what the learned and inquisitive are doing or have done in physick, mathematicks, mechaniks, optics, astronomy, medicine, chymistry, anatomy, both abroad and at home. (cited in Andrade, 1965, p. 12)

Hooke's Baconian description closely anticipated the shape the journal actually took when first published in 1665. What Hooke did not mention, however—and what proved crucially important in establishing the journal's character in its formative years—was the role of Henry Oldenburg.

The German-born Oldenburg had first visited England as a private tutor; he later returned as a diplomat to Cromwell's government, staying on when his term was up and finding employment first with Boyle's sister as tutor to her son, and later with Boyle himself. At some point in the early-to-mid-1650s, he was briefly at Oxford, where he fell under the influence of the Oxford-based group that prefigured the Royal Society. Then, while with his pupil in continental Europe from 1657 to 1660, he began what became the dominant work of his life—a massive correspondence for the purpose of exchanging scientific information.

Returning to England in 1660, Oldenburg was put up for membership in the Royal Society and elected at its founding in that year. This distinction was due, no doubt, to the influence of his patron Boyle, but must also have reflected a broader appreciation of Oldenburg's scientific contacts and communicative skills. He was then appointed one of the Society's two secretaries in 1662. The role of secretary was similar to that of register-keeper in the Society's original design: Secretaries recorded goings-on at meetings, and managed correspondence between the Society and outside parties. In addition, one of the secretaries usually read selections from this correspondence at Society meetings.

It was left to Oldenburg, however, to turn these seemingly mundane duties into an art; in so doing, he in some ways *invented* the scientific journal (Bazerman, 1988, chap. 5; Shapin, 1987). As mentioned previously, Oldenburg had already established a formidable network of correspondents among devotees of the new science abroad, a correspondence based on the active trading of scientific "intelligence" between Boyle's Oxford circle and Oldenburg's continental contacts. But although scientific correspondence of a private or semiprivate nature was popular at this time among individuals or small groups, it was Oldenburg who first institutionalized it on a large, and increasingly public, scale. He was aided by the fact that, as natural philosophers throughout Europe became aware of the Royal Society's existence and Baconian agenda, they began to bombard it with letters seeking or offering scientific information, letters which it fell largely to Oldenburg as secretary to answer. Oldenburg responded to this challenge enthusiastically, writing ever-increasing numbers of letters from 1663 on.[7]

Given these several conditions—broad international interest in scientific knowledge exchange, the Royal Society as a magnet for such correspondence, and an industrious corresponding secretary—it might appear, from a late 20th-century perspective, that the printing of a public version of this correspondence was inevitable. Yet retrospective inevitability does not do justice to the complex of factors that led to the establishment of the *PTRS,* or to its successful continuation in the critical early years.

On the one hand, Oldenburg brought to this task personal qualities and social skills that significantly enhanced the flow of information between the Royal Society and the outside scientific world. First, Oldenburg consistently encouraged individual scientific activity through the liberal use of flattery and a diplomatic reluctance to criticize; at the same time, he was adept at asking questions that might push interesting research forward. Second, and somewhat paradoxically, Oldenburg actively fomented controversy among his correspondents, a strategy that proved a major stimulus to scientific work. His goading of Hooke, for instance, into public dispute with the French astronomer Auzout is only the best known example of Oldenburg's role as *agent provocateur*. Third, Oldenburg was a "linguist" (in the lay sense of being a polyglot) of considerable talent.[8] Fluent in all the major European languages and a highly accomplished Latinist, Oldenburg performed a critical function in a period when vernaculars were coming into common use in academic communication. Thus, French, Italian, and German letters were all "English'd" by Oldenburg for the early *PTRS*, although communications in Latin still appeared mainly in that language.

On the other hand, however, the *PTRS* also succeeded for reasons quite apart from Oldenburg's personal attributes. Thus, publication in the journal as a reliable means of establishing priority and assuring a public audience for discoveries was an irresistible attraction to many; it was largely for these reasons that researchers like Leeuwenhoek and Malphigi reported virtually all their findings in the early *PTRS*. Also crucial was the strong attraction of the Society's identification with the Baconian goal of a cooperatively constructed universal natural history.

Whatever the exact constellation of factors that paved the way for the *PTRS*'s early success—and these are impossible to know with precision—the general sequence of events accompanying its introduction is clear. In the minutes of the Royal Society's council (i.e., its executive body) for March 1, 1665, the order is recorded:

> That the Philosophical Transactions, to be composed by Mr. OLDENBURG, be printed the first Monday of every month, if he have sufficient matter for it; and that the tract be licensed by the council of the society, being first reviewed by one of the members of the same; and that the president be desired now to license the first papers thereof, being written in four sheets in folio, to be printed by JOHN MARTYN and JAMES ALLESTRY, printers to the society. (cited in Andrade, 1965, p. 13)

Subtitled "Giving some ACCOMPT of the Present Undertakings, Studies, and Labours of the INGENIOUS in many considerable Parts of the WORLD," the first issue appeared forthwith on March 6. It began with a dedication by Oldenburg to the Royal Society, in which allusion is made to the notion that the journal was Oldenburg's personal project rather than an official publication of the Society.[9] The Baconian vision of cooperative science is also invoked in Oldenburg's desire "[t]o spread abroad Encouragements, Inquiries, Directions, and Patterns, that may animate, and draw on Universal Assistances." This point is further elaborated upon in Oldenburg's short introduction that follows the dedication.

The issue itself is 16 pages long and contains 10 items of what might loosely be called "scientific news." Three of these report astronomical observations, a fourth describes field tests of pendulum watches, and a fifth provides a brief outline of a book by Boyle. The remaining five items concern topics in 17th-century natural history, including whaling in Bermuda, mining in Germany, and the stillbirth of a monstrous calf. To call any of these short pieces "articles" would be anachronistic—they are more like the digested news items common to the newspapers of the period. Oldenburg's role as compiler and intermediary of these items is plainly evident; except in one case, little of the original authors' language remains.

Following this first issue, the *PTRS* was printed on a mostly monthly basis for the next 12 years. By 1675, however, it had expanded significantly: Issues were now typically 24 pages long, but occasionally ran to 40. In addition, reports had taken on the characteristics of authored articles (cf. Bazerman, 1988, chap. 3)—they were titled and typically presented in the original authors' own words. Substantial book reviews, in most cases written by Oldenburg himself, occupied the latter pages of many issues, although this trend had been well underway by the close of the first volume.[10]

In September 1677, Oldenburg died. The *PTRS* had suspended publication some 3 months previously, and the next issue did not appear until the following February. In the 12 months after that only five issues were published; these were edited by Oldenburg's replacement as Society secretary, Nehemiah Grew, who had sent out a formal request asking Oldenburg's correspondents to continue writing letters. But most of the work eventually published by Grew had been in preparation when Oldenburg died.

From February 1679 to January 1683, the journal was replaced by the *Philosophical Collections,* edited by Robert Hooke (*qua* Society secretary) and composed mostly of correspondence from abroad. Then in 1683 the *PTRS* was reinstated under the Society's new secretary, Robert Plot, and published without interruption until 1687. In that year the journal ceased publication, remaining moribund—a state paralleling the Society's own lack of vitality in these years—until 1690. At that point, the Society determined under new leadership to revive the *PTRS*. It accordingly appeared over the next 4 years under the editorship of then-secretary Richard Waller, but with a much smaller circulation and less frequently than previously. The editorship was then taken over in 1695 by Sir Hans Sloane, who remained editor until 1713 and restored the journal to a generally healthy condition. Except for the notably unstable period of transition from Oldenburg's death to 1690, the journal has remained in continuous publication up to the present day.

THE NEWTONIAN PERIOD AND ITS AFTERMATH: THE ROYAL SOCIETY AND THE *PHILOSOPHICAL TRANSACTIONS*, 1700–1750

Historians of the Royal Society have traditionally treated the 18th and early 19th centuries as an especially undistinguished stage in its institutional genesis and scientific achievement. Thus, Lyons (1944) characterizes this period as one in which most members were not scientists, with the result that comparatively little scientific research was undertaken, or "scientific progress" made. Although assessments like Lyons' are highly anachronistic in that they are based on present-day judgments of what counts as scientific activity, they also contain a kernel of truth. The 18th and early 19th centuries *were* times in which there was significant stability in all areas of the Royal Society, whether leadership, general membership, financing, intellectual interests, scientific activity, or methods of scientific communication. Perhaps as a result, there was little impetus for change.[11]

However, historical descriptions of this period, which began with Newton's election to the Society presidency in 1704, also belie the received view. Thus, Newton and his colleagues revitalized the Royal Society, giving it direction at least until his death in 1727. They did so by taking an active and highly political role in managing the Society, including placing allies in positions of power, underwriting research falling within the Newtonian paradigm, and fomenting opposition within the Society to Newton's competitors on the Continent.

Although the same strong sense of renewal may not have extended to the *PTRS* in this period, Sloane's assumption of the editorship in 1695 brought it the continuity and stability it had lacked since Oldenburg's death. In the 10 years prior to 1695, no single secretary had published more than two volumes in a row, and in many cases they apparently printed whatever came most easily to hand. Like Oldenburg, Sloane was exceptionally energetic, and deeply committed to the success of the Royal Society. Unlike Oldenburg, he was an elite M.D. and an avid natural historian, whose specialty was the collection and classification of plant specimens. Sloane must therefore have brought somewhat different priorities to the editing of the *PTRS*.

Apart from its sporadic appearance in the period preceding Sloane's editorship, one indicator of the journal's poor health had been the decline in foreign contributions. According to Heilbron (1983), articles by non-Englishmen amounted to 40% of the total in the 1660s, but had fallen to 20% by the 1690s. This decline was directly related to the neglect of foreign correspondence by the secretaries following Oldenburg, a problem Sloane immediately set out to solve. Soon, due partly to increasing foreign contributions, the *PTRS* had grown to about three times the number of pages it had contained before Sloane's advent, publishing approximately 400 pages per year through 1700.

Yet although Sloane had restored the *PTRS* to a solid footing by the turn of the century, there was discontent both within and beyond the Royal Society over his editorship. This was made manifest in 1700 with the circulation of an anonymous pamphlet viciously lampooning the journal. Entitled *The Transactioneer with some of his Philosophical Fancies: In Two Dialogues,* and actually written by a non–Royal Society lawyer, William King, it por-

trayed the *PTRS* as a collection of outlandish miscellanea, written in a
confused style. Sloane himself was characterized as a pompous, muddle-
headed collector of natural knickknacks who delighted in obscure speech
and even more obscure writing.

This satire had an apparently strong effect on Sloane and his colleagues
at the Royal Society, perhaps because it carried enough truth to injure.
Sloane *was* a great collector of miscellaneous objects (the British Museum
was later established largely on the basis of his personal collection), and
his impulse to collect without discrimination extended to his editing of the
PTRS.[12] In retaliation, Sloane accused two Royal Society fellows of complicity
in the satire, but they were exonerated by the Society's council. A probable
second effect of the satire was a reduction in the size of the *PTRS* in the
years following 1700; it averaged about half the 400 pages it had for the first
5 years of Sloane's tenure.

An additional (but probably related) problem for Sloane in this period
was his growing conflict with Newtonian elements in the Royal Society. As
a natural historian and avid collector, Sloane's version of science was not
particularly congenial to that of Newton's followers, such as Edmond Halley
and J. T. Desaguliers, who had been given important positions within the
Society's leadership. Sloane's hold on the secretaryship was further weakened in 1709–1710, when King published a second spoof of the *PTRS* and an
unsuccessful attempt was made to remove Sloane from his post. By this
point, Newton himself was reportedly at odds with Sloane, and the latter
was voted out as secretary in 1713 and replaced by Halley.

Sloane's replacement by Halley marks the beginning of a 14-year period
in which the editorship of the journal was controlled by Newtonians. Halley
presided from 1713 to 1721 in what was probably an unremarkable tenure,
since it is given little attention by the Society's chroniclers.[13] The journal
came out on a quarterly basis for most of this period, although Heilbron
(1983, p. 41) suggests that Halley, unlike Sloane, did not use his own financial
resources when necessary to ensure prompt publication.

In 1718 the Society, or elements within it, published a pamphlet designed
to advertise its accomplishments, and to encourage communications from
outside parties.[14] This short work is of much historical interest in that it
indicates what were considered important topics for research and publication in this period. After reminding readers that the Society did not coun-
tenance assertions based on "anything but what ocular demonstration would
allow to be matter of fact, in spite of the hypothetical [i.e., given to groundless
theorizing] influence of Aristotelians, Cartesians, Adepts, Astrologers, and
common Longitudinarians," the pamphlet went on to describe the kinds of
research the Society wanted to encourage:

> It were, therefore, to be wish'd, that such as have Opportunity, Capacities,
> and the Advantage of good Telescopes, would be pleased to communicate all

Astronomical and other Observations, whether of the Spots in the Heart of the Sun, of their situations and variations therein; of their increase and decrease; or of the Nebulae mentioned by that universal scholar, and most acute Philosopher, Dr. Halley, in the *Philosophical Transactions;* of new and strange Stars appearing, or of others disappearing; of Comets, and of all Eclipses, whether of the Sun, Moon, Stars, or Satellites.

No less acceptable would be accurate accounts of all uncommon appearances in the Heavens; such as *Aurorae Boreales,* Thunder and Lightning; particularly noting the time between the *Flash* and the *Crack,* and the like *Phenomenas:* also Registers of Winds and Weather, of the Thermometer and Barometer, of the quantity of Rain that falls upon any space of ground, though but a foot square; of the constant Flux and Reflux of Tides. . . .

All new Discoveries in Natural History would be also very acceptable and desirable; such as good descriptions of Quadrupeds, Birds, Reptiles, Insects, Amphibious Animals, Fish . . . of Plants, Minerals, Fossils, or the like, that are met with but rarely, ill treated by the authors who write of them, or that have hitherto pass'd unregarded; whether they may be of any advantage to man-kind as Food or Physic. . . .

Dissections of Morbid Bodies, whether human or of other Animals, are highly wanted by the Society, with particular Relations of the Parts decay'd or affected; and all Anatomical Discoveries.

New experiments, either in Chymistry, such as those of the learned Dr. Freind . . . or in Pharmacy; such as what Medicines are easily incorporated together, and what not. . . .

Improvements in Agriculture would be in like manner gratefully received, such as the best and most commodious ways to water high grounds, drain the more wet and low, to meliorate the barren, and to enrich even fertile land.

No less valuable would be new Inventions, or Improvements, in Mechanicks, with Descriptions of Machines, Engines, Instruments, or the like; with exact Histories of all sorts of curious and beneficial Trades in any Country. (cited in Weld, 1848, Vol. 1, pp. 425–426)

This list—except for several notable omissions regarding Newtonian subjects such as optics and perhaps electricity—gives an accurate sense of topics studied by members of the Society in this period, and consequently treated in the *PTRS.* Directly following this passage, the pamphlet lists specific papers in the *PTRS* as models of how such research should be written.

In 1721, James Jurin succeeded Halley as editor of the *PTRS.* Even more than Halley, Jurin was a loyal Newtonian: His early work involved improving Newton's edition of a treatise by Varenius, and experimental confirmation of Newton's theory of forces. Besides giving Newtonian science a large place in the *PTRS,* Jurin also supported meteorological research by offering to lend measuring instruments to observers at home and abroad, and encouraged early research on inoculation. His work on the latter subject, as well as that of others, appeared frequently in the *PTRS* in this period.

On March 20, 1727, Newton died. Sloane, who had stayed active in the Society after losing his secretaryship, was chosen interim president. The Newtonians, however, prepared for a fight, and at the annual November elections they put forward Newton's protégé Martin Folkes for president, and Jurin again for secretary. But these candidates were soundly defeated after a tumultuous campaign. Bad feelings were running high, however, and the Society's newly elected council initially refused to give the customary vote of thanks to Jurin for his 7 years of work. Partly in revenge, Jurin dedicated his final volume of the *PTRS* to Folkes, lauding Newton's hand-picked successor for his allegiance to "manly" Newtonian science. Jurin then went on to recapitulate Newton's dismissal of natural history as a science:

> That Great Man was sensible, that something more than knowing the Names, the Shape and obvious Qualities of an Insect, a Pebble, a Plant, or a Shell, was requisite to form a Philosopher, even of the lowest rank. . . . We all of us remember that Saying so frequently in his Mouth, *That Natural History might indeed furnish Materials for Natural Philosophy; but, however, Natural History was not Natural Philosophy;*. . . . It was not that he despis'd so useful a Branch of Learning as *Natural History;* he was too wise to do so: But still he judg'd that this humble Handmaid to Philosophy, tho' she might well be employ'd in amassing Implements and Materials for the Service of her Mistress, yet must very much forget her self, and the Meaness of her Station, if ever she should presume to claim the Throne, and arrogate to her self the Title of the *Queen of the Sciences.* (Preface, 1726–1727; italics in original)

Jurin's immediate successor was William Rutty, but he presided over the editing of only one volume of the *PTRS*. He was replaced in 1730 by Cromwell Mortimer, who, like Jurin and Sloane before him, was a medical doctor, but one more sympathetic to Sloane's scientific interests.

The *PTRS* under Jurin had appeared for the most part either every other month or quarterly, and averaged about 210 pages per year. A single volume appeared every 2 years, with medical, astronomical, and articles on Newtonian subjects predominating. Under Mortimer, however, there was a greater emphasis on natural history and antiquities, at the expense of Newtonian subjects and astronomy; medical articles held steady at around 20% of the total (Potter, 1943, p. 172).

In 1741, Sloane's advancing age forced him to give up the Society presidency, and Folkes was chosen to replace him the following November. Although Folkes had earlier been a follower of Newton and a promising mathematician in his own right, his interests at this point—as demonstrated by the fact that he was simultaneously president of the Society of Antiquaries—were primarily archeological and literary. It was doubtless partly for this reason (as the president held undeniable power in all Society activities throughout the 18th century) that the journal now came under attack once again for the perceived triviality of its contents. This attack appeared in the form of at least two publications: Little is written about the first, but the second, by the apothecary John Hill, came out in 1751 under the title *Review of the Works of the Royal Society of London: Containing animadversions on such of the Papers as deserve Particular Observation*. This work resembled the earlier *Transactioneer* in that it presented summaries of what Hill considered to be "the more trivial and downright foolish articles" (Preface, cited in Stimson, 1968, p. 142) that had appeared in the *PTRS*. Hill also "dedicated" his book to Folkes, laying the blame for the journal's low standards directly at his feet, and repeatedly attacking him in the book's main text.

Once again, sharp public criticism from without appears to have had a strong and immediate effect on the Society. In 1752, the governing council voted to remove the *PTRS* from the stewardship of a single secretary, and to make its editing the direct responsibility of a committee, whose job it was to:

> assemble together and select from the said papers . . . such of them as they should think proper to be printed, and to order that no other papers should be published in the *Philosophical Transactions* than such as shall have been so selected by the said Committee. (Royal Society "Journal-book," cited in Weld, 1848, vol. 1, p. 519)

The Society's president (as chair), vice-president, and secretaries made up the committee's permanent membership, which, along with 18 other members, represented the whole governing council. The expedient of placing the fate of submitted articles into the hands of such a committee—a committee also empowered to refer papers to noncommittee fellows if their expertise was needed—is widely considered to be the first step in the innovation of the modern journal–referee concept.[15]

As mentioned earlier, up to this moment the *PTRS* had been published—at least officially—solely on the private initiative of one of the two Society secretaries (but see note 9). Thus, by directly taking over the journal, the Society was significantly altering its public stance vis-à-vis the *PTRS*. This change was prominently noted in an "Advertisement" published in the *PTRS*'s next volume, which began by offering the official version of the historical relationship between Society and journal:

> the Society, as a body, never did interest themselves any further in their publication, than by occasionally recommending the revival of them to some of their Secretaries, when . . . the *Transactions* had happened for any length of time to be intermitted. (cited in Weld, 1848, vol. 1, p. 520)

It then went on to state a rationale, although an incomplete one given the probable effects of Hill's satire, for the new relationship:

> But the Society being of late years greatly enlarged, and their communications more numerous, it was thought advisable, that a Committee of their Members should be appointed to reconsider the papers read before them, and select out of them such as they should judge most proper for publication in the future *Transactions*. (cited in Weld, 1848, vol. 1, p. 521)

The "Advertisement" also explained that papers were to be judged for publication on the basis of "the importance or singularity of their subjects, or the advantageous manner of treating them" (Weld, 1848, vol. 1, p. 521). As an official statement of the relationship of the Royal Society to its main publication, this short text was reprinted at the beginning of every volume of the journal for the next 205 years, until 1957.

AGE OF STABILITY: THE ROYAL SOCIETY AND THE *PHILOSOPHICAL TRANSACTIONS*, 1753–1820

Although 1752 was an important year for the *PTRS*—the year in which it both officially became a Royal Society publication and began to be edited by committee—this date represents merely an arbitrary (if convenient) break-point in the Society's general history. As mentioned previously, the 18th century was a period of pronounced stability in the Royal Society, a period often characterized as one in which little scientific "progress" was made. But although that characterization was accepted above as having some validity, it was also regarded as having serious drawbacks. In the following paragraphs I attempt to specify these drawbacks, and to describe the Society's 18th-century context in a less anachronistic way.

Like their 17th-century predecessors, 18th-century British scientists were by and large members of the upper classes.[16] Most notable among them were those who pursued science as dedicated amateurs, and, in so doing, made substantial contributions; thus, in the second half of the century the aristocratic Henry Cavendish helped establish the pre-Lavoisierian basis of modern chemistry. More commonly, however, support for science among the upper echelons of society was related to its status as a fashionable and acceptable genteel pastime, and to some degree to faith in the utilitarian ends of such activity. Sustained attention to describing the natural world was, therefore, by no means an expected outcome of gentlemanly scientific pursuits.

The only sense, in fact, in which science could be considered even slightly professionalized in this period was the degree to which it was undertaken by academics, medical doctors, and to some extent public performer–lecturers; Newton's coterie during his presidency of the Royal Society, for instance, came substantially from these three groups. But they were the exceptions—the overall character of the Royal Society strongly reflected the genteel and amateur scientific community at large.

Given, then, this *zeitgeist* of gentlemanly, amateur science—which continued in a gradually weakening form up to and beyond the age of Darwin—it is not legitimate to judge the 18th-century Royal Society in terms of our present-day understanding of "scientific activity" or "scientific progress." By many other measures, the 18th century was a time in which science evolved demonstrably, leading, for example, to the development around the century mark of both modern physics and chemistry. At the same time, however, 18th- and late 20th-century conceptualizations of science diverge substantially, as much perhaps as they overlap.

The Royal Society in the mid-18th century represented a firmly established and by most measures successful cultural institution. Membership was up more than threefold from the beginning of the century (to an average of 510 between 1751 and 1755), the Society was in excellent financial shape, and the *PTRS* had a nearly 60-year record of regular publication and a widespread readership and reputation. The critics' attacks on the journal and the Society (in the person of its president) in the early 1750s had been serious but hardly mortal blows: The shift in editorial responsibility for the journal and Folkes' departure from the presidency brought apparently immediate relief.

Folkes was replaced in 1753 by the Earl of Macclesfield, an aristocrat thought to have been instrumental in bringing about the new editorial policy at the *PTRS* while on the Society's governing council. Macclesfield was himself a practicing mathematician and astronomer, and published papers in the *PTRS* in both areas. He was also a notable patron of individual scientists, the astronomer James Bradley being an early protégé.

The Society launched the first in a long string of government-funded expeditions during Macclesfield's presidency, sending astronomers to two islands in the South Atlantic to observe the 1761 transit of Venus. The use of government money to finance this expedition set a precedent that had profound repercussions in the long term for the professionalization of British science. Other publically financed Society-led expeditions followed in quick succession: a second transit of Venus in 1769; Captain James Cook's first trip to the South Seas in 1772; a naval search for the North Pole in 1773; a large-scale investigation of the earth's magnetic pull on a Scottish mountain in 1774; and Cook's expedition to Hawaii in 1776–1779, during which he lost his life. As this list suggests, these expeditions were motivated substantially by politically and economically inspired empire-building.

Macclesfield died in 1764, and was replaced by another science-minded aristocrat, the Earl of Morton. But Morton held office for only 4 years, being replaced first by a president pro tem, and in the next year by a regularly elected president. This was James West, whose interests tended rather to antiquarianism (he was a notable collector of manuscripts, old coins, and medals) than more purely scientific pursuits. West's interests, in fact, reflected those of a substantial portion of the Society membership at this time, as signified by a broad cross-membership in the Society of Antiquaries (D. P. Miller, 1989). Like Morton before him, however, West held the Presidency for only 4 years, dying in 1772. He was replaced the next year by John Pringle, a well-connected military doctor who was also personal physician to King George III. Pringle continued in the presidency for 6 years.

A major controversy within the Society took place during Pringle's presidency, with the main public forum of debate being the *PTRS*. Because it indicates the vital role of the journal as a medium for scientific debate in the 18th century—and because it exemplifies the sometimes bitter infighting that was a prominent feature of the Society from its beginnings, no matter how "genteel" its character—this controversy is described next.

The origins of the dispute were in a committee, convened by the Royal Society at government request, to determine the best way of protecting government gunpowder magazines from lightning. A leading member of the committee was Benjamin Franklin, who had earlier discovered the protective power of the lightning rod. Franklin believed that pointed rods were far more effective than blunt ones, and when the committee published its report in the *PTRS*, pointed conductors were recommended at all magazine sites. Appended to the report, however, was a vigorous protest by another committee member, Benjamin Wilson, to the effect that pointed conductors in fact *increased* the chances of lightning damage, and Wilson followed up his protest with a separate article in the journal. The ensuing controversy threw the Society into turmoil over the "pointed versus blunt" question, and both weekly meetings and many pages of the *PTRS* were devoted to debating its particulars.

The resolution of this debate took place in 1777. In that year a powder magazine protected by pointed conductors was slightly damaged by lightning, leading Wilson to renew his efforts. He submitted to the government a report of experiments that he took as conclusive proof of his position; but the report was turned over to a newly formed Royal Society committee, which determined against Wilson's findings. At this juncture, the dispute became overtly political, with George III stepping in to declare for Wilson, apparently on the grounds that Franklin was one of the American enemy and therefore not to be trusted. This action brought a formal end to the controversy, but Pringle's resignation shortly thereafter is thought to have indicated the Society's collective unhappiness with the solution.

Pringle was replaced by Joseph Banks, the enormously wealthy scion of an influential land-owning family. Banks had taken part in four voyages of discovery with Cook and others in the 1760s and 1770s, and had a national reputation as a tropical botanist. He was therefore an ideal choice for Royal Society president in both his social status and scientific attainments, though only 35 years old at the time. His subsequent 42-year reign was the longest and probably most influential of any Royal Society president.

Although modern historical scholarship paints differing portraits of Banks, the most common is that of "the autocrat of science." Banks took an active and even intrusive role in all aspects of Royal Society business during his presidency; from the beginning he stacked the Society's ruling council with his supporters, and, perhaps more unusually, took it upon himself to screen candidates for Society membership. He also attempted to suppress certain newly constituted specialist scientific societies, apparently in the belief that they would attract members and support away from the Royal Society.

But Banks' authoritarian actions also reflected the interests of those conservative elements holding ultimate power in both the Royal Society and Britain at this time. Their common source can be seen in the close relationship that developed between Banks and the British government during his presidency, especially in colonial matters. Banks had concerned himself with cataloging potentially exportable plant materials during his early voyages, leading him to become an authority on imperial trade. Along with his elevated social status and Royal Society presidency, this fact propelled Banks in the 1780s and 1790s into the role of indispensible government adviser. As described by Mackay (1985):

> he was virtual director of Kew Gardens [the government-supported botanical gardens in which exotic plant specimens from throughout the empire were kept and studied], he advised the Board of Trade on the supply of cotton, naval stores, explosives and dye-stuffs. He gave advice on the whaling, fishing and textile industries. He played a crucial role in developing new coinage and in organising supplies of grain in times of dearth. In 1797, in recognition of his hitherto unofficial services, he was made a Privy Councillor so that he could regularly serve the Board of Trade and work on its specialist committees. *Banks was the government's foremost adviser on colonial affairs in the period 1780 to 1800* and became the East India Company's acknowledged counsellor on all matters pertaining to botany and vegetable products. No other man outside the government in the last 20 years of the eighteenth century exercised such a pervasive influence over such a wide area of government activity. (p. 22, italics added)

In addition to his service to the government, Banks cultivated his ruling-class connections by awarding positions on the Royal Society's council—an important cultural attainment—to politically powerful individuals. Such influence-peddling helped in turn to ensure the continued success and stability of the Royal Society in what were socially unsettled times. Equally importantly, the government was led to provide relatively generous financial support to Society projects and expeditions.

In 1784, Banks faced a serious challenge to his authority, one that revealed ongoing tensions in the Royal Society between essentially nongenteel Newtonian science and genteel natural history. Banks, after all, was a Baconian, a natural historian of the type that Newtonians had belittled in the first half of the century. Continued adherence to Newtonian science by a minority in the Royal Society therefore created natural opposition to his rule. The initiating event in the controversy was the council's rejection in 1781 of two candidates for Society membership who specialized in mathematics. When several non-Banksian council members objected strenuously, Banks set about having them removed from the council: The first to go was Charles Hutton, the "foreign secretary" in charge of international correspondence. To a person, the offending council members were part of a group of neo-Newtonians who were nongenteel in most cases socially and in all cases scientifically, in the sense that they were professional mathematicians. The nongenteel character of this group, and their supposedly poor behavior in the controversy, became one of Banks' main arguments against his council opponents, and against admitting more such individuals to the Society.[17] In response, the disaffected party leveled a number of charges, one major one being that, because it was composed largely of genteel amateurs:

> [The ruling council in its role as collective *PTRS* editors was] incapable of examining or even perusing the various papers on mathematical, mechanical, astronomical, optical, and chemical subjects, etc. that may come before them. . . . [and under such a council] this house, instead of being a resort of philosophers, [would] become a cabinet of trifling curiosities, and degenerate into a virtuoso's closet decorated with plants and shells. (Glenie, cited in Heilbron, 1993, p. 86)

A number of highly divisive meetings of both the whole Society and its ruling council eventually followed, with a vote of confidence on Banks' presidency being held at one of the former. Although Banks won the vote decisively, he did so at the price of completely alienating the mathematical group, including the Astronomer Royal, Nevil Maskelyne, and both a former and a then-secretary of the Society, Samuel Horsley and Paul Maty, respectively, the latter of whom soon resigned. Although no further challenges of any magnitude were made to Banks during his administration, the attempt to unseat him, and the resurfacing of friction between Newtonians and natural historians, can be seen as precursors of 19th-century moves to alter substantially the scientific character of the Society. Indeed, this very dispute rankled well beyond Banks' tenure, having consequences for Society reform after 1830.

A more protracted (but not unrelated) problem for Banks during his administration was what to do about newly established specialist scientific societies and public scientific institutions. The first of the new societies to be founded was the Linnean Society, established in 1788, whose stated purpose was to focus purely on natural history. This group had many of the same trappings as the Royal Society—a transactions, regular meetings, a largely genteel membership, and an extensive collection of specimens—and Banks was in fact one of its founding members. Its establishment was followed by that of the Royal Institution in 1800; the Horticultural Society in 1804; the Geological Society in 1807; the Society for Animal Chemistry in 1809; and the Astronomical Society in 1820.

In the first, second, and fourth cases, Banks again took an apparently supportive role. Thus, he was present at the founding of the Royal Institution, whose aim was the application of scientific findings to practical problems, although a contemporary observer also recorded a "violent attack" by Banks against the concept; and the Society for Animal Chemistry was established as an affiliate, or "assistant," society of the Royal Society. In the third and fifth cases, however, Banks vehemently opposed foundation.

In the case of the Geological Society, Banks' opposition was brought on partly by the failure of a plan to make the newer society an affiliate of the Royal Society. But it was also the by-product of a split among the Geological Society's founders regarding whether to follow a more genteel-style, natural history-type agenda with practical goals (known as "mineral history"), or a specialist program based on an independent science of geology (Rudwick, 1963).

In the case of the Astronomical Society, which was founded in the final year of his life, Banks declared that it would be "the ruin of the Royal Society," and actively discouraged two leading Royal Society members from taking up its presidency. This opposition was in no small part due to the fact that the Astronomical Society was dominated by neo-Newtonians, but can perhaps be more generally attributed to the fact that, like the Geological Society, the Astronomical Society represented a substantially independent structure. That is, both the Geological and Astronomical Societies were made up of individuals who, although they may often have held membership simultaneously in the Royal Society, were unlikely to share its vision of genteel, amateur, basically nonspecialist science. Nor—at least in the case of the Astronomical Society—did these individuals share the primary interest of Banks and many other Royal Society fellows: natural history. The establishment of independent specialist societies can therefore be seen as an important development in the evolution of British science.

One major point of contention between Banks and the newly formed specialist societies was the latters' desire to publish their own "Transactions." The Linnean Society had done so from the start with Banks' blessing, while the Society for Animal Chemistry published its research in the *PTRS*. But the right to publish independently had been a point of continuous wrangling with the Geological Society, and to a lesser extent the Astronomical. In negotiations with Banks, the former's organizers would not agree to give up their plans to publish their own separate and independent transactions, although they assented to giving the Royal Society the right of first refusal of all scientific papers sent them. This plan, however, was not adopted, and the *Transactions of the Geological Society* came out as an independent journal starting in 1811. One effect of the new journals, according to A. B. Granville in his 1830 critique, was that relatively fewer papers on zoological, geological, and astronomical topics were published in the *PTRS* in the first 30 years of the 19th century, and none whatsoever (by Granville's count) on botany.

Like its parent society, the *PTRS* itself maintained a notably stable existence between 1750 and 1820, although it showed a gradual overall increase in number of pages printed per year. And whereas before midcentury the journal had produced full volumes only every other year, by 1763 volumes were regularly being issued on a yearly basis.

In terms of content in the second half of the century, the journal leaned somewhat more toward natural history than it had in the first half, with medical case reports being featured with almost equal prominence as formerly, and astronomy and other Newtonian subjects also appearing regularly. Electricity in particular was a common topic, as were earthquakes, the discovery of Herculaneum, and the transits of Venus. Carter (1988, p. 572) gives figures indicating that 72% of articles printed in the *PTRS* between 1781 and 1820 were on "nonbiological" topics, while the remaining 28% were on "biological" topics, but such statistics may mask considerable variability in preferred topics across time. Moreover, Carter's assignment of papers to the categories "biological" and "nonbiological"—a division of scientific endeavor that did not actually obtain at the time—compels caution in the interpretation and use of such statistics.[18]

M. B. Hall (1984a) gives this useful description—based on a review of records kept during Committee of Papers meetings—of how the *PTRS* was edited in the period preceding the 1830s:

> [The Committee] met regularly (usually half a dozen times a year between January and July) and kept careful minutes which show that all papers received serious consideration, and by no means all the papers read at meetings were thought worthy of publication. Those rejected were usually either irrelevant or trivial: the Society never took seriously the seemingly endless stream of English and foreign papers and letters offering solutions to such problems as the trisection of the angle, the quadrature (squaring) of the circle or perpetual motion, although some hopefuls wrote in the belief that the Society offered premiums for such solutions; nor did it accept naive accounts of 'monstrous births' as mere objects of curiosity. (pp. 9–10)

A count of papers considered for publication in the *PTRS* for the 3 years 1824–1826 reveals that, of the 37 papers considered on average per year, just under 27 were printed, while approximately 9 were determined unpub-lishable. These three volumes of the *PTRS* therefore had an average rejec-tion rate of just over 23% (cf. note 28 for rough corroboration of this statistic in the period 1800–1830).[19] This figure should certainly not be taken, how-ever, to mean that the Society viewed submissions as in direct competition with one another; as mentioned in the previous quotation, papers were denied a place in the journal only when judged seriously wanting from a "scientific" point of view.[20] As in most other periods of the Society's history, the *PTRS* therefore fulfilled more the function of a proceedings/transactions-type publication—as a record of Society goings-on—than that of a modern-day, competitive scientific journal.

"THE TROUBLES" AND THEIR RESOLUTION: THE ROYAL SOCIETY AND THE *PHILOSOPHICAL TRANSACTIONS,* 1820–1850

At the death of Joseph Banks in June 1820, the Royal Society suddenly found itself in an unstable situation. There was a staunch establishment composed of members who either actively or tacitly supported a Banksian view of gentlemanly science, while against them were arrayed at least two disaf-fected factions. These were comprised, roughly, of members of the Astro-nomical Society (itself made up of two groups of mathematical physicists, one from Cambridge and the other from London) and Geological Society, respectively. Of these, the mathematical faction supported, at least to some degree, a *professionalized* (and to that degree nongenteel) version of science based on a Continental model, while both groups proclaimed their right to pursue research exclusively in their own specialties. Additionally, in the case specifically of the London faction of the Astronomical Society, there were grievances going all the way back to the 1784 incident, described previously. Over the next 15 years, increasing tensions between these groups and the conservative party in the Society were acted out in sometimes dramatic fashion, while over the approximately 15 years following that the tensions were significantly resolved. By the 1850s, the Royal Society repre-sented a rather different institution—at least in terms of its overall purpose and goals—than it had at Banks' death.

In keeping with his iron-fisted administration of the Society, Banks had provided for a wealthy protégé, Davies Gilbert, to be appointed president on his death. Gilbert, however, was opposed by many Society members including the two minority factions mentioned above, who instead threw their support to W. H. Wollaston, a Society stalwart and well-known fellow of the Geological Society with unimpeachable scientific credentials. Wollas-ton, however, agreed to fill the position only until the next regular election in November. A third candidate for the presidency (among several others) had been Humphry Davy, one of the outstanding scientists of his time and himself a protégé of Gilbert. Representing something of a compromise candidate, Davy was again put forward in November, and after a period of uncertainty was elected.[21]

Unlike most of the conservative supporters of Banksian science in the Royal Society, Davy was a self-made man. He had begun as a surgeon's apprentice, but early brilliance in the study of chemistry enabled him to procure a lectureship (and later more important positions) at the Royal Institution. Despite being in this way a nongenteel *professional* scientist, however, Davy also relied heavily on the patronage of several influential gentlemen; and his marriage to a wealthy, aristocratic widow helped to cement these upper-class connections. Still, Davy's working-class pedigree and status as a professional scientist made him something of an unknown quantity on assuming the Society presidency in 1820.

Davy started well: In his first annual address to the fellows he pledged noninterference and cooperation with the specialist societies, and moved quickly to bring members of the Cambridge group of mathematical physicists and (to a lesser extent) the Geological Society back into the fold. Thus, Charles Babbage, Francis Baily, John Herschel, and James South—all radically disaffected members who advocated purging the Society of "nonscientific" members—were soon included for the first time on the Society's ruling council, with Herschel being elevated to a Society secretaryship in 1824. Davy also made an important symbolic move in the direction of the London mathematicians: He asked Charles Hutton, whose removal by Banks in the 1784 incident had been a perennial rallying point for dissent, to rejoin the council, even though Hutton was old and in failing health.

Other reform-minded steps taken early in Davy's administration included restricting new membership so that scientific attainment became a more important criterion for membership. Steps were also taken to restructure two quasi-governmental bodies overseen by Royal Society appointees that had been under heavy criticism, the Royal Observatory and the Board of Longitude. But when little substantial progress resulted from any of these moves, disaffection in the Society grew even stronger.

Most of the above-mentioned steps was taken early in Davy's tenure; as his presidency progressed, however, it became clear that Davy also identified significantly with the genteel, conservative party in the Society. Thus, he was seen to depend increasingly on this group's patronage to gain government financial support for the Society, and his appointments to posts in the Society hierarchy suggested that Davy favored personal patronage over scientific attainment. By 1826, the opposition was once again seriously aggrieved, and in the following year Davy resigned.

Starting with the election of Gilbert as Davy's successor, inter-party dissension within the Royal Society came gradually to a head. Gilbert had been appointed to fill out Davy's term until the year's annual elections, but did not himself appear to be in the running for the presidency. Instead, he put forward Sir Robert Peel, momentarily out of political office, as his candidate. In the final days before the election, however, Gilbert apparently convinced Peel to revoke his candidacy, threw his own hat into the ring, and was easily elected.[22]

Gilbert's presidency was rocky from the start. He disbanded a council committee looking into electoral reform in the Society and, probably as a result, Herschel quickly resigned his secretaryship. As the main leader of the more powerful of the two disaffected factions, Hershel's resignation was a bad sign. A second significant problem arose in 1828 regarding the awarding of the recently instituted Royal Medals, which were to be given (at least nominally) "for the most important discoveries or series of investigations" conducted in the past year. When members of the Astronomical Society proposed the work of an exceptional young German scientist, the council first voted to give him the medal, but then retracted its decision and awarded it to Wollaston instead. Once again, the Royal Society establishment was seen by its critics as an oligarchical gentlemen's club, based on personal relationships and ignorant or uncaring of what constituted real science.

Other problems added to the tension: The fate of the quasi-governmental Board of Longitude and allegations of the scientific uselessness of its *Nautical Almanac* were among the more serious. In 1829, there also commenced a series of public attacks against the Royal Society in the print media. These initially concerned the election to the Society of an allegedly incompetent M.D., but were quickly widened to criticize the power of various Society constituencies, including medical men.[23] At the same time, members especially of the Astronomical Society increased the volume of their criticism that British science in general, and the Royal Society in particular, were in a sorry state. In this atmosphere, Charles Babbage's *Reflections on the Decline of Science in England* was published in 1830.

Babbage's book—a combination of well-known grievances against the Royal Society and wild personal attacks against certain members—brought the rift among the Society membership clearly into public focus, with immediate effect. Thus, members of the ruling council moved to expel Babbage from the Society, but could not find sufficient support. In response, Babbage demanded that all discussion concerning his expulsion be expunged from the minutes of the meeting in which it took place—this also came to nothing. Charges and countercharges, praise and blame were bandied back and forth by Society members in the press, and reports were leaked of council meetings in which reforms were debated (the meetings being closed to all but council members). When canvassing got underway for the annual November election, Society members steeled themselves for a divisive campaign.

The establishment's proposed candidate in the 1830 presidential election was Augustus Frederick, the Duke of Sussex, younger brother of King George IV. Sussex was a perfect candidate in the conservative, gentlemanly tradition—powerful by virtue of his royal blood and therefore sure to have influence with the government, courtly, above politics, and a patron of the arts and science. Gilbert and those surrounding him believed that, because of his exalted position, Sussex would proceed unchallenged in the election. They also believed that, once elected, he would serve but a figurehead role, with Gilbert managing the Society from behind the scenes.

On November 4, a letter was presented to the council demanding that secret correspondence between Gilbert and certain council members be made available to the letter's 33 signatories—the subject of these communications was proposed personnel changes on the council after the elections. The council acceded to this demand and a meeting was held to view and discuss the letters, resulting in a resolution that new council members be chosen solely for their scientific attainments. More charges and counter-charges followed this meeting, including two publications by members which, although they disagreed on a solution, both portrayed the Society as badly out of date and needing reform.[24]

Much to the distress of Gilbert and his followers, and in spite of their candidate's special status, Herschel was put forward as an opposition candidate for the presidency (cf. note 21). In a highly charged election, Sussex received 119 votes to Herschel's 111, leaving the defeated party bitterly denouncing the outcome as the death of British science. At the same time, Sussex began a presidency which was notable for its steady, if slow, efforts at bringing rapprochement among the warring groups in the divided Society.

Little if any constitutive change came out of the new president's 8-year tenure. Rather, a gradual shift in power took place due to an enlightened policy of inclusiveness on the part of Sussex and a combination of other factors including generational change, the founding of a powerful new scientific institution—the British Association for the Advancement of Science (BAAS)—and the influence of much larger political currents of democracy and reform.

Sussex, for his part, revealed a desire to share power that was distinctly lacking in his predecessors. Thus, whereas earlier presidents had appointed only two vice-presidents per year, and from among their strongest supporters, he chose six from the widest spectrum of council members. He also made the council more representative of the Royal Society rank-and-file, including on it a large number of Herschel's supporters. Even more power devolved on the vice-presidents and council after 1834, when Sussex was unable to attend most meetings due to poor health. Perhaps most importantly, reports of Society meetings—including detailed, still-private reports of all council meetings—were for the first time published, giving the Fellows at large a sense of involvement and influence they had earlier lacked.

The BAAS was founded in September 1831 partly as an alternative organization for disaffected members of the Royal Society. Although it changed in character over the next few years, the Association's early identity as a refuge for alienated Society fellows took some of the pressure for immediate reform off the Society, providing a space in which important changes could come about more deliberately.[25] The BAAS also gave something of a scientific voice to members of the rising mercantile and professional classes, and thereby defused some of the class conflict underlying the issue of amateurs versus professionals in the Royal Society. At the same time, however, the Royal Society and the BAAS maintained good relations, as well as a significantly overlapping membership.[26]

Finally, the larger context of national politics and political reform must be considered when describing change within the Royal Society at this juncture. European politics in general was progressing fitfully toward democratization in the first half of the 19th century, and this movement was reflected in all facets of British political life. Thus, the Reform Act of 1832—a milestone in the development of the present British political system—was passed after years of struggle and agitation, and more radical currents of change like the Chartist movement began to appear at this time. As a member of Parliament, Sussex's predecessor Gilbert had staked his career on opposing all such liberalization by and within the government, just as he had opposed liberalizing reforms within the Royal Society.[27] Sussex, on the other hand, sympathized with moderate political reform, although as a royal family member he was not permitted to give his political feelings free rein.

In a notably uneventful election for the period, Sussex was succeeded in 1838 by another member of the royal family, Spencer Compton, the 2nd Marquis of Northampton. Northampton had been recommended by the council, was supported across the board by the Society membership, and so was elected, in effect, without opposition. The Society of which he was elected president, however, was in important ways in transition relative to the one inherited by his predecessor. By the late 1830s, it was widely accepted that serious reform was imminent, especially regarding the importance of scientific attainment as a criterion for membership and the absolute power of the president.

Although there were minor moves toward reform in the early 1840s, the pace of change began to quicken in 1846. In the spring of that year the council appointed a committee to review the Society's royal charter, and to recommend changes as needed. The committee came back with one major recommendation: to limit the election of new members to 15 a year, with prospective candidates first being screened by the council and then voted on by the Society at large. This was seen as an indirect way of preventing nonscientists from joining the Society—an uncomplicated alternative to changing the Society's charter. The recommendation was soon adopted by the council, as was a separate proposal that, along with 10 alternates, the list of current council members be submitted to a vote of the whole Society during the annual elections. In a single year, two reforms long sought by Society members had come about at last.

The *PTRS* under Banks, like the Royal Society in general, had enjoyed a period of stability and prosperity. In some senses it continued to do so from 1820 to 1850, although it, too, eventually came in for its share of criticism and controversy. In 1820, the *PTRS* was nominally under the editorship of Taylor Combe, an antiquarian and the last of several secretaries to hold office simultaneously in the Royal Society, the Society of Antiquaries, and the British Museum. At the same time, the Society's Committee of Papers— wholly coterminous with the ruling council, as mentioned above—had effective control over what was published. This state of affairs led to strong criticism from numerous individuals, only some of whom can be identified as Society reformers. Two problems noted, for example, by A. B. Granville in his *Science Without a Head, or The Royal Society Dissected* (1830/1969) were that papers submitted to the *PTRS* were judged by committee members with no expertise on the papers' topics, and that the committee as a whole never explained why papers had been rejected. These problems led, in Granville's view, to the loss by the *PTRS* of many scientifically worthy reports.[28] Another criticism voiced by Granville was that very few of the Society's members had in fact published in the *PTRS*, and could not therefore be considered real scientists.

Reforms that took place in the Society between 1830 and 1850 therefore also encompassed the *PTRS* to some degree. Thus, probably in response to critics like Granville, the selection procedure for papers was modified in 1831 to include more direct recourse to outside referees. According to Moore (1995), the new procedure stipulated that:

> those [papers] failing to gain a majority vote on two meetings of the Committee were rejected, but the Committee could call upon any Fellow to present a written report to assist the process of deliberation before the second meeting. This system of assessment commenced in December 1831, and soon became the norm for most papers. (p. 26)

Then in 1838 seven "sectional committees" covering the main areas of scientific activity were appointed, and these committees assumed the all-important task of refereeing papers.[29] But this latter system lasted only a decade, finally collapsing under the gravity of charges that several of the committees were hopelessly biased. A major scandal concerning the awarding of the Royal Medals (another task of the sectional committees) and involving P. M. Roget, one of the two secretaries of the Society, added circumstantial weight to these attacks.

In 1832, an initiative was undertaken by the Society that eventually had significant consequences for the *PTRS*. In that year the *Proceedings of the Royal Society* was first published, incorporating Society news and the abstracts of papers published in the *PTRS*, starting retrospectively with the year 1800. Over the next approximately 75 years the *Proceedings* developed into a scientific journal in its own right, although without fully losing its function as a Society news organ. Obituaries, medal awards, and meeting minutes were published in the *Proceedings,* along with abstracts, research notes, shorter articles, and articles otherwise thought unfit for the *PTRS*.

STABILITY REGAINED: THE ROYAL SOCIETY AND THE *PHILOSOPHICAL TRANSACTIONS,* 1848–1900

Northampton resigned the presidency of the Society in 1848, with no stated preference for a successor. At the full Society's request Herschel was quickly approached, but his response was negative. The next petitioned accepted, however: William Parsons, 3rd Earl of Rosse, a nobleman in the conservative presidential mold but also a serious astronomer. But unlike past presidents, Rosse assumed the presidency of a Royal Society in which the council had a much expanded role. Of almost equal importance, therefore, was the choice of a new secretary—this was Thomas Bell, a physiologist whose election has been taken to represent "a spontaneous demand for more official recognition of biological subjects" (M. B. Hall, 1984a, p. 91), as the other secretary at the time was a practicing physicist.

Rosse's presidential tenure, which lasted until 1856, was marked by no single great event. At the same time, the council's newfound power caused the president and some conservative members discomfort: Rosse's choice for at least one important position in the Society, for example, was turned down, and his desire to include politically influential nonscientists on the council was disappointed. The heyday of political patronage, which Banks had institutionalized so successfully in the Royal Society, was now past, although the practice of coopting aristocracy at the presidential level was still pursued.

The next president, John, Baron Wrottlesley, was a nobleman astronomer much like his predecessor, although Wrottlesley had played an important role in the Astronomical Society when many of its members were in full voice for reform in the Royal. His presidential tenure was shorter than Rosse's—from 1854 to 1858—but more lively. One major event involved controversy over the Government Grant, in retrospect a monumentally important development in British science as it represented the first fully institutionalized government support of that science. Strictly speaking, the Grant had been established in 1850 at the amount of £1000 per year for the Society to distribute among researchers, but apparently for a limited period and with an underspecified purpose. Wrottlesley was instrumental in turning a temporary beneficence into a permanent fund by arguing against government opposition that the Grant played a critical role in encouraging scientific research. Together with the later Government Fund, the Grant supported 2,314 research projects by 938 scientists between 1849 and 1914 (MacLeod, 1971), when it was superceded by a more modern system of professional funding.

Wrottlesley was replaced in 1858 by a well-known surgeon and chemist, Benjamin Brodie, but Brodie was forced to retire after 3 years due to poor health. Some wrangling over competing candidates took place prior to the next election, with the nonaristocratic and more scientifically distinguished candidate, General Sir Edward Sabine, being elected. Sabine presided for 10 years (1861–1871) over the Society in what was generally a peaceful period, although there was once again tension between president and council over presidential prerogatives of appointment. When Sabine retired in 1871, it was partly at the behest of the council, who felt he had stayed in office too long. In the same year the council considered, but did not adopt, a resolution to limit future presidents to 5 years in office; despite this formal rejection, the sentiment for term limitations was clear, and Sabine was the last president to hold office for more than 5 years.

Sabine's replacement was George Biddell Airy, Astronomer Royal, who resigned after 2 years, citing the pressure of his other professional commitments. Airy was the last in the "elder statesman" mold to hold the presidency in the 19th century, which henceforth fell to younger men nearly all from the postreform generation. From 1885 on they were, in addition, all professional scientists, including two great ones—Kelvin and Lister—T. H. Huxley having also served in this period. The presidency they assumed also continued to change as described previously, becoming more of a figurehead position, with the actual management of the Society falling increasingly to its council and officers. Society politics was generally peaceful at this time, although accusations arose in the press regarding favoritism toward the Society's "biological" side, the apparent successor to the natural historians, at least in some critics' eyes. Numerous personal attacks and complaints about publication practices were also heard in this period, but had little serious impact.

As admission to the Society had become more desirable across the first half of the 19th century, and while there were still no strict standards for membership or annual limits on new inductees, the number of members had steadily risen, reaching a peak of 771 by 1846. The reforms of that year had the immediate effect of halting this rise, and by 1860 the total was down to 630 and still falling.[30] Lyons (1944) gives an interesting breakdown of the membership into "scientific" and "nonscientific" fellows in this period, finding the former in the majority for the first time in 1860, having increased by 117 since 1830 to 330, while the nonscientific fellows had decreased by 146 to 300.[31] At the same time, Galton (1874/1970; cited in MacLeod, 1983, note 111), in an analysis of 180 Society fellows alive in 1874, found that 120 of them came from only 13 well-to-do families, thus substantiating the belief that the Royal Society remained a haven for gentleman scientists.

An important development in this era was the establishment in 1877 of the Government Fund. A government commission, the Royal Commission for Scientific Instruction and the Advancement of Science, had finished its 5-year period of study in 1875, and its final report included a recommendation to increase the level of government funding for scientific individuals and institutions. Given that an ideology of extreme individualism had dominated British science up to at least 1850, however, this proposal was by no means supported in all quarters. The former Society president and still Astonomer Royal Airy, for example, stated the genteel/conservative but still popular view that:

> Successful researches have in nearly every instance originated with private persons, or with persons whose positions were so nearly private that the investigators acted under private influence, without the danger attending connection with the State. Certainly I do not consider a Government is justified in endeavouring to force, at public expense, investigations of undefined character, and, at best, of doubtful validity: and I think it probable that any such attempt will lead to consequences disreputable to science. (cited in MacLeod, 1971, p. 340)

The commission's recommendation was nonetheless adopted by the government, and the Royal Society was again given a major role in administering the funds—originally set at £4000 per annum. Competition for this money in the form of grants and stipends increased greatly in the next few years, with a disproportionate amount going to London-based members of the Royal Society. Like the smaller Government Grant, the Government Fund was continued up to 1914.

Regarding the history of the *PTRS* in the second half of the 19th century, there was substantial activity and change. Some of these developments concerned the growing number of papers read at meetings and submitted for publication to the Society, and others related to the reforms introduced before 1850.

One early change indirectly concerning the role of the journal in the Society was that, after about 1840, prior publication in the *PTRS* became an important criterion for membership. This development is in keeping with the Society's evolution into an organization of full-time scientists. It can be seen in the treatment of the certificates of application that members filed on behalf of candidates—those stating that candidates were *PTRS* authors usually stood the best chance of being approved (Crosland, 1982). A modification made to the statutes of the Society in 1834 had also served to distinguish authors from nonauthors; starting in that year new Fellows were charged £60 to join the Society if they had not published in the journal, but only £40 if they had. Although this policy was given up in 1871, a "P" continued to be printed in membership lists next to the names of fellows who had contributed to the journal until 1887.

As mentioned previously, the Royal Society's *Proceedings* had been established in 1832 as an organ for circulating abstracts of papers and reporting Society news. By the early 1850s, full papers began to be published in the *Proceedings,* although news and abstracts also continued to appear there. Over the next two decades the *Proceedings* gradually became the main outlet for shorter papers and those of less scientific interest or originality, the last of these criteria, especially, being a common focus of referees' comments when directing a paper to the *Proceedings* instead of the *PTRS.* Eventually, however, a paper's length became the main criterion by which its place of publication was decided.[32]

Statistics based on submission records for 1874–1876[33] show an average of just under 97 papers submitted for publication yearly. Of these, approximately 62 were accepted for the *Proceedings*, and 22 for the *PTRS.* Just under 10 manuscripts per year were archived, withdrawn, or returned to their authors or communicators (nonfellows had to submit their papers through a member–communicator), while just under 4 papers per year had no decision recorded for them or were unclassifiable. These averages reveal three key developments in the Society's publications in the latter part of the 19th century: (a) the extreme growth in numbers of paper submissions, such that almost three times more were submitted in 1874–1876 than in 1824–1826; (b) that the *Proceedings* was now publishing the lion's share of submissions to the Society, outdistancing the *PTRS* by approximately three-to-one; and (c) that many fewer papers were being rejected than had been earlier in the century, when the *PTRS* was the only vehicle of Royal Society publication. Thus, whereas about 23% of the papers considered for publication had been rejected in 1824–1826, only 10% fell into this category from 1874–1876. Among other things, these findings indicate that, while the two Society publications were still functioning together as proceedings-type records of current Society activity, the *Proceedings* took on a relatively greater part of this role, with the *PTRS* tending to be reserved for papers which were special in some way.

In 1887, an important change in the printing of the *PTRS* was effected, although the idea had been aired by the then-president, Joseph Hooker, at least 12 years earlier. In this year the journal was divided into two sections, each published under separate cover: the *Philosophical Transactions A* series, representing "Mathematical and physical papers," and the *Philosophical Transactions B* series, comprising "Biological papers"—the journal has continued in this format up to the present day. A second major change took place in 1896, when the manuscript review process was once again handed over to sectional committees. Two years later, it was agreed that the names of paper referees would no longer be kept in the Society journal book, thereby ensuring the anonymity of reviewers.

MODERNITY: THE ROYAL SOCIETY AND THE *PHILOSOPHICAL TRANSACTIONS* IN THE 20TH CENTURY

Although the character of the Royal Society had evolved in the 19th century from one in which amateur scientists and gentlemen prevailed to one in which bona fide scientific credentials (as we understand science today) were the key to entry, the nature of this change was gradual and smooth rather than radical and discontinuous. Such ongoing "conservative change" (see chap. 6) has had notable consequences for the Society, leading it to retain in the present century at least some of its former character. Lord Todd, Royal Society president from 1975 to 1979, for example, remembered the late 1930s as a time when:

> the Royal Society seemed like a rather exclusive gentlemen's club where occasional rather ill-attended meetings were held at which short scientific papers were read and after which the Fellows dined together at the Royal Society Club. ("Anniversary Address," 1979; cited in Rowlinson & Robinson, 1992, p. 29)

This description was intended partly to show how far the Society had come in the intervening years. Todd's successor Florey, however, appears to have been altogether less confident that such progress had in fact been made: He is said to have remarked that he was "not so highbrow as my predecessors," and that one goal of his presidency was "to carry the Royal Society kicking and screaming into the 20th century" (Rowlinson & Robinson, 1992, p. 11).[34]

Statements such as these point to the continuing conservative nature of the Society in the 20th century, including its ongoing identification with elite interests. The latter is also patent in the growing relationship between the British government and the Society during the present century, a relationship that can partly be quantified in economic terms.

From 1876 to 1900, the Society had received a steady £5000 from the government as an annual grant-in-aid (administered in two parts, as described in the previous section). In 1920 this total was increased to £6000, but it was not until 1939, under the pressure of British entry into World War II and the attendant need for war-related research, that the amount increased substantially, this time to £15,500. By 1980, however, £3.72 million was being contributed annually by the government; by 1990 the corresponding amount was £11.64 million; and, in the last budget available at the time of writing (1995–1996) the amount was at £21.28 million. This striking infusion of public monies into an organization that earlier prided itself on its autonomy and collective free thinking has obviously brought with it profound change.

Even prior to substantial increases in government funds, however, the Royal Society was assuming a larger role in scientific administration at the government's behest. Thus, above and beyond its continuing role as extraordinary government consultant and advisor, the Society took on the management of the newly established National Physical Laboratory in 1900, and had direct or indirect executive functions in many of the major public scientific institutions of Britain: the Imperial College of Science and Technology (established 1905); the Medical Research Council (established 1913); the Department of Scientific and Industrial Research (DSIR, established 1915); and the Advisory Council on Scientific Policy (founded in 1940). The latter two bodies were fully integrated into the government bureaucracy, and in them the Royal Society was especially influential; thus, seven of the eight original members of the DSIR's Advisory Council were Royal Society fellows, with all members being "appointed by the lord president [of the Privy Council], acting for the government, after consultation with the president of the Royal Society" (Alter, 1986, p. 208). In the case of the Advisory Council on Scientific Policy, three of the six original members were Society officers.

The founding of the National Physical Laboratory (NPL) in 1900 marked a crucial event in the developing symbiosis of government and scientific communities in 20th-century Britain (Alter, 1986, chap. 3; Moseley, 1978). Given the *laissez-faire* attitude of the British government throughout much of the 19th century, and the staunch ideology of independence and self-sufficiency both within and beyond the Royal Society at that time, it is not surprising that this new relationship was a difficult one. In fact, the Society relinquished full control over the NPL in 1918, citing insufficient support by the government, while maintaining supervision of the laboratory's scientific efforts. Extreme disagreement surfaced again between the two parties during the interwar years, this time over support for basic research in the NPL. Nevertheless, a new and different relationship between government and science had been irreversibly established with the founding of the NPL.

At the same time as it was being assigned increased administrative duties by the government, the Society was also filling the role, much more than previously, of Britain's national science academy. This function became especially prominent following World War II, with the growth of international bodies like the United Nations and Common Market. The Royal Society was in fact one of the chief agitators for a UNESCO-type organization within the UN, which in an earlier conception had not included science at all; at the latter's founding in 1947, the Royal Society became its official cooperating body for Britain. In the preceding year, and supported by government funds, the Society sponsored the enormous Empire Scientific Conference, bringing scientists from the current and former British colonies together with their British counterparts for several weeks of meetings in London. In 1953, the European Organization for Nuclear Research (or CERN, best known for its later discoveries in high-energy physics) was founded with the crucial support of the Society, while over the next 30 years the Society established formal relationships and academic exchanges with national scientific academies in a number of nations. The Royal Society has therefore taken on the character of a supernational scientific body in the 20th century, while in no way relinquishing its guiding role in British science.

The Society's journals have likewise undergone substantial development in the 20th century, while remaining part of a long-lived and conservative tradition. In 1905, the division of labor between the *Proceedings* and the *PTRS* was finally formalized: The *Proceedings* printed shorter scientific papers up to 24 pages, and the *PTRS* printed longer and more elaborate papers, especially those with lots of illustrations (see note 32). Also at the same time, the *Proceedings* was divided into two series along the lines adopted for the *PTRS* almost 20 years earlier, Series A carrying "Mathematical and physical papers," and Series B, "Biological papers." At this point, the two journals in a sense became one by dividing the labor of printing original research more or less equally between them, all papers continuing to be refereed by sectional committees reporting to the Committee of Papers.

Further important changes in both journals' modes of publication have taken place in more recent years. In 1968, responsibility for refereeing papers and recommending publication was removed from the various sectional committees, which had operated in that capacity continuously since 1896. In their place, the two Society secretaries—the nominal (and technical) editors of the Society's journals, as previously—were assigned a cadre of specialist associate editors to assist them. This arrangement lasted for just 15 years, however; in 1983 two full-time editors were appointed, one each for the A and B sides of the journals. Additionally, the Committee of Papers was dissolved in 1989, and new bylaws were adopted which stipulated a set term and payment for the editors, and the appointment (and payment) of editorial boards to assist them.

Finally and most recently, it has been announced that starting in July 1997 "research papers will no longer be accepted for consideration in *Philo-*

sophical Transactions B. Instead they will be transferred for consideration by the Editor of *Proceedings* B" *(PTRS* Series B, 1997, p. 255). Instead, *PTRS* B will become a vehicle for printing theme-based series of review articles, or "monographs on a single topic" (p. 255), as well as continuing to publish research papers presented in special Discussion meetings in which experts in particular areas come together in a seminar format. For its part, *Proceedings* B will consider for publication all regularly submitted research papers, but these will be limited in most cases to a maximum length of seven pages, with an option of accompanying appendices being made available via the Internet. This decision, by which the two journals "will adopt clearly separated tasks" (p. 255), also extends to the *PTRS* and *Proceedings* A series.

Statistics drawn from the most recent available publication records of the Society indicate striking developments in numbers of submissions to the journals as compared with the years 1874–1876, while rejection rates remained approximately the same.[35] For the 3 years from 1957 to 1959, approximately 325 papers were submitted for consideration per year, with 289 being accepted. Approximately 30 papers were withdrawn yearly, and 7 papers per year had no decision recorded for them or were unclassifiable. Although these averages mask extreme variation in terms of the numbers of papers submitted in the A versus B series (240 for Series A vs. 85.6 for Series B) and accepted by them for publication (A: 217.3; B: 71.6), they do indicate vastly increased submissions, more than three times the number received by the combined journals in 1874–1876. At the same time, overall rejection rates have held steady—at 9% in 1957–1959 (vs. 10% in 1874–1876).[36]

Despite these changes, however, the *PTRS* and *Proceedings* have managed to maintain a not-insignificant place in current science. Thus, measurements based on the Science Citation Index show that the *Proceedings* was the 20th most highly cited scientific journal for the year 1969, and the 32nd most highly cited journal for 1974 (Garfield, 1976, 1977b). Although the *PTRS* itself is not listed among the top 150 journals in this regard, it still maintains an important place in specific fields, as 40th on the list of scientific journals most frequently cited in 1981 by "core" earth sciences journals (Garfield, 1983), 56th on the list of journals most cited by journals of geology and geophysics from 1961 to 1972 (Garfield, 1977a), and as one of the "top 30 significant journals of mathematics" for the year 1974 (Garfield, 1976).

SUMMARY: THE *PHILOSOPHICAL TRANSACTIONS* OF THE *ROYAL SOCIETY* TRADITION IN CONTEXT

In this chapter, I have attempted to provide both a broad historical background for and more specific information regarding the *PTRS* tradition of the Royal Society of London. The journal has evolved over the last 328 years in tandem with its parent Royal Society and British science as a whole. It was begun under the aegis of Baconian science by Henry Oldenburg, and for much of the 17th and 18th centuries reported an eclectic mix of articles covering topics ranging far beyond the borders of science as we know it today. The *PTRS* eclecticism, however, was in keeping with contemporary notions of science/natural philosophy. From 1752 until quite recently, the journal was for all intents and purposes edited by the executive council of the Royal Society.

In the 19th and early 20th centuries, the *PTRS* developed along the lines of discipline-innovating, professionalizing British science, although both the conservative nature of the Society and its commitment to an all-encompassing (as opposed to a disciplinary) scientific focus caused it to move slowly in this regard. By 1905, however, the labor of reporting original research was being divided between two journals—the *PTRS* and the *Proceedings*—each further broken down into separate "A" (Mathematics and Physical Sciences) and "B" (Biology) publications. This arrangement continued until 1997.

Some of the biggest scientific controversies of the last three centuries have been featured in the *PTRS*, as has a significant part of the most important research. The *PTRS* is generally acknowledged as, if not *the* most, then one of the two or three most influential scientific journals in the history of Western science. And, although it has lost its formerly preeminent position in the present century, it continues, along with the *Proceedings*, to be a force to be reckoned with in scientific journalism.

ENDNOTES

[1]An articulated portrait of the context of any text(s) is certainly a necessary condition for its valid understanding. In this chapter, I attempt to provide such a portrait of the Royal Society and its *Philosophical Transactions* over the 300-year period of study. At the same time, I conceive of this activity as doing more than simply supplying "context," or background information (see chap. 1, section entitled "Discourse and Discourse Analysis"). Rather, I think of this chapter as moving toward—but by no means fully representing—a description of the larger forms of life, or Discourses (Gee, 1990), that existed in the Royal Society from 1675 to 1975 (see chap. 1, note 6).

In some cases the details given in this chapter may not appear immediately relevant to this study's concerns, but I would claim that this description represents approximately the minimum necessary for a holistic understanding of the texts, textworlds, and (with the previous qualification) Discourses being investigated.

This chapter is based on historical studies and selected records of the Royal Society and *PTRS*. It therefore reflects the unevenness of the historical literature, with earlier periods and more controversial topics receiving relatively better coverage. In keeping with this chapter's purpose of providing a broad historical portrait, I have opted for a continuous narrative over a more "academic" exposition; sources are therefore listed below for the topics and periods regarding which they were consulted, and are only occasionally cited in the text itself. It should also be noted that the unpublished manuscript sources consulted are mentioned in individual endnotes rather than in the following list, which is limited to published works (Moore, 1995, provides a full description of the Royal Society's manuscript source collection). Finally, I need to make clear that in writing this chapter I have in no way attempted a comprehensive, professional history of the *PTRS*. As noted by Hunter (1989, chap. 7, note 17), a serious history of the Royal Society's journal tradition remains to be written.

- *The Founding of the Royal Society:* M. B. Hall (1991); Houghton (1942); Hunter (1981, 1989, 1990); Lyons (1944); Purver (1967); Shapin (1994); Shapin and Schaffer (1985); Stimson (1968); Weld (1848, vol. 1). The paragraph beginning "In several significant ways" is based heavily on Hunter's (1989) introduction.
- *The Birth and Early History of the Philosophical Transactions, 1665–1700:* Andrade (1965); Bazerman (1988, chap. 5); Bluhm (1960); Gross (1990); M. B. Hall (1965, 1975, 1991); A. R. Hall and M. B. Hall (1965); Hunter (1981, 1989, chap. 7, 1990); Johns (1991, to appear); Kronick (1976); Lyons (1944); Paradis (1987); Shapin (1987); Weld (1848, vol. 1).
- *The Newtonian Period and Its Aftermath: The Royal Society and the Philosophical Transactions, 1700–1750:* Heilbron (1979, 1983); Lund (1985); Lyons (1944); Potter (1943); Stimson (1968); Thomson (1812); Weld (1848). The parts of this section on the editorships of Halley and Jurin rely heavily on Heilbron's (1983) account.
- *Age of Stability: The Royal Society and the Philosophical Transactions, 1753–1820:* Cantor (1983); Carter (1988); Golinski (1992); M. B. Hall (1984a); Heilbron (1993); Lyons (1944); Mackay (1985); MacLeod (1983); D. P. Miller (1983, 1989); Rudwick (1963); Sorrenson (1996); Weld (1848, vol. 2). I have relied on Weld's account for the years 1750–1778 as few other comprehensive historical accounts exist for this period. The description of the 1784 challenge to Banks' rule depends substantially on Heilbron's (1993) account.
- *"The Troubles" and Their Resolution: The Royal Society and the Philosophical Transactions, 1820–1850:* Anderson (1993); Gleason (1991); Granville (1830); M. B. Hall (1984a); Lyons (1944); D. P. Miller (1983); Moore (1995); Stimson (1968); Weld (1848, vol. 2). I have depended significantly on M. B. Hall (1984a) as the only current synoptic treatment of the Royal Society in the 19th century.
- *Stability Regained: The Royal Society and the Philosophical Transactions, 1848–1900:* Crosland (1982); M. B. Hall (1984a); Heyck (1982); Lyons (1944); Morrell and Thackray (1981); Royal Society (1940); Stimson (1968); Weld (1848). As previously, I have depended significantly on M. B. Hall (1984a).
- *Modernity: The Royal Society and the Philosophical Transactions in the 20th Century:* Alter (1986); Crawford (1990); Garfield (1976, 1977a, 1977b, 1983); Krige (1990); Moore (1995); Moseley (1978, 1980); Rowlinson & Robinson (1992); Royal Society (1940, n.d.).

[2]The coverage of the term *individuals* here was obviously of limited scope in 17th-century Britain, because it would not have included women, men of dependent means (cf. Shapin, 1994, chap. 8), people of color, and so on. Still, the openness of the Society, even within these limitations, differed in kind from all known preceding scientific groupings.

Haraway (1997, chap. 1) takes the position that early modern science as practiced in the Royal Society not only excluded women, but actively constituted itself in opposition to them.

[3]Although early writers on the Society and some Society records describe an interest in "experimental philosophy" and "physico-mathematical learning," it is clear from other records—not the least of which is the early *PTRS* itself—that the interests of Society fellows and their correspondents were much wider than these terms might suggest to most moderns. In fact, what distiguished experimental from other versions of science was not at all clear in the 17th century, as recent accounts (e.g., M. B. Hall, 1991) have perhaps unwillingly found. Pumfrey (1995, pp. 139–140) discusses some of the problems with what counted as an "experiment."

[4]An additional allegedly revolutionary feature of the early Royal Society should be considered here. Elements associated with the early Royal Society (most notably, its official apologist, Thomas Sprat, 1667/1959) claimed that the Society adopted a "close, naked, natural

way" of communicating about science that was in marked contrast to the "amplifications, digressions, and swellings of style" of other natural philosophy writers, especially the scholastics. Such pronouncements have been taken uncritically by some scholars (e.g., Shapiro, 1983) as heralding a revolution in prose style. However, others (e.g., Dear, 1985; Hunter, 1989, chap. 2; Vickers, 1985; cf. Wood, 1980) have argued persuasively that the "plain style" was partly a rhetorical construction of Sprat and his colleagues rather than a simple historical fact. Vickers (1985) uses evidence from the writings of the apologists themselves to show that the norms of 17th-century writing were alive and well within the Royal Society. Recently updated standard treatments of the history of English (e.g., Baugh & Cable, 1993, chap. 9) are also more cautious about the influence of the Royal Society on "the plain style" than they have perhaps been in the past.

[5]Virtually all sources discussing the history of the Royal Society and *PTRS* support the view that the journal has been in the first rank of publications reporting scientific research since its founding. Some of these same authors report an even more important role for the *PTRS* in the development of modern science—as an archetype of the present-day system of formal scientific communication. A selection of modern-day evaluations of the *PTRS* at various points in its history follows, but many more such exist than can be included here (e.g., Crawford, 1990, p. 256; George, 1952, p. 320; Golinski, 1992, p. 252; M. B. Hall, 1975, p. 190; Kronick, 1976, p. 148; Meadows, 1974, pp. 67, 70; McClellan, 1985, p. 54; Stimson, 1968, p. 146; Thornton & Tully, 1971, p. 263; Walker & Hurt, 1990, p. 27):

- Barnes (1937): "Though over 300 such [early learned] periodicals were founded before 1730, the most important, judged by duration and content, were the *Journal des Sçavans,* the *Philosophical Transactions,* and the *Acta Eruditorum*" (p. 155).
- Bazerman (1988): "The *Philosophical Transactions of the Royal Society of London,* the first scientific journal in English, carries the main line of the development of scientific journal writing in English through the 19th century" (p. 63).
- Hunter (1981): "[After its founding in 1665, the *PTRS*] soon established itself as the leading European scientific periodical. . . . In some ways its influence surpassed that of the [Royal] Society. It certainly reached a wider audience than did direct knowledge of the Society's activities: Virtuosi, particularly in the country, often wrote to the publisher . . . rather than to the Society. It was also badly missed whenever its publication was interrupted. . ." (p. 51).
- McKie (1948): "In the [19th-century] physical sciences it [the *Philosophical Magazine,* established 1798] was to become second in importance only to the 'Philosophical Transactions' of the Royal Society of London" (p. 131).

For evidence that the *PTRS* tradition has maintained something of its former reputation, see the statistics regarding citation frequencies given in the section of the present chapter entitled "Modernity: The Royal Society and the *Philosophical Transactions* in the 20th century."

[6]There is some debate on the exact date of Hooke's letter. One scholar even places it *after* the initial publication of the *PTRS*, although this seems unlikely (see Andrade, 1965, p. 12).

[7]The following counts have been given based on Oldenburg's extant correspondence (both incoming and outgoing) in the 15 years preceding his death: 1662—9 letters; 1663—52 letters; 1664—59 letters; 1665—115 letters; 1666—114 letters; 1667—151 letters; 1668—318 letters; from 1669 to 1677—approximately 250 letters per year (Bazerman, 1988, chap. 5; Hunter, 1989, chap. 7). These counts represent only a partial record of Oldenburg's correspondence.

[8]Of Oldenburg's spoken English, for example, Milton wrote, "You have indeed learnt to speak our language more accurately and fluently than any other foreigner I have ever known" (cited in M. B. Hall, 1975, p. 278).

[9]The private enterprise character of the early *PTRS* (up to 1752, when the Royal Society officially took it over) has been emphasized by many historians who treat its first 100 years. This view presents something of a paradox: On the one hand, the journal is universally acknowledged to be a primary instrument of the early Royal Society's activities and interests, and manifestations of an intimate connection between the Society and the journal are many. On the other hand, the journal is often characterized as an essentially private endeavor, as officially (if retrospectively) announced in the 1752 "Advertisement," and Oldenburg constantly complained in his letters to others (including the Royal Society leadership) that the financial burden of the *PTRS* was great, and sometimes even too much to bear. What I believe this paradox indicates is that the Society found it useful to have an ambiguous relationship with the journal, a relationship that gave the Society an opportunity to air or propagandize for its vision(s) of science while maintaining for both the Society and the journal an atmosphere of impartiality and lack of close involvement. Shapin (1987), among others (e.g., Heilbron, 1983), develops a rationale for such an interpretation.

[10]All in all, for the 151 months from March 1665 until his death in September 1677, Oldenburg published 136 issues of the journal. Brief lacunae in its run included 3 months at the height of the London Plague, and the 2 months when Oldenburg was briefly imprisoned (for unknown reasons) in the Tower of London. There was also at least one instance of two issues being printed in the same month: On the occasion of the London hot spell of July 1666, Oldenburg published an issue at midmonth comprised largely of Boyle's directions for cooling water by chemical means. In defense of this extraordinary printing, Oldenburg prefaced the issue with: "the Publisher of these Tracts [i.e., Oldenburg] never meant so to confine himself to a Set time, as not to retain the Liberty of taking any other, when there is occasion."

[11]The view of the 18th century as a time when there was comparatively little achievement within and around the Royal Society (and in fact in British science at large) has led to a limited literature on the institution in that period. This makes the task of writing a historical account from secondary sources rather more difficult. It is also part and parcel of a chicken-and-egg situation: The view of 18th-century science as intellectually arid leads to a limited literature, which in turn perpetuates the view that the period was devoid of interest or progress. The active Newtonian research tradition in the Royal Society in the first part of the century contradicts the assertion that the 18th century was a period of scant historical interest, as does the work of Priestley (cf. Golinski, 1992), Cavendish, Black, and their contemporaries in the latter part of the century.

[12]On the other hand, Heilbron (1983, p. 12) defends Sloane against the view that his editorship of the *PTRS* weakened the scientific character of the Royal Society in this period. Heilbron points out that: (a) the number of fellows actively engaged in scientific research *actually increased* at this time; and (b) Sloane, rather than making a special point of publishing reports of trivial and outlandish happenings in the *PTRS,* had few other options but to print from what was submitted.

[13]Halley had actually been the de facto editor of the *PTRS* briefly once before, in 1691, when the journal was brought back after 4-year period of moribundity. At this time, however, Halley's official position was that of clerk to the secretaries.

[14]D. P. Miller (1989) attributes this passage to one Thomas Clerk.

[15]This claim does not take into account the historical tradition of the *Edinburgh Medical Journal* (cf. D. Atkinson, 1992; Kronick, 1978), in the 1733 incarnation of which a similar proto-referee system was proposed:

Several Collections of Observations communicated to some considerable Men by their Correspondents have been published, and seemed to promise more Accuracy and Candour, by passing thro' the Hands of a Censor equal to the Task; but even in these we find plain Marks of the Publisher's too great Complaisance, or of his Fear to offend.

. . . But allowing these Collections to be put in the best Plan, it might be presumed that a Society of which every Member has his particular Task assigned him, to be executed behind the Curtain, would be as free from a faulty Complaisance or Fear, and as capable of performing the Work to Advantage, as one Gentleman who is engaged in private Practice, and publickly known for the Author. (Preface, *Medical Essays and Observations,* 1733, pp. x–xi)

It can also be noted that, although referring submitted papers to noncommittee referees in the Royal Society was theoretically a possibility from 1752, it appears to have happened only rarely. The first official record of such a referral is in 1780, and the next in 1831, when the practice appears to have become regularized (Royal Society, 1940, chap. 2).

[16]Sorrenson (1996, p. 36) gives the following percentages of Royal Society fellows by social rank/occupation from 1735 to 1780. These counts are based on an analysis of all election certificates submitted for new Fellows at 5-year intervals between 1735 and 1780:

Peer	20%
Baron/Knight, Military Officer, Government Official	15%
Gentleman	15%
Lawyer	5%
Physician	16%
Surgeon/Apothecary	9%
Cleric, Bishop, Schoolteacher	16%
Other	4%

All of these categories except for "Surgeon/Apothecary," "Schoolteacher," and "Other" fall under one definition or other of 18th-century aristocrats or gentlemen, since the law, military, and medicine were frequent career choices for younger male progeny of genteel families (e.g., Perkin, 1969, p. 24). Hunter (1994, cited in Sorrenson, 1996, p. 36) gives the following highly comparable statistics for all British Fellows elected to the Royal Society in the 17th century (Sorrenson has reworked some of Hunter's categories to make them more directly comparable to his own), concluding on their basis that the social makeup of the 17th-century Society was predominantly upper-class.

Aristocrat	14%
Courtier and Civil Servant	20%
Gentleman	15%
Lawyer	4%
M.D.	16%
Surgeon/Apothecary	—
Divines, Scholars, Writers	20%
Merchant	7%
Unknown	3%

It should also be mentioned, however, that gentility in the 17th century was an issue of considerable debate and contestation. For a discussion of the complexities of this issue, see Shapin (1994, chap. 2).

[17]Statements made by Banks' followers to this effect include:

The Man who, though he may not have confined his Studies to any Single Branch of Science, in his large Grasp embraces Knowledge of every kind; courting it, not for a

pitiful Subsistence, but through real Love . . . ; he, Sir, is an Honour to the Royal Society.
. . . A profound Knowledge of the Mathematics is not the Qualification most requisite in
the Secretary of the Royal Society . . . ; a general Acquaintance with the Sciences and
classical Learning are of much more Consequence. (Anonymous, *Canons of Criticism,
Extracted from the Beauties of "Maty's Review," and the Oratorical Powers of Dr Horsley,*
cited in Heilbron, 1993, p. 88)

and:

It was not sufficient to be a Mathematician, to be a Fellow of [the] Society; there were
other qualities requisite, social qualities, the lack of which might make a man unfit,
however competent he might be in learning. (Anguish, in Banks, "Notes," RS, MM. 1, 46a,
cited in Heilbron, 1993, p. 86)

[18]Carter's (1988, p. 572) full statistics are as follows:

Astronomy	17.25%
Mathematics	6.3%
Chemistry	21.38%
Physics	36.4%
Meteorology	5.47%
Geology	3.61%
Geography	2.89%
Metallurgy	1.18%
Engineering	1.08%
General Botany	3.82%
General Zoology	3.61%
Comparative Anatomy	11.98%
Comparative Physiology	2.79%
General Medicine	2.99%
Oriental Studies	0.83%

[19]These figures are based on an examination of the Committee of Papers' Minute Book for
1825 (RS MS. CMB 90B). The Minute Books list all papers considered by the Committee of Papers
by year, and decisions regarding whether or not to print them. These records exist off and on
from the mid-1700s, but not for the years 1774–1776.

[20]My own further examination of the Committee of Papers' Minute Book for 1825 (RS MS.
CMB 90B), however, does not fully confirm Hall's description of the kinds of papers that were
excluded from the *PTRS* in this period. Of the 10 papers withdrawn or archived, for example,
at least half were by well-reputed researchers. One, James Pond, was even himself on the
Committee of Papers at this time, although his research was, in fact, controversial.

[21]It should be mentioned here that Royal Society presidential elections such as that of Davy
in 1820 were largely pre-determined; that is, once a consensus candidate had emerged there
was a "gentleman's agreement" to vote for him. This usually led to lopsided, and occasionally
unanimous, votes. This state of affairs was part of the background that made the election of
1830, described farther along in this section, so divisive.

[22]A radically different account of Gilbert's election is given by Gleason (1991). My description
follows that of D. P. Miller (1983).

[23]"Medical men" had been an important constituency in the Royal Society since its inception
(see note 16). However, having the initials "F.R.S." affixed to one's professional title took on
special social significance for physicians in the 19th century, social significance that translated

into professional success and stature (cf. MacLeod, 1983). Probably not coincidentally, doctors were one of the groups that was constantly singled out in the contemporary periodical press (especially the crusading, rabble-rousing medical journal *Lancet*) as lining up on the conservative, antireformist side in the Royal Society.

[24]One of these publications was by Granville (1830). Some of his criticisms are discussed farther along in this section.

[25]Some of the disaffected members of the Royal Society who were instrumental in founding or supporting the BAAS were Babbage, David Brewster, Roderick Murchison (also president of the Geological Society, 1831–1833), and Francis Baily.

[26]Morrell and Thackray (1981) point out how the BAAS, originally envisioned as an alternative to gentlemanly science, quickly came to be controlled by the very elites it had sought to counter.

[27]As might be imagined, the Royal Society—or at any rate its leadership and their followers—came down squarely on the side of conservative forces in these revolutionary times in almost all instances in which it was involved, at least until 1830. Gilbert, for his part, had had the following reaction to a bill supporting universal education that was placed before Parliament in 1807, and such attitudes were perhaps typical of those conservative elements in the Society that supported genteel interests (cf. Berman, 1978, p. 27):

> [G]iving education to the labouring classes of the poor . . . would in effect be found to be prejudicial to their morals and happiness; it would teach them to despise their lot in life, instead of making them good servants in agriculture, and other laborious employment to which their rank in society had destined them; instead of teaching them subordination, it would render them factious and refractory, as was evident in the manufacturing countries; it would enable them to read seditious pamphlets, vicious books, and publications against Christianity; it would render them insolent. (cited in Winterowd, 1989, p. 4)

[28]Granville (1830) also gives interesting statistics on a number of other characteristics of the Society and the *PTRS*, although it is sometimes difficult to judge the accuracy of his figures. For the period 1800–1830, for example, he finds that approximately three out of every four papers submitted to the journal were accepted for publication; in this case, the numbers agree substantially with my own.

[29]These seven sectional committees were: astronomy, chemistry, geology and mineralogy, mathematics, physics, and physiology, the latter "including the Natural History of organized beings" (M. B. Hall, 1984a, p. 68). The idea for such committees came out of proposals made in 1827 for Society reform by a committee convened for that purpose.

[30]By 1875, membership was down to around 500, finally leveling off at around 450 at the beginning of the 20th century. It should be noted that the numbers reported here (from Lyons, 1944) exclude foreign members, who held steady at between 40 and 50 per year from around 1810 onward. Changes in bylaws had limited the number of foreign members to 100 in 1776; their number was further reduced to 50 in 1823.

[31]As mentioned earlier in this chapter, Lyons' sense of who and what merited the attribute "scientific" in 18th-century Britain was highly anachronistic. For periods closer to his own time, however, when science had substantially taken on its modern form, his judgements are doubtless more valid.

[32]Printed referee-report forms, first appearing in 1898, included the following instructions (called there "Standing Orders," presumably being orders of the Committee of Papers or Society as a whole) in reference to the question, "Should [the paper] be published in the 'Philosophical Transactions' or the 'Proceedings'? (see Standing Orders on opposite page.)":

The 'Proceedings' shall be the medium of publication for papers of approved merit not more than twenty-four pages in length, and not containing numerous or elaborate illustrations, provided that the Council may in exceptional circumstances, on a report from a Sectional Committee, order papers of greater length to be printed in the 'Proceedings.' The 'Proceedings' shall also contain short abstracts of papers to be published in the 'Philosophical Transactions' . . . , and such other matters as the Council may judge desirable to insert.

The 'Philosophical Transactions' shall be the medium of publication (a) for papers of approved merit which contain numerous or elaborate illustrations, or which cannot without detriment to their scientific value be condensed into the space reserved for papers in the 'Proceedings'; (b) for such reports or investigations carried out by a Committee of the Society as the Council may order to be printed in the 'Transactions.' (RS Referee's Report No. 20, 1925)

It may also be mentioned here that "Instructions to Authors" did not appear in either of the two journals until 1934. Also, up to 1989 these instructions still specified that papers had to be transmitted to the journal for submission by a Society fellow, a practice retained from the 18th and 19th centuries.

[33]These counts were made from the Society's "Register of Papers" (RS MS. 421, 1853–1887). These are records of the receipt and disposition of all papers received for publication by the Society, and exist from 1853 onward. It should be noted that they are not strictly comparable to the Minute Books of the Committee of Papers (on which my earlier counts of papers considered in the years 1824–1826 were based, as the "Register of Papers" did not exist at that time), but that, for present purposes, approximate comparisons can be made.

[34]A third president in the mid-20th century, Adrian (president from 1951 to 1955), expressed the conservative viewpoint that the Society's main function was "to exist and to perpetuate its existence by electing new Fellows" (cited in Rowlinson & Robinson, 1992, p. 9).

[35]The Royal Society keeps a 30-year embargo on all its records. In itself this should mean that the last available statistics on article submission, acceptance, and rejection rates would come from the year 1966. However, because volumes of the "Register of Papers" (see note 33) can run for many years, and typically end in different years for the A and B series, the last 3-year period for which full statistics were available was 1957–1959.

[36]The exact significance of these statistics is not clear. One interpretation is that they indicate that the *PTRS* and *Proceedings* were still substantially fulfilling a proceedings-type recording function in the Society at this time, since the rejection rates are so low. But it is not known, among other things, whether papers submitted to the journals were still first being read at Society meetings. Also, current journal submission rejection rates in the hard sciences are generally low (e.g., Zuckerman & Merton, 1971, wherein an analysis of 12 hard scientific journals showed an average rejection rate of 24%), although 90% acceptance rates would be quite unusual.

3

Methods of Analysis and Description of Text Corpus

The two main analytical methods employed in the present study derive from two conceptually distinct traditions of discourse analysis. The first is the tradition of rhetorical text analysis, which has a well-established history of use in university English departments in the United States and Britain. This approach has found a contemporary place in nonliterary studies of written language with the advent of rhetoric/composition as a more or less distinct academic discipline (Lauer, 1984; Phelps, 1988), and a "rhetorical turn" in the humanities and social sciences. The second main tradition of discourse analysis informing the present study is that of sociolinguistic register research (e.g., Biber & Finegan, 1994a; Ferguson, 1983; Halliday, 1988). In particular, this study adopts the Multidimensional (MD) approach to register analysis developed by Douglas Biber (Biber, 1986, 1988), and subsequently used in a number of synchronic and diachronic studies of discourse variation and change (e.g., Biber, 1987, 1989, 1991, 1992, 1994; Biber & Finegan, 1988, 1989, 1992; Besnier, 1988; D. Atkinson, 1992, 1996; Kim & Biber, 1994; Biber & Hared, 1994).

These two approaches to discourse analysis are complementary in significant respects. Most importantly, the former approach (which I will call *rhetorical analysis*) focuses on the highly contextualized microanalysis of rhetorical features in and across individual texts; it is therefore a "bottom–up" and context-sensitive type of analysis, from which results are "emergent."[1] In terms of the approach to written discourse laid out in chapter 1, rhetorical analysis operates at the textual level of genre. The latter approach, on the other hand (which I will call *MD analysis*), represents a powerful form of "top–down" macroanalysis, in that it begins with an explicit set of categories of linguistic functionality in texts—as well as specific sets of linguistic features performing these functions—and proceeds to characterize the particular texts under analysis empirically in these terms (Biber, 1988, p. 61). In regard to the concepts discussed in chapter 1, MD analysis operates at the textual level of register. However, as described in chapter 1, register is, in practice, also an inextricable component of genre. From this perspective, the two types of analysis employed in this study are complementary and convergent.

As described in chapter 1, but not yet fully integrated into the discourse–analytic methodology described in this chapter, there is a third level of discourse analysis represented in this volume. That is, what I frequently call "context" in this work should properly be seen as more than that, if by "context" is meant primarily "background information" relevant only as an aid to interpretation. Current theories of discourse (e.g., Fairclough, 1992; Gee, 1990) view a wide range of social practices as bound organically together into particular "forms of life," or Discourses (Gee, 1990)—Discourses in which language use is thus an important but by no means especially privileged contributor. The historical account given in chapter 2 of this volume, as well as the more Discourse-focused sociohistorical descriptions given in chapter 6, therefore represent an integral part of the approach to discourse analysis set forth in chapter 1 of this volume, although this approach is not yet fully realized at the methodological level.

The combination of diverse analytic methodologies and data has been a frequently stated desideratum for social—including language-related—research (e.g., DeWalt & Pelto, 1985; Eisner & Peshkin, 1990; Kirsch, 1992; Labov, 1971; Lazaraton, 1995; Nunan, 1992). The sociolinguist Labov (1971), for example, believes that:

> good linguistic work will draw upon several types of data and methods in approaching a given problem. Since different methods will have different sources of error, even a partial convergence in the results will lead to a higher degree of confidence than we can give to work with one kind of data and one way of dealing with it. (pp. 478–479)[2]

Yet while the use of distinct methodologies in combination—especially where one is qualitative and the other quantitative—has been called for repeatedly, it has only rarely been undertaken in the study of language. As pointed out in the introduction to this volume, scientific writing research is no exception to this pattern: It has depended heavily on rhetorical text–analytic methods, at least in the study of the history of such writing. The present research design is therefore an attempt to bring independent but complementary methodologies of discourse analysis together in order to describe the development of scientific research writing more fully and adequately.

In particular, by supplementing the rhetorical text–analytic approach with MD analysis, an important quantitative linguistic dimension is added to the rapidly growing body of knowledge concerning the textual aspects of historical and modern-day scientific research writing.[3]

RHETORICAL ANALYSIS: GENERAL DESCRIPTION

Bazerman (1988, chap. 1, note 1) characterizes the methodological approach that he originally took to studying scientific writing as follows:

> Primarily it consists of close textual reading and historical contexting. The textual readings are all framed by recognition of traditional literary devices, and have been intensified by new critical insistence on the text in itself. However, other modes of criticism have suggested the application of interpretive frameworks from other disciplines, such as linguistics, psychology, sociology, anthropology, and philosophy. Such imported frameworks are justified in two ways: Either they represent fundamental truths so that they cannot help but influence texts, or the writer on some level was aware of such ideas and constructed parts of the text upon them.
>
> Historical contexting has served a variety of functions, from simply providing a decorative framework . . . to offering a complete account for the creation and meaning of a historically bound text. On occasion text and context have been drawn more tightly together to view the text as a historical event within the unfolding context. . . .
>
> An extended repertoire of concepts and tools has also come out of the teaching of writing. The rhetorical approach to the teaching of writing has been particularly concerned with public argument; an approach loosely labelled composition has been concerned with the formal prescriptions of the school essay, but has in recent years also taken on a concern for the process of writing, as approached through a cognitive psychology model.

Following this basic description, Bazerman discusses the concepts he added to his methodological repertoire as his research progressed. Rather than any one analytical technique, these additions reflected a deepening appreciation of the embeddedness of written texts in their social, historical, and disciplinary contexts, as revealed by research in the fields mentioned in the above quotation.

I have introduced Bazerman's description of rhetorical analysis at length because it represents perhaps the fullest account of this method as applied in the historical study of scientific writing. In describing my own uses of this approach, I will limit myself mostly to highlighting and elaborating on Bazerman's points.

First, rhetorical analysis is *eclectic.* That is, concepts that aid analysis are borrowed from any of a number of approaches to the study of language, mind, and society. The only requirement for such borrowing is that the analytical concepts thus obtained have potential to shed new light on the object or objects of study.[4]

As Bazerman states in the previous quotation, his approach to rhetorical analysis has its roots in a wide range of fields—basically any discipline that has concerned itself with the study of communication, society, and mind in recent times. In my own version of rhetorical analysis many of the concepts in fact originate in linguistic and applied linguistic research (e.g., D. Atkinson, 1991; Ferguson, 1994; Swales, 1990), although others derive from the work of literary theorists, philosophers, and historians and sociologists of science. As mentioned by Bazerman, rhetoric/composition research has also proven to be a rich source of rhetorical text–analytic concepts, as evidenced, for example, in Phelps' (1985) illuminating discussion of textual coherence (for which, see note 9). To give some added concreteness to this discussion, concepts which I have found useful in performing rhetorical analysis,are listed in the notes to this chapter, along with citations of studies in which these concepts have been fruitfully discussed or employed.[5]

A second point of elaboration on Bazerman's description is that rhetorical analysis is *contextual.* That is, it depends on an articulated knowledge of the workings of the discourse communities in which the texts under study are or historically were situated. Where the discourse community is presently in existence, researchers therefore often engage in some level of participant observation (Denzin, 1989): Recent studies of situated literate practices both in the sciences and beyond (e.g., Brown & Herndl, 1986; Freed & Broadhead, 1987; Heath, 1983; Knorr-Cetina, 1981; Latour & Woolgar, 1986) provide strong exemplars for this approach. Where, on the other hand, the discourse community is a historical one as in the present study, researchers must immerse themselves deeply in the available historical sources and secondary literature. It is only in this way that they can hope to gain the articulated understanding necessary to perform an analysis of situated linguistic and rhetorical practice.[6]

A third point of elaboration on rhetorical analysis is the converse of the foregoing. That is, although rhetorical analysis depends on close attention to and articulated knowledge of sociorhetorical context to elucidate the text(s) under study, the researcher can also "read off" important aspects of the surrounding context from the text itself. Just as "an animal's wings, gills, snout or hands describe an animal's environment" (Michaels & Carello, 1981, cited in Rogoff, 1990, p. 30), the written word is assumed to reflect its complex environments of production and consumption. This assumption is made explicit in recent text-focused rhetorical research (e.g., Bazerman, 1994, p. 93; MacDonald, 1994, p. 7)—in the present work I attempt to stabilize it in the notion of *social indexicality* (Ochs, 1990, 1992, 1996), that is, that certain uses of language tend to point to or *index* certain insider perspectives and social practices or ideologies. My reliance on this concept will be especially apparent in the section of chapter 4 entitled "Discourse Community." It should be added, however, that the analytical reading of texts as deeply embedded in their sociohistorical contexts and the "reading off" of such contexts from the texts themselves are mutually supporting, dialectically related activities.

Fourth, rhetorical analysis is a *bottom–up,* or inductive type of analysis, from which results are *emergent.* Mishler (1990) describes work in a cross-disciplinary paradigm he calls "inquiry-guided research"—work in which the object of analysis emerges gradually in relation to a growing qualitative understanding of its organic existence within its rich and variegated contexts of occurrence. This paradigm has been powerfully informed by the hermeneutic and phenomenological perspectives disseminated in recent years throughout much of the Western academy, and accords closely with the approach to rhetorical analysis taken here.[7]

Fifth and finally, rhetorical analysis as used in this study depends heavily on the theoretical notion of genre. But because this concept has been described in detail in chapter 1, it will not be considered further here.

RHETORICAL ANALYSIS: PROCEDURES

In the present study, rhetorical analysis was performed according to the following procedures. First, all "original articles" from all volumes under study were photocopied.[8] Starting with the 1675 volume, I then read through each article in each volume, noting all potentially relevant text features, and writing brief commentaries on each article. On finishing an analysis of each volume's original articles, I next wrote a summary characterization of these articles in terms of their rhetorical text features. On completing this procedure for all seven *PTRS* volumes under analysis, I then compared the summary characterizations of each volume's material, identifying the most prominent recurring features and developmental trends. Finally, I checked these overall impressions against my commentaries on the individual articles in each volume, and, where necessary, the actual articles themselves.

In accordance with the context-embedded nature of rhetorical analysis described previously, the actual analysis occurred after I had done a large amount of reading of similar kinds of texts across the period of time studied here (see, e.g., D. Atkinson, 1992), and a substantial amount of reading in the history of British science and the Royal Society of London. My contextualized understanding of the texts I analyzed is partly captured in chapter 2 of the present work.

In performing the rhetorical analysis, I was further guided by six broad questions focusing on rhetorical issues that had been considered in past investigations of scientific writing:

1. What different text types or genres of scientific research writing are identifiable within each sampling period? What are the formal and semantic characteristics of these genres?
2. To what degree do these genre types appear to be standardized, or *conventionalized* (D. Atkinson, 1991) within each period?
3. What is the relationship of theory to data in each of the articles examined? How stable does the relationship appear to be within and across periods?
4. What are the principles of "design coherence" (Phelps, 1985) or "top-level" discourse structure (Horowitz, 1987; Meyer, 1985) within and across articles?[9]
5. What aspects of the scientific "discourse community" (Swales, 1990; chap. 1, this volume) appear to be indexed in texts across periods? That is, what can the rhetoric of the articles themselves tell us about the social relationships among their authors and other researchers?
6. Are there formal aspects of articles which appear to be shaped by the cultural "thought styles" (Fleck, 1979) or "conventions for construing reality" (Bizzell, 1982) that constitute the discourse community's base of scientific knowledge and activity? That is, do there appear to be links between standardized rhetorical form(s) and scientific epistemology or epistemologies?

MD ANALYSIS: DESCRIPTION AND PROCEDURES

At the second, or linguistic level of analysis, the methods used were those developed by Biber (1986, 1988; Biber & Finegan, 1989, 1992) for sociolinguistic and sociohistorical register analysis. This approach to the analysis of language in use—fully described in Biber (1988, chaps. 4 and 5)—is based on four key theoretical assumptions: (a) that linguistic registers derive their distinctive characteristics from inherent *co-occurrence patterns of linguistic features* (Ervin-Tripp, 1972; Stubbs, 1996); (b) that these co-occurrence patterns may be characterized for particular social member-defined genre groupings of texts (e.g., newspaper editorials, mystery fiction) as discrete numerical values on underlying *dimensions of variation*—continuous, empirically determined scales on which a wide range of texts have been shown to differ significantly (cf. Biber, 1988, and Table 3.1 and Fig. 3.1); (c) that these dimensions themselves can be interpreted in terms of the social, psycholinguistic, situational, and text-functional roles that their constitutive linguistic features have been found to play in the extensive literature on linguistic functionality (see Biber, 1988, Appendix II); and (d) that it is necessary to characterize all text genres on multiple dimensions of variation in order to capture the complex, *multidimensional* nature of textual variability.

Methodologically, MD analysis depends on both the computerized identification/counting of linguistic features and the multivariate statistical technique known as factor analysis (Gorsuch, 1983; Lauer & Asher, 1988) to analyze large, representative text corpora. The MD analysis used in the present study itself consisted of two parts, which I referred to in the introduction as the "baseline analysis" and the "target analysis."

The baseline analysis was performed by Biber (1988) in six overall steps. First, a computer program was written to "tag" (i.e., identify) and count occurrences of 67 linguistic features that were known to be functional in discourse, as determined by earlier research. This program was written in the programming language PL/1, and relied substantially on a 50,624-word online dictionary derived from the "Brown Corpus" (Francis & Kucera, 1979, 1982), a previously hand-tagged corpus of standard written (American) English. More specifically, the program matched open-class forms (e.g., nouns, adjectives, verbs) found in the texts under analysis with entries from the online dictionary, and closed-class forms (e.g., pronouns, prepositions) with those included in purpose-written algorithms. It also used additional context-sensitive disambiguating algorithms (based on Quirk, Greenbaum, Leech, & Svartvik, 1985) to tag ambiguous usages. Items that the tagger had trouble tagging accurately (e.g., various uses of the lexeme "that") were checked by hand and retagged where necessary.[10] A straightforward example of one of the 67 functional discourse features automatically tagged is the simple past tense form of the verb, which numerous linguists (e.g., Labov, 1972, chap. 9) have identified as a prototypical marker of narrativity.

Second, the tagging/counting program was run on a large computerized corpus of English speech and writing comprising 481 texts in 23 different genre categories—a set of texts designed to represent the full range of genres of standard modern-day English. These texts represented the bulk of the two major computerized text corpora available at the time: the Lancaster–Oslo–Bergen (LOB) Corpus of British English (Johansson, Leech, & Goodluck, 1978) and the London–Lund Corpus of Spoken English (Svartvik & Quirk, 1980).[11]

In step 3 of the baseline analysis, feature counts across these texts were factor-analyzed. Factor analysis is a multivariate statistical technique which, according to Lauer and Asher (1988, p. 247; cf. Gorsuch, 1983), is designed to "extract an underlying, reduced set of major conceptual variables from a set of real, observed, and interrelated variables." In the present case, factor analysis of the original 67 linguistic features yielded five smaller *factors*—sets of features that grouped together at a high rate of frequency across texts.

In step 4, the five factors were interpreted. That is, according to commonalities in the linguistic functions of the particular features making up each of the five factors, each was given an interpretive label. To exemplify: One feature set identified by the factor analysis consisted of simple past tense verbs, third-person personal pronouns, perfect-aspect verbs, and "public verbs" (i.e., verbs that express a publicly observable communicative act—e.g., *claim, report*). Based, once again, on past linguistic research into the functional roles of the individual linguistic features making up this factor, it was interpreted as constituting a parameter of discourse variation in the functional domain of narrativity.

In step 5 of the baseline MD analysis, all 481 texts in the corpus had individual *factor scores* computed for them; these scores were then averaged for all texts by genre, giving a single average (or *mean*) factor score for each genre. The factor scores for individual texts were themselves determined by counting all occurrences of each feature on a particular factor in each text, and adding these counts together.[12] Thus, for the "narrativity" factor described previously, a text with 50 past-tense verbs, 25 third-person personal pronouns, 25 perfect-aspect verbs, and 25 public verbs would receive a dimension score of 125. In actuality, however, factor scores are never this large due to two operations carried out to insure the comparability of feature counts across texts: Feature counts are *standardized,* thereby putting all counts on a common (standardized) scale, and text lengths are *normalized* to a length of 1,000 words, allowing feature counts from texts of widely varying lengths to be uniformly expressed in *counts per 1,000 words.*

Finally, in step 6 of the baseline analysis mean factor scores for each of the 23 genres analyzed by Biber were scaled relative to one another on each of the five factors, according to these genres' factor scores. This gave a way of directly comparing different genres in terms of the degree to which they quantitatively "participated" in a particular factor, that is, how much or little of the linguistic functionality represented by a particular factor was present in a particular genre of text. For this purpose, the factors were conceptualized as *dimensions,* or continuous scales on which the genre scores could be arrayed vis-à-vis one another. For example, in regard to the "narrativity" factor described previously, genres (e.g., romantic fiction) in which the features making up the factor co-occurred frequently received a high "narrative" factor/dimension score vis-à-vis other genres, and texts in which the features occurred seldom if at all (e.g., official documents) received a markedly "nonnarrative" score. The five dimensions of functional variation arrived at in this way, with their factor labels construed where possible as binary oppositions, were: (a) *Involved versus informational production;* (b) *Narrative versus nonnarrative concerns;* (c) *Situation-dependent versus explicit reference;* (d) *Overt expression of persuasion;* and (e) *Nonabstract versus abstract information.* Results of this final step in the baseline analysis were then displayed in graphic form, as in Fig. 3.1, which is a composite of Biber's (1988) five dimensions. (More information is given later on the five dimensions, including the linguistic features comprising them.)

In the target analysis, following Biber (e.g., 1995; Biber & Finegan, 1989) and D. Atkinson (1992, 1996), the dimensions developed by Biber (1988) were used to measure change across time within one particular written genre, the scientific research article. That is, instead of studying how different genres of texts varied one from another on the five functional dimensions at a single point in time, the task here was to see *how text groups from the same historical genre varied one from another on the five functional dimensions across time.* This extension of MD analysis into the historical domain assumes the overall stability of functionality for individual linguistic features (e.g., the "narrative" nature of simple past tense verbs), and the overall integrity of functional feature groups across the 300-year period of study. The actual procedures employed in carrying out the target analysis basically repeated steps 2 and 6 of the baseline analysis. In the former, a modified version of Biber's (1988) tagging program was run on the 70 *PTRS* texts under analysis;[13] in the latter, dimension scores for each of the five factors were computed for each period, and then arrayed on dimension scales to show how they changed over time.

Although it is true that MD analysis minimizes attention to individual texts as cultural and rhetorical artifacts in order to maximize descriptive adequacy and comparability of a more general nature, a considered approach to its use significantly diminishes this problem. Thus, the results of MD analysis should properly *lead the analyst back to the individual texts or groups of texts under consideration,* with the goal of relating its powerful macroscopic generalizations to the individual textual phenomena from which they are derived. And the analyst returns to the texts better equipped than formerly: Besides having five precise characterizations of how much, in relation to other texts, a particular text or text group "participates" in a particular dimension, the analyst has in addition five major sets of functional linguistic features—features that can now be studied in detail within and across texts both singly and in terms of their relationships and text-building potential.

In addition, as mentioned at the start of this chapter, the combination of this form of (largely) macroscopic analysis with the (largely) microscopic approach of rhetorical analysis creates a situation in which there is both significant overlap and complementarity of discourse–analytic methods. Whereas neither analytical method is in itself fully adequate to the task of describing discourse change across large spans of time, in tandem—and especially when augmented by the third level of discourse analysis introduced in chapter 1 and brought to bear (although less than fully) in chapter 6—they hold out the potential for a richer, more complete description.

MD ANALYSIS: LINGUISTIC MAKEUP OF DIMENSIONS

The five main dimensions of variation which Biber has identified in his research, and the linguistic features which comprise them, are listed in Table 3.1.[14] In this table, all features which are *above* the dashed line group together—or significantly co-occur—on the dimension under which they are listed, while those feature groups listed *below* the dashed line co-occur in inversely proportional distribution, in terms of frequency, with those above the line on the same dimension. Furthermore, where the dimension has both a two-part label (e.g., Dimension 1, *Involved vs. informational production*) and *additionally* has feature groups in inverse distribution, the feature group above the dashed line represents the text style characterized in the first half of the label, whereas that below the line represents the style denoted in the label's second half. Thus, for Dimension 1, we can speak of the features above the dashed line as "involved" (strictly, "involved production") features, and those below the line as "informational" (strictly, "informational production") features.

The relative positions of some modern-day written genres on these dimensions (from Biber, 1988) are presented in Fig. 3.1.[15] Scores for selected spoken genres are also given there, in order to indicate as much of the full range of textual variation found by Biber (1988) as possible. Zero on each of the five dimensions shown in Fig. 3.1 represents the mean score of group mean scores on that dimension for each of the 23 spoken and written genres studied by Biber (1988). This artificial calibration of mean dimension scores at 0 is the outcome of standardizing all feature frequencies, as noted previously. The genre scores themselves (e.g., the score of −10.0 for editorials on Dimension 1) represent mean scores based on the standardized factor scores of each individual text in that genre group.

CONSTRUCTION OF TEXT CORPORA

Two closely related corpora of scientific research articles were employed in this study. Both were constructed from the first bound volumes of the *PTRS* for the years 1675, 1725, 1775, 1825, 1875, 1925, and 1975. For the years 1925 and 1975, articles from the *PTRS* were supplemented with those from first bound volumes of its companion journal, the *Proceedings of the Royal Society of London* (hereafter, *Proceedings*). Originally established in 1832 for

TABLE 3.1
Major Dimensions of Register Variation: Interpretations and Constitutive Linguistic Features of MD Analysis

DIMENSION 1 Involved vs. Informational Production	DIMENSION 2 Narrative vs. Nonnarrative Concerns	DIMENSION 3 Explicit vs. Situation-Dependent Reference	DIMENSION 4 Overt Expression of Persuasion	DIMENSION 5 Abstract vs. Nonabstract Information
Private verbs	Past tense verbs	WH-relatives on object position	Prediction modals	Conjuncts
That deletion	3rd person pronouns	Pied piping	Suasive verbs	Agentless passives
Contractions	Perfect aspect verbs	WH-relatives on subject position	Conditional subordination	Past participial WH-relative
Present tense verbs	Public verbs	Phrasal coordination	Necessity modals	clause deletions
2nd person pronouns		Nominalizations	Split auxiliaries	Other adverbial subordinators
Demonstrative pronouns				By-passives
General emphatics				
1st person pronouns				
Pronoun it				
BE as main verb				
Causative subordination				
Discourse particles				
Indefinite pronouns				
General hedges				
Amplifiers				
WH-questions				
Possibility modals				
Non-phrasal coordination				
WH-clauses				
Final prepositions				
		Time adverbials		
		Place adverbials		
		Other adverbials		
Nouns				
Word length				
Prepositions				
Type/token ratio				
Attributive adjectives				

Note. Adapted from Biber, 1988.

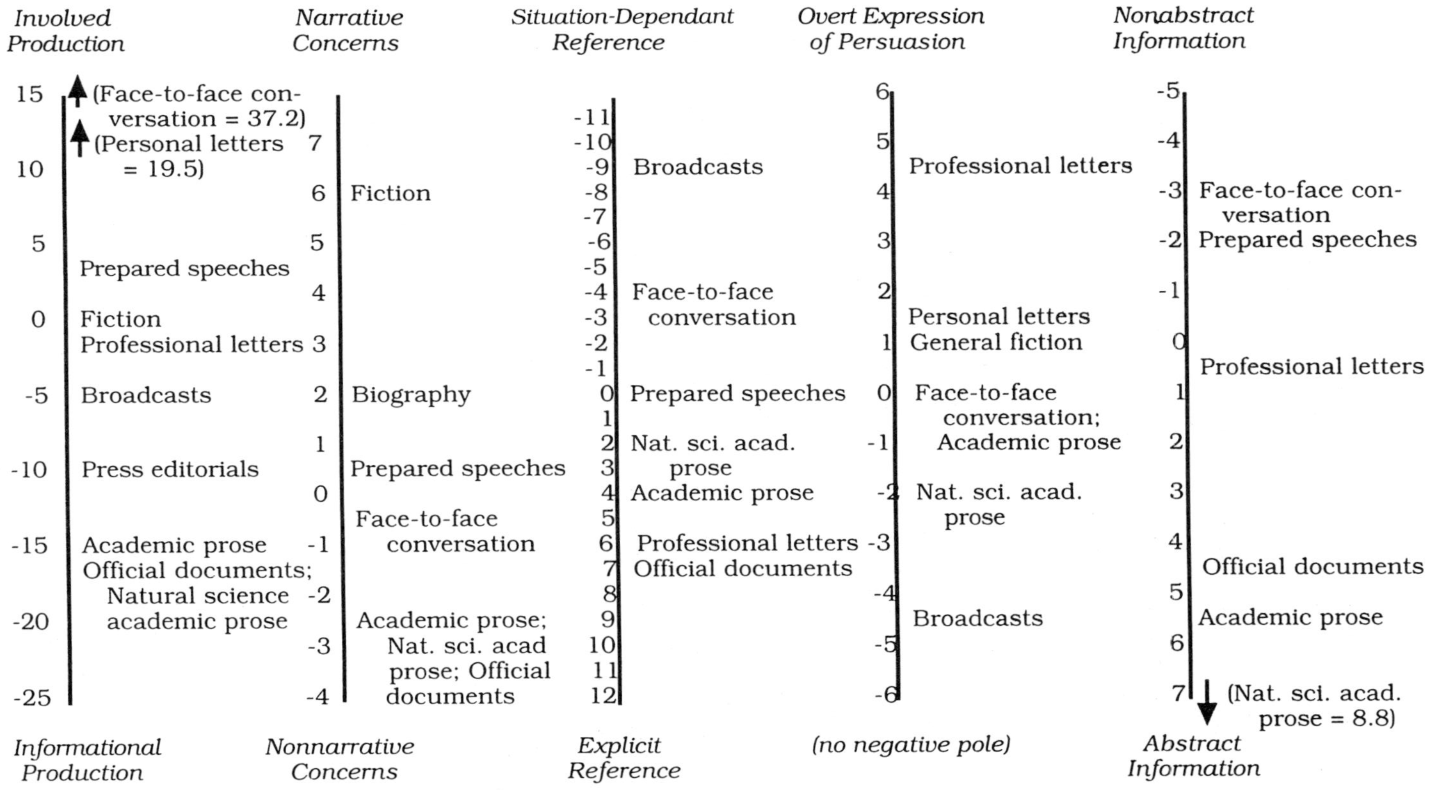

Involved Production

Score	Genre
15	(Face-to-face conversation = 37.2)
	(Personal letters = 19.5)
10	
5	Prepared speeches
3	Professional letters
0	Fiction
-5	Broadcasts
-10	Press editorials
-15	Academic prose; Official documents;
-16	Natural science academic prose
-20	
-25	

Informational Production

Narrative Concerns

Score	Genre
7	
6	Fiction
5	
4	
2	Biography
1	Prepared speeches
0	Face-to-face conversation
-1	Academic prose
-2	Official documents; Natural science academic prose
-3	Academic prose; Nat. sci. acad prose; Official documents
-4	

Nonnarrative Concerns

Situation-Dependant Reference

Score	Genre
-11	
-9	Broadcasts
-4	Face-to-face conversation
0	Prepared speeches
2	Nat. sci. acad. prose
4	Academic prose
6	Professional letters
7	Official documents
12	

Explicit Reference

Overt Expression of Persuasion

Score	Genre
6	
5	Professional letters
2	Personal letters
1	General fiction
0	Face-to-face conversation; Academic prose
-2	Nat. sci. acad. prose
-3	Professional letters
-4	Official documents
-5	Broadcasts
-6	

(no negative pole)

Nonabstract Information

Score	Genre
-5	
-3	Face-to-face conversation
-2	Prepared speeches
0	Professional letters
4	Official documents
5	Academic prose
7	(Nat. sci. acad. prose = 8.8)

Abstract Information

FIG. 3.1. Five major dimensions of register variation, with mean dimension scores from MD analysis of selected modern-day text genres (from Biber, 1988).

the purpose of printing abstracts of papers read before the Society and summaries of meeting minutes (see chap. 2, section entitled " 'The Troubles' and Their Resolution" for a fuller account), the latter journal was included in the present study because it gradually came in the later 19th and early 20th centuries to share the function of reporting original scientific research with the *PTRS*. Thus, in order to make accurate comparisons among volumes of the *PTRS* from both before and after the period in which the *Proceedings* assumed a research-reporting function, it was necessary to include the latter journal in the present analysis.[16]

Corpus A: The first of the two corpora used in this study (hereafter referred to as *Corpus A*) was made up of all original articles in the first bound volumes of the *PTRS* from the seven target dates listed previously, and first bound volumes of the *Proceedings* for the years 1925 and 1975. This corpus represents the material that was subjected to rhetorical analysis in the present study, and was collected specifically for that purpose.

Construction of Corpus A took place as follows. First bound volumes of both the *PTRS* and *Proceedings* (as described previously) for the years under study were located in the libraries of the University of Southern California and the University of California at Los Angeles, and these volumes were photocopied. Next, all articles in these volumes that were *not* original articles (see note 8) were excluded from further analysis. All remaining articles were then rhetorically analyzed according to the general principles set forth in the section entitled "Rhetorical Analysis: Procedures."

Corpus B: The second corpus used in this study—that employed in the MD analysis part of the project—represented a subset of the articles comprising Corpus A. It was also part of a larger corpus constructed under the direction of Douglas Biber and Edward Finegan, and known as "A Representative Corpus of Historical English Registers," or ARCHER (Biber, Finegan, Atkinson, Beck, Burges, & Burges, 1993; Finegan & Atkinson, 1993). This is a 2-million-word corpus made up of texts representing 10 historical written and speech-based genres of British and American English, generally sampled in 50-year segments between 1650 and 1990. The present project utilized the scientific research report subcorpus of this larger corpus, although modifying it in various ways.

The original (i.e., ARCHER) scientific report subcorpus was constructed in the following manner. First, a "universe of texts" was defined, in this case as all articles in first bound volumes of the *PTRS* from 1650 to 1990, supplemented by similar articles in the *Proceedings* from 1880 onward. Second, a sampling interval was chosen, in this case 50-year intervals starting in 1675. The year 1675 was chosen because it was the 10th year after the journal's establishment, and thus represented a point at which the journal could be expected to have developed a more-or-less conventionalized form and content. Third, a random sampling rubric was devised for choosing 12 samples from each targeted year/volume of the *PTRS*.[17] This was effected by dividing the number of pages in each targeted volume by the number of texts needed for each sampling period (e.g., 480 pages divided by 12 articles yields a page-sampling interval of 40 pages). Taking this information, I went to the actual volumes, opened them to the page number corresponding to a two-digit number picked "blind" from a random numbers table, and then chose the next complete article to occur in the volume as I paged forward from that point. On finding an article in this manner, I recorded the information and skipped forward in the volume the number of pages indicated in the sampling interval, and there began paging forward again for the next (eligible) complete article. When 12 articles were not obtained by paging through a volume once in this manner, I cycled through the volume again as necessary (although in practice almost never more than once) to obtain the requisite number of texts. In this way, a total of 70 texts (10 texts per period—see note 17) was obtained for the original ARCHER scientific research report subcorpus. The titles and authors of all texts in Corpus B are given in Appendix A.

This original subcorpus was modified for the purposes of the present study in several ways. First, it was "stratified" to reflect the actual frequencies of occurrence of articles in three content domains of scientific activity in the journal across its history. This stratification was considered necessary in order to permit later comparison of results from the rhetorical analysis with those from the MD analysis—the pure random sampling methods employed in the ARCHER project did not allow for this sort of comparison. Stratification of the samples took place in the following way. A three-way categorization for distinguishing article types was first devised based on: (a) the modern two-way categorization of scientific research writing in Royal Society journals (see chap. 2, section entitled "Stability Regained") into *Series A: Mathematical and Physical Science* and *Series B: Biological Sciences* (see D. Atkinson, 1993, Appendix 1, for the history of this distinction); and (b) a preliminary review of all articles in Corpus A, as well as of scholarly sources on the historical categorization of the sciences.

The resulting categorization had the following three divisions: (A) *physical and mathematical sciences;* (B) *biological/life sciences;* and (C) *other.* All articles in Corpus A were then categorized according to this system, and the numbers of articles falling into each category for each sampling period were recorded. Based on these raw numbers, percentages of each article type's frequency of occurrence per volume were next computed. These percentages were used as guidelines for the number of articles to be selected from each category per period (for a total of 10) for MD analysis, and then texts were actually chosen from the ARCHER subcorpus using this information, or where enough texts did not already exist to fill a category,

TABLE 3.2
Article Types Chosen for MD Analysis[a]

Date	A	B	C	Totals
1675	20 (43%) 4	10 (22%) 3	16 (35%) 3	46 (100%)
1725	15 (54%) 5	10 (38%) 4	1 (8%) 1	26 (100%)
1775	22 (46%) 5	15 (31%) 3	11 (23%) 2	48 (100%)
1825	13 (54%) 5	7 (29%) 3	4 (17%) 2	24 (100%)
1875	14 (64%) 6	7 (31%) 3	1 (5%) 1	22 (100%)
1925[b]	N/A (50%) 5	N/A (50%) 5	N/A (0%) 0	N/A (100%)
1975[b]	N/A (50%) 5	N/A (50%) 5	N/A (0%) 0	N/A (100%)

[a]This table indicates percentage frequencies of occurrence, and corresponding numbers of texts chosen for MD analysis for three article types in *Philosophical Transactions:*

A = *Physical Sciences and Mathematics* (including astronomy, physics, mechanical philosophy, chemistry, geology, geological natural history, math, meteorology, scientific instrumentation)

B = *Biological/Life Sciences* (including physiology, anatomy, botany, morphology, embryology, zoology, biological natural history, taxonomy, medicine)

C = *Other* (including nonbiological and nongeological natural history, technology/inventions, applied research)

[b]A superscript *b* signifies that the *PTRS* and *Proceedings* were divided in these periods into A and B editions, which corresponded to the A and B article-type division used here. Therefore no stratified sampling was performed in these sampling periods. Instead 5 articles (3 per period from the *PTRS* and 2 per period from the *Proceedings*) were drawn respectively from the A and B editions of these journals.

the ARCHER text-selection procedures described previously were reapplied. Table 3.2 displays the results of these stratification procedures: actual numbers of texts in each category per year; percentages of frequency of occurrence per category; and the number of texts actually chosen for each category. For the final two sampling periods, when the Royal Society journals were actually being published in separate A and B series (as noted previously and in chap. 2), five texts from each of the first two categories were simply selected without computing frequencies of occurrence, because all articles printed had presumably been preselected according to the physics/mathematics versus life sciences organization of the journals.

A second change made in the ARCHER scientific report subcorpus was the inclusion of whole texts up to a total of 6,000 words, whereas ARCHER text samples were comprised of a maximum of 2,000 words. From 1925 onward—when the standard Introduction–Methods–Results–Discussion rhetorical format for current experimental scientific research writing first appeared in force—texts longer than 6,000 words were additionally sampled so that approximately equal sections of 2,000 words were selected from the beginnings, middles, and ends of texts.

Third and finally, two types of texts disqualified from inclusion in ARCHER were judged necessary to be included in the corpus used here, in order to capture the full range of textual variation in the historical *PTRS*. These were: (a) articles that had been explicitly translated from other languages; and (b) articles, such as those on musical theory, which could not be construed as falling within a broad 20th-century definition of "science and technology."[18] All other selection criteria adhered to in the construction of ARCHER were also followed in assembling the B corpus used in the present study. The 70 texts chosen in this manner totaled 243,304 words.

ENDNOTES

[1]In using the term "emergent," I do not mean to suggest that there is any such thing as a system of discourse analysis which is totally "theory neutral." Rather, by this term I intend to denote analysis which is relatively open-ended, in the sense that it is not guided by a precise set of theoretical postulates that a priori determine what is or is not interesting or fruitful to examine. As for the theoretical basis of rhetorical analysis, I attempt to make this as explicit as possible in the two sections concerned with describing it in this chapter.

For a discussion of the theory-laden nature of all human perception, see Gee (1990, chap. 1), wherein it is argued that because all perception *is* highly theory-laden, the best course is for humans (including scientists and linguists) to try to make their "theories" of seeing the world explicit, and then to change these theories if they are found to be harmful to others. This is a course of conduct, according to Gee, which should not only guide human behavior but should also underlie the study of discourse analysis. I have briefly tried, at the end of the introduction to this volume, to locate my work within this tradition, but a fuller articulation must take place elsewhere.

[2]I am grateful to Edward Finegan for pointing out this quotation to me.

[3]MacDonald (1994, pp. 147–148) argues for a similar combination of linguistic and rhetorical analysis in the study of professional writing.

[4]The pragmatic—even ad hoc—eclecticism of rhetorical analysis, however, is often at odds with more committed forms of interdisciplinarity.

[5]The following concepts, and the discussions of them in the accompanying citations, are among those I have found useful in the rhetorical analysis of scientific and medical research writing.

- Voice and vocality (Bakhtin, 1981; Bowden, 1991)
- Social indexicality (Ochs, 1990, 1992, 1996)
- Persona (Cherry, 1988)
- Intertexuality (Bennett, 1982; J. E. Porter, 1986)
- Metadiscourse (Crismore, 1989; Crismore & Farnsworth, 1990)
- Discourse conventions (D. Atkinson, 1991; Ferguson, 1994; Tannen, 1987)
- "Psychological" writing (D. Atkinson, 1992)
- Top-level discourse structure (Horowitz, 1987; Meyer, 1985; Phelps, 1985)
- Special attention to openings and closings
- Subtitles and text-sectioning conventions (D. Atkinson, 1991; Bazerman, 1985; Ong, 1982, chap. 5)
- "Constructing" the reader/reader-position (Brandt, 1990; Kress, 1989; Latour, 1987; Myers, 1990; Ong, 1982; Scollon & Scollon, 1981)

- "Constructing" the author/writer-position (Barthes, 1977; Foucault, 1977; Kress, 1989; Scollon & Scollon, 1981)
- Narrative structure (Gee, 1990; Scollon & Scollon, 1981)
- Discourse community (Bizzell, 1982, 1992; Harris, 1989; Killingsworth, 1992; Rafoth, 1988; Swales, 1990, 1993)
- "Distanced" and "effaced" author norms (D. Atkinson, 1992; Brandt, 1990; Kress, 1989; Trimbur, 1990)
- Authority (Dear, 1985; Kress, 1989)
- Author (Barthes, 1977; Foucault, 1977)
- Subject-positioning (Fairclough, 1989; Kress, 1989)
- Schemas and cultural models (Adams & Collins, 1979; Gee, 1992; Holland & Quinn, 1987)
- "Conventions for construing reality" (Bazerman, 1988; Bizzell, 1982; Fleck, 1979; Kuhn, 1970)
- Design coherence versus flow coherence (Phelps, 1985)
- Multifunctionality of linguistic features (D. Atkinson, 1991; Halliday, 1985; Ochs, 1992)
- Rhetorical "moves" (Swales, 1990)

[6]As I hope I have indicated earlier in this chapter, and chapter 1, I regard context as playing more than simply a background, interpretative role in discourse analysis. It does seem typically to occupy such a role in the version of rhetorical analysis I describe here, though the work of rhetoricians such as Jarratt (e.g., 1994) seems to signal an attempt to move beyond restrictive views of context.

[7]Bazerman (1988, pp. 64–65) also attaches the following caveat to his own rhetorical analysis of experimental articles in the *PTRS* from 1665 to 1800, a caveat that I wholeheartedly endorse, as well, in the case of the present study:

> The story I will be presenting thus has been filtered several times through my own personal, interpretive, selective, and synthetic judgments. I will present detailed evidence from the texts to illustrate and support the story I present, but I will not be presenting all the trees in the forest. If I were to tell more I would risk the reader losing sight of the shape of the forest I believe I have found. On the other hand, I have no more impersonal way of either reconnoitering the shape of the forest or communicating and demonstrating that shape. This is always the dilemma of attempting to make sense of historical and literary material which incorporates the complex actions of many individuals. In terms of persuasion, this essay must rest in the short term only on the impression it gives of a plausible story and in the long term only on whether others crossing the same terrain find the shapes presented here recognizable and useful.
>
> Another consequence of working from individual accounts of the products of many individuals, each reacting to specifics of individual situations, is that the overall trends are likely to wash out many individual variations as well as to appear more uniform than they in fact are. When looking at all the trees in the forest, I find a somewhat more ragged shape than will emerge here, although I will attempt to indicate where the raggednesses are.

[8]"Original article" is a historical and current standard designation for scientific research reports that covers the report types thought to be generically central to the field (cf. Kronick, 1976; Rudwick, 1963, p. 319). Because the *PTRS* has never explicitly marked original articles as such (in contrast to other historical scientific and medical journals—see D. Atkinson, 1992, note 7), original articles were operationally defined in this study as all articles to which authorship was attributed, whether the actual name of the author was given or not (e.g., some articles in the 17th and 18th centuries are attributed to "anonymous") .

[9]Phelps (1985, p. 23) defines "design coherence" as the "fully realized and relatively fixed coherence [of a text] as a meaning object." Thus, design coherence is largely a function of the top-level "architectural" structure of written text, as opposed to more local coherence-maintaining devices such as cohesion markers, which Phelps characterizes as contributing to a sort of online, or "flow," coherence (cf. Brandt, 1990). Meyer's (1985) concept of "top-level text structure" is basically synonymous with Phelps' design coherence.

[10]The development and implementation of the original tagging program is described in more detail in Biber (1988, Appendix II.2).

[11]All written genres but two analyzed by Biber—a total of 15—came from the LOB corpus and amounted to a total of 324 texts and approximately 675,000 words; all spoken genres came from the London–Lund corpus, totaling 141 texts and approximately 280,000 words. The two additional written genres, personal letters (6 texts) and professional letters (10 texts), were added by Biber to the written part of the corpus, since the LOB corpus included only published writing (see Biber, 1988, chap. 4 for further details of his corpus).

Although the online dictionary used by the tagging program was based on American English, while the texts analyzed at this stage of MD analysis were from two corpora of British English, Biber (1988, Appendix II.2) found only minimal levels of mistagging due to such differences. He further points out that, to the degree to which it occurred, such mistagging was spread evenly across all varieties of texts, so that MD relations among these text groups were not disturbed.

[12]Where *two* inversely co-occurring sets of linguistic features are present on the same dimension, as described later in this section and as seen on Dimension 1 (see Table 3.1), feature counts for each of the two sets are first summed as described here, with the smaller of the two sums then being subtracted from the larger to arrive at the individual factor score.

[13]The version of the tagging program used in the target analysis was an improved version of the earlier PL/1 tagging program. Unlike the earlier program, it also included a probabilistic tagger whereby tags could be assigned on the basis of probability to grammatical and lexical forms not included in the online dictionary on the basis of information regarding the surrounding linguistic context. A second program was used to check the problematic items that had been checked by hand in Biber's (1988) study. In my use of MD analysis I aim for 90% tagging accuracy, which is validated by random 100-word checks of tagged texts (see Biber, 1988, Appendix II.2).

[14]The feature types listed here are explained and exemplified in Biber (1988, Appendix II.3), and in selected cases in chapter 5 of the present study. It should be noted that whereas Biber's original computer program identified and counted 67 linguistic features, a smaller number of features actually emerged on the factors produced by the original factor analysis.

It should also be noted here that historical and British spellings deviating from the modern American spellings represented in the online dictionary employed in the tagging procedure were modified when the actual texts under study were first being digitalized (i.e., at the point at which the texts were first typed or scanned into the computer).

[15]Two of the genre descriptors in this figure have been shortened for the sake of formatting. The shortened forms are: "academic prose," which is referred to in Figs. 5.1, 5.5, and 5.6 as "general academic prose"; and "broadcasts," which are referred to in Fig. 5.5 and the text surrounding that figure as "non-sports radio broadcasts." The subgenre of "natural science academic prose" has also been added.

[16]Volumes of the *PTRS* from 1665 to 1780 are widely available in reprinted form (e.g., by Nieuwkoop Publishers, Amsterdam). Volumes from 1781 onward are available only in the original, but these can be found in major research libraries in the United States. There is also an abridged series of *PTRS* volumes from around 1780 on, but it was not consulted for this project. The *Proceedings* is available in major research libraries from 1887 onward. Earlier volumes of the *Proceedings* are less easily available.

[17]Although only 10 samples were actually used in the corpus for each period, by initially selecting 12 samples allowance was made for the possible disqualification of texts according to some of the selection criteria mentioned in this section.

[18]"Science and technology" here includes medical science. Despite the decision to include these two kinds of texts, however, very few actually occurred in the sample: The only clear examples were two translations occurring in the 1675 volume of the *PTRS*.

4

Rhetorical Analysis

In this chapter, I describe the results of rhetorical analysis of *PTRS* articles at seven 50-year intervals from 1675 to 1975. The chapter is divided into five sections: this short introduction; three longer sections, each characterizing a major aspect of rhetorical variation across the 300 years studied; and a short summary. The section following this introduction focuses on the way authors position themselves in their texts; that is, whether the author is indexed as an important actor in the events depicted in the text, or, at the opposite extreme, is largely "effaced" or "distanced." The second longer section deals with preferred genres and discourse structures employed in reporting research in the *PTRS*, and changes that took place in them. The third longer section examines the changing character of the "discourse community" in which *PTRS* texts were situated, as that community is itself represented in the texts.

Although it would be foolish to claim that every important parameter of rhetorical variation appearing over the last 300 years in the *PTRS* has been described in this chapter, each of the foregoing categories does reflect a major axis of change. It would be equally foolhardy to purvey this or any analysis of the *PTRS* as an objective and definitive description of the textworld in question; instead, the present analysis should be read in conjunction with others that cover some of the same territory, such as Allen, Qin, and Lancaster (1994), Bazerman (1988, chap. 3), Dear (1985), Katzen (1980), Paradis (1987), and Valle (1997).

THE PLACE OF THE AUTHOR[1]

Generally speaking, the place of the author is seen to change across time in the *PTRS*, from one in which he or she occupies a central position in the text, to one in which the author is "effaced" or "distanced."[2] This phenomenon can be related to the crucial role a strong authorial persona played in the rhetoric of early modern scientific writing (see chap. 6), and to the gradual replacement of that early modern rhetoric with one that emphasized an impersonal or "object-centered" orientation.

The "author-centered" approach is well-represented in the *PTRS* of 1675. Most articles have a prominent authorial persona, which is indexed linguistically through the frequent use of first person personal pronouns and, to a lesser extent, active-voice verb constructions. Thus, articles frequently begin in ways like the following:[3]

> Sir,
> It may seem, by the curious Remarks sent to you from Scotland, that we are yet to seek out the Causes and original Source, as well as the Principles and Nature, of *Frosts*. I wish, I were able to name all the circumstances that may be causative of Frosts, Heats, Winds, and Tempests. I know by experience, that the Scituation of the place is considerable for some of these; but, after much diligence and troublesome researches, I cannot define the proximity or distance, nor all the requisites, that ought to be concurrent for all the strange effects I have observ'd in them. (Beal, 1675, p. 357)

Some of the author-centered character of this opening can be attributed to the fact that the article is also a letter, as indeed were many *PTRS* reports in this period. (Epistolary articles are treated in the following section.) At the same time, it cannot be the *only* explanation for this approach, as it also appears in articles that are not letters. The generalized nature of the author-centered approach in this period is shown in the following passage, taken from the middle of a nonepistolary "experimental discourse":

> I doubt not but what I have related and hinted has given you a Curiosity to know somewhat further of this Mercury: And I confess, that if there be any truth in what some of the most approved *Spagyrists* have deliver'd about a Solvent of Gold that seems of kin, and perhaps is not much Nobler than one that I had; it seems allowable to expect, that even ours should be of more than ordinary use, both in *Physick* and *Alchymy*. But the misfortune I had to have lost a considerable quantity of it, being afterward increased by the almost sudden death of the only Operator I trusted in the making of it; I was altogether discouraged from repeating such a troublesom preparation, especially being diverted by Business, Removes, Sickness, and more pleasing studies. (Anonymous, 1675, p. 515)[4]

This passage also gives plentiful evidence of a second common aspect of author-centered discourse—the use of language to portray the subjective states and psychological processes of the author. Thus, besides "doubt[ing]," "expect[ing]," and "trust[ing]," the author here describes himself as suffering a "misfortune" which "discouraged" him from reformulating a "troublesom" compound.

Other rhetorical characteristics of the early *PTRS* co-occur with the "author-centered" approach. These include: (a) *witnessing,* that is, the naming of (typically important) persons who were present at the scientific event being reported; (b) *indexes of modesty and humility,* such as stance markers,[5] by means of which researchers showed their diffidence and caution in the interpretation of natural phenonema (cf. Shapin, 1984; Shapiro, 1983); (c) a *tendency toward miscellaneity,* such that digressions are frequent, and some articles are patchworks of unconnected observations; and (d) *elaborate politeness,* as when articles open with encomia to the Royal Society membership, or when fellow researchers or their discoveries are referred to as "ingenious" and "intelligent." (Most of these characteristics are treated further below; cf. Dear, 1985; Shapin, 1984).

What happens to the author-centered approach after its pervasive appearance in the 17th century? It occurs with nearly equal strength in the 18th, although the highly mathematical nature of several long articles in the 1725 volume—when the Royal Society was fully under the sway of Newton— seems temporarily to have diluted it.[6] In 1775, though, no less influential a scientist than Joseph Priestley can be found operating fully within the author-centered discourse, as indeed did most other authors:

> The nitrous acid I have exhibited in the form of air [i.e., gas], though only, as it were, for a moment; since no fluid, that I am acquainted with, is capable of confining it. The more I consider the nitrous acid, the more wonderful and inexhaustible the subject appears. The kinds of air which it forms, according to its various combinations with *phlogiston,* are, I believe, more numerous than all the kinds that can be formed by the other acids. Many of the phaenomena which have lately occurred to my observation relating to it are, to me, altogether inexplicable; though I perceive certain analogies among some of them. (Priestley, 1775, p. 386)

Although the author-centered approach taken by Priestley represented the overwhelming norm in 1775, there are a few signs that a different, essentially *object-centered* rhetoric was also beginning to assert itself. This rhetoric can be seen in isolated passages of articles, particularly where the methodology and conduct of experiments are described. Thus, the pioneer physiologist John Hunter is found detailing experiments on "plant and animal heat" in a rather modern-looking, object-centered way:

IV. A leaf taken from a growing bean was put into the cold mixture, and frozen, and afterwards thawed, which served as a standard. Another fresh leaf was taken and bent in the middle upon itself; a small shallow leaden vessel was put upon the top of the cold mixture, and the two leaves put upon its bottom; but one-half of each leaf was not allowed to touch the vessel by the bend; the cold mixture was between 17° and 15°, and the atmosphere at 22°. (Hunter, 1775, p. 451)

The choice of the agentless passive as the nearly exclusive finite verb form in this description seems distinctly modern; at the same time, accounts of other experiments in this article show that Hunter was not averse to a more author-centered style when it suited him:

I. The first experiment was made on two carp. They were put into a glass vessel with common river water, and the vessel put into the freezing mixture; the water did not freeze fast enough; and therefore, to make it freeze sooner, we put in as much cooled snow as to make the whole thick. The snow round the carp melted; we put in more fresh snow, which melted also; and this was repeated several times, till we grew tired. . . . (Hunter, 1775, p. 447)

Finally, an important marker of modesty in this passage that frequently occurred in association with the author-centered approach should be noted: the reporting of experimental difficulties or failures (cf. Shapin, 1984).

As mentioned previously, instances of an essentially object-centered style of discourse can be found only rarely in 1775, and this holds as well for 1825, the next period sampled. Generally speaking, the author-centered approach again predominates across all types of articles, although they show revolutionary change in other areas (see, in particular, section entitled "Orientation to Discourse Community" below). Likewise, earlier correlates of the author-centered approach such as witnessing, modesty, and honoring introductions, while less foregrounded in this period are still frequently represented. By 1875, however, most author-centered prose is being used for specific rhetorical purposes, or is confined to specific textual locations in reports; only 4 out of 22 articles (18%) in this volume take a generalized author-centered approach. Instead, the norm is for discourse which focuses on others' research findings—exhaustive reviews of literature are common—or which describes phenomena, whether in terms of experiments or observations, in a basically object-centered way. Consider, for example, this description of tooth development in two species of reptiles:

Anguis fragilis and *Lacerta viridis*—The description of these two forms may be most conveniently taken together, as no differences of importance have been recorded between them. The area of tooth-development exists in them as a sharply defined region, bounded on its inner side by connective tissue, just as in the newt and the frog; but although it is not restricted by extraneous causes, such as the antagonism of the upper and lower jaws, it nevertheless is not widely extended as in the newt, but contains only one advanced tooth-sac at one time (Plate 47, figs. 16, 17, 18). (Tomes, 1875, p. 292)

One major rhetorical use of author-centered discourse, however, also appears in descriptions such as this: where it is used to index the author's uncertainty, or unique position, vis-à-vis some aspect of the text's content (cf. Tarone, Dwyer, Gillette, & Icke, 1981). Thus, in the paragraph directly following that just quoted, and which continues the description begun therein, the discourse for a brief moment becomes author-centered:

> The enamel-germ appears to be given off from that of the preceding tooth-sac (fig. 19); at least a process is very often discoverable at the side of this latter, although the connexion with the oral epithelium is not lost and appears to be tolerably direct (see figs. 18 & 16): *I am inclined to think* that the enamel-germs do not arise from the oral epithelium quite *de novo* for each tooth-sac, but that they may be justly described as successive branches of a common stem. An early stage of a tooth-sac is represented in fig. 20, in which the dentine-papilla is seen to be distinct in its origin from the enamel-organ . . . (Tomes, 1875, p. 292, italics added)

This specialized use of the author-centered approach can perhaps also be seen, in primitive form, in the second passage by Hunter quoted previously.

A second function of author-centered style in 1875 is to begin articles or specific sections within them; this use may be a holdover from the particularly concentrated author-centered approach often seen at the beginning of articles in earlier periods. Just as frequent in this period, however, are articles in which the author is either distanced at article beginning through the use of such devices as third-person reference, or seemingly left out of the discourse altogether.

Finally, articles from 1925 and 1975 show continued development of distanced and effaced author norms. This is particularly clear in article beginnings, a textual location where indexes of the author were once nearly universal:

> Early in 1923 it was shown that a tungsten filament heated to 1200° K or more in saturated caesium vapour converts all caesium atoms which strike it into caesium ions. Thus when the filament is surrounded by a negatively charged cylinder a positive ion current flows from the filament, which is independent of the filament temperature (above 1200° K) and independent of the applied potential, if this is sufficient to overcome the space charge effect of the positive ions. At lower voltages the currents follow the $\frac{3}{2}$ power law, and the currents are smaller than the corresponding electron currents obtainable from the

same filament in the ratio of the square roots of the masses of the electrons and caesium ions. (Langmuir & Kingdon, *Proceedings,* Series A, 1925, p. 61)

That this is more than just non-author centered discourse—that direct indexes of the author are in fact being *avoided*—is made clear by the fact that "it was shown" in the first line refers to earlier work done by these very same authors. In other cases, authors refer to themselves exclusively as "the author," extending this form of self-reference even into article-ending acknowledgments:

> The author desires to express his indebtedness to those who have assisted at various times in the experimental work which forms the basis of the fore-going paper. Many of the earlier photographs with the large quartz spectrograph, including those reproduced in Plate 2, were taken by Mr. J. S. Clark . . . (Fowler, *PTRS,* Series A, 1925, p. 40)

However, despite the fact that articles have patently become more object-centered and impersonal in the 20th century, those that substantially include authors in the events they describe have not completely vanished from the scene. One article type in which the author's role is given comparatively direct expression seems even to be a creation of the 20th century: the purely theoretical paper written by nonexperimental physicists or mathematicians. Besides their obviously nonempirical content, these papers differ from other work presented in the *PTRS* in that their topics are rarely contextualized within an active research tradition, nor are they formatted according to the conventional Introduction–Methods–Results–Discussion (IMRD) format of modern experimental reports. (See section entitled "Orientation to Discourse Community" below for more on theoretical reports.) An even smaller number of articles—three in 1925 and one in 1975, all biological—retain a generalized author-centered rhetoric that resembles in a muted way the dominant author-centered approach of the preceding three centuries. But both of these exceptional article types, although interesting, do nothing to diminish the fact that by far the larger number of articles in 1925 and 1975 include few if any direct indexes of the author. Where such indexes do occur, they usually function to indicate either a unique choice or significant uncertainty on the part of the author in what is otherwise highly object-centered discourse.

PREFERRED GENRES AND DISCOURSE STRUCTURES

Although a large number of apparent *genre names* occur in the titles of *PTRS* articles over its first 200 years, finding enough evidence from articles to distinguish one such supposed genre from another is usually impossible.

Instead, it appears that such names were assigned to articles almost indiscriminately. In 1775, for example, 18 separate category names are used in article titles, and even those names that appear multiple times (i.e., *Account, Observations, Description, Experiments and Observations, Experiments*) seem to be applied to widely different types of articles.[7] Thus, a 1775 article entitled "Account of a Musical Instrument, which was brought by Captain Fourneaux from the Isle of Amsterdam in the South Seas to London in the Year 1774, and given to the Royal Society" is a four-page description of the instrument and the tonic system of its users. The 1775 volume's final article, on the other hand, "An Account of Observations made on the Mountain Schehallien for finding its Attraction," reports in 42 pages a major research project undertaken by the Society to determine the gravitational attraction exhibited by large geological structures such as mountains.

The converse situation is also true: Articles that appear generically similar in form and function are typically given different kinds of titles. The first of the two "accounts" mentioned just previously, for instance, is clearly made up of a letter and an accompanying explanation, as is the article—by the same author on a closely related subject—which immediately follows it. The latter, however, is entitled "*Remarks* on a larger System of Reed Pipes from the Isle of Amsterdam, with some Observations on the Nose Flute of Otaheite" [italics added].

Spanning the period 1675–1875, then, there appear to have been mostly loose sets of co-occurrence expectations of form, style, and content for reporting research in the *PTRS*, rather than highly conventionalized genres and discourse structures. Two sorts of articles which occur widely throughout this period, however, may be considered partial exceptions: (a) articles published in the form of letters; and (b) reports of experiments.[8] In the following two subsections I characterize these article types and the changes they exhibit over time.

Letters. The single most common generic form in which articles appeared between 1675 and 1875 was the letter. As suggested previously, this form had close connections to the author-centered style of discourse. An overall sense of the changing frequency with which letters were used to report research in the *PTRS* can be gained by considering some statistics. In the 1675 volume, 51% of all *PTRS* articles appeared in letter form, while in 1725 only 33% were letters. In 1775, 48% of articles appeared as letters, and in 1825 29% appeared in this form. It was only a little more than 100 years ago then—in 1875—that the letter is seen to have dropped completely out of the repertoire of reporting genres in the *PTRS*.[9]

As mentioned just above, articles in the 1675 volume of the *PTRS* appear in letter form roughly half of the time. These letters themselves occur in varying forms and are published in varying degrees of completeness: Most commonly, (apparently) full letters were reprinted, but about one quarter of all letters are called "extracts" in their titles, although what has been left out is not always apparent.[10] A second form in which letters sometimes appear is interlarded with or framed by editorial comments. This phenomenon accords closely with the historical portrait of Henry Oldenburg as a highly intrusive editor, although correspondents acting as intermediaries between Oldenburg and the actual letter writers are also seen to have played the role of commentator.

Most commonly in this period, letters are prefaced with the salutation "Sir." They usually begin with a paragraph honoring the addressee and/or the Royal Society, who are virtually always addressed with the second person personal pronoun, placing the writer in a typically humble or petitionary role. The following example, addressed to Oldenburg, is more involved than most but otherwise representative:

> Honoured Sir,
>   Having long understood the freedom of address, you have allowed to any candid and unprejudic'd persons, whose general good wishes to the Commonwealth of Learning make 'em ambitious to impart something, whereby they may promote the Empire of Man above other Creatures; I flatter'd my self, it would be no unpardonable presumption, to communicate some of my thoughts unto you, on such a subject, as that the usefulness of the matter may keep me from seeming altogether impertinent, and the smalness of my performance, argue the greatness of my desires to serve you. This I resolved to do by way of Animadversions on the two last *Philosophical Transactions;* and though I performed nothing more, I hop'd at least, my Observations may do them the kindness, as shades intermixt with light, to render them more conspicuous. In hopes of this, I shall draw up my thoughts under the general Title of *Some Philosophical Observations on some passages in the two last Months Transactions,* viz. for *Decemb.* and *January.* (Anonymous, 1675, p. 533)

This opening, honoring the Royal Society and humbling the author, shows the elaborate politeness identified in the preceding section as associated with an author-centered rhetoric. Following this opening the article displays a second characteristic mentioned earlier and common also in letters of this period: a tendency toward miscellaneity or digression. Thus, the author devotes himself to commenting on articles on a wide variety of subjects in the two immediately preceding issues of the journal. At least one third of the letters in 1675, most on natural history topics, show similar evidence of miscellaneity.

Finally, letters in this period are commonly quite short, with the majority not exceeding three printed pages. It should also be noted that many of the characteristics described here as typical of letters also occurred (although less frequently) in articles from 1675 *not* appearing in letter form.[11]

In the next period, 1725, letters comprise exactly one third of all articles. This substantial drop in their relative numbers can partly be attributed to the dominance of a Newtonian research agenda in the Royal Society at this time: Newtonian science does not seem to have favored the letter form, given as the latter was to comparative brevity and miscellaneity.[12] Rather, the research approach modeled by Newton appears to have resulted in longer and more elaborately organized articles, such as the three very long mathematically oriented articles by Desaguliers in this volume on the shape of the earth.

Of the nine articles in the 1725 volume that *are* letters, few show the honoring introductions and miscellaneity that were characteristic of letters in 1675. Three of the nine are medical case reports (the editor at this time, John Jurin, was a practicing physician), and only two concern natural history topics, per se.

By 1775, some of the characteristics noted for 1675 letters have reappeared. Epistolary articles typically begin "Sir" or "Dear Sir," and frequently have polite and honoring introductions, although the length and elaborateness of these introductions are much reduced. Digressions are also again in evidence, although usually restricted to positions close to the ends of papers. Near the end of a 47-page epistolary article on basalt formations in France and Italy, for instance, the author writes:

> Having often had occasion to speak of Abano in the course of this paper, I cannot conclude it without mentioning an extraordinary phaenomenon in the animal kingdom, which is observable there. Notwithstanding the heat of those waters, in which FAHRENHEIT'S thermometer rises to eighty-eight degrees, a particular species of *buccinum* breeds and lives in them, and is found in great plenty. (Strange, 1775, p. 45)

It should also be mentioned that this article, like others of its time, is organized in a contingent, bottom-up way. Thus, detailed descriptions of basalt columns in one location are followed by those of columns in another according to no apparent overall scheme.[13] This style of arrangement, oddly enough, is even signaled in an "advance organizer" near the beginning of the paper: "I shall, first, briefly explain the two drawings [of basalt columns near Venice]; and then add such observations as have occurred to me, upon considering more particularly the curious originals which they represent" (pp. 5–6).

New uses of the epistolary form also appear in the 1775 volume of the *PTRS*. Thus, a few articles have short "cover letters" accompanying longer, typographically separated articles. These letters are usually a single paragraph in length, and are typically polite in an understated way. A second innovation in this period is the article made up of multiple letters, with each printed in its own (apparently original) discrete form. For example, Priestley's article on "air," quoted previously, is made up of three separate letters. Finally, 1825 is the last period in which letters appeared in the *PTRS* volumes analyzed here.[14] Although they still represent roughly one third of all articles, letters in this period show important differences compared with those from the two preceding centuries. First, letter beginnings are only sometimes honoring—they are just as likely to "get straight to the point":

> DEAR SIR,
> It is more than two years since, in a conversation I had with you [i.e., Royal Society secretary John Herschel] on subjects connected with magnetism, you enquired what effect I thought might result from giving to an iron ball a rapid rotation? The subject however dropped, and it did not occur to me again, till in some speculative views in which I was lately engaged, as to the cause of the rotation of the earth's magnetic poles, the apparent irregularity of the terrestrial direct powers, &c. I was led to consider that, probably, rotation might have a certain influence. (Barlow, 1825, p. 117)

While this letter retains a personal tone, the emphasis here, as in other article introductions in this period, is most directly on the topic at hand. A second characteristic of letters in 1825 is their much greater length (as with articles generally in this period), although short letters are still occasionally printed. Finally, less than half the letters in this period are on natural history subjects: Three of the seven letters in this volume concern magnetism, a topic of great interest to Royal Society physicists at this time, and a fourth deals with actuarial statistics.

Experimental Reports. Apart from letters, the only long-lived type of research writing approaching a discrete generic form in the pre-1875 *PTRS* was the report of experimental research.[15] Experimental articles, however, are only loosely governed by genre norms in this period—even synchronically they exhibit substantial variation in form. It is also the case that a relatively small percentage of *PTRS* articles overall reported experiments in the 17th and 18th centuries (cf. Bazerman, 1988, chap. 3). In the present study, such reports amount to 16% of all articles in 1675, 19% in 1725, and 23% in 1775. It was only, then, in the 19th century that experimental reports became a journal staple, representing exactly 50% of all articles in 1825. In 1875, however, there is a large drop—only 17% of articles report experiments in this year—although the corresponding percentages for 1874 and 1876, 43% and 42% respectively, suggest that the drop is an anomaly. By the 20th century, experimental reports are clearly the most frequent article type, constituting 63% of all articles in 1925 and 59% in 1975.

The seven experimental articles appearing in the 1675 volume are all written by two sets of authors. Five articles report a series of experiments

by Christiaan Huygens and Denis Papin, a well-known Dutch–French research team, and there are two by Robert Boyle (one of these having
appeared anonymously—see note 4). Within the limits of a restricted range
of authors, then, some generalizations concerning these articles can be
ventured.

First, six out of the seven reports are extracts from longer works—in the
case of the Huygens–Papin experiments all appear to have been extracted
from a single book published in French. Although extraction was a relatively
common means of procuring material for the *PTRS* in the 17th century, and
particularly material of foreign origin (Katzen, 1980), its exact textual consequences are not clear. One possible outcome is that the Huygens–Papin
reports typically begin by "diving straight in" to experimental narratives:[16]

> To know, whether the *Vacuum* would be of use to the *Preservation of Bodies,*
> I took an Apple, and included it with such a *Cover,* as is described formerly
> in our Method of taking away an exhausted Recipient from off the Engin. The
> Apple I chose, had a little speck of rottenness, and I did purposely include
> some water in the same Recipient, thereby to promote the corruption in case
> any should come to pass. But I have not found that any change happened to
> this Apple since the third of *April,* 1673 [punctuation unclear] which was the
> day on which I included it. (Huygens & Papin, 1675, p. 492)[17]

The five Huygens–Papin articles are largely collections of such short,
author-centered experimental narratives, with the exception of one article
that extensively discusses experimental methods. In almost all cases, the
narratives are connected only loosely via temporal conjunctive expressions,
for example, "Another time I . . ." or "After this I . . ."; the average number
of experiments reported in these five articles is 11. Of the remaining two
articles, both by Boyle, the first reports a string of 10 such experiments, and
the other is a more theoretical and discursive piece, reporting only 2 experiments discretely. Both have elaborate (unmarked) introductions and
discussion/conclusions, and are the only articles in the volume showing
signs of explicitly marked top-level discourse structure.[18]

Experimental reports in the next period, 1725, differ in several ways from
those of 1675. Of the five appearing in this volume, three report no more
than two experiments each. Of these, one reports mostly brief narratives
similar to those in the 1675 volume, and the other (in Latin) has a lengthy
theoretical section followed by 11 experimental narratives. In each of the
latter two cases, individual experiments are explicitly marked off via subtitles from those surrounding them. A second difference is that four of the
five articles deal with purely physical, rather than biological, phenomena.
A third characteristic differentiating experimental reports in 1725 is that
they generally describe results in more quantitative terms than formerly,

as seen in the following comparison of passages from 1675 and 1725, respectively:

Experiment the Fifth.

We took some Filings of Copper, and putting them together with a *Mercurial gage* in a Conical Glass fitted with an exactly ground stopple of the same matter, (which was Crystalline) we poured on the Filings as much rectified *Spirit* of *fermented Urin* made *per se,* as sufficed to swim an inch or better above them; then carefully stopping the Glass, coming to look on it many hours after, we perceived that the Mercury in the seal'd leg was considerably deprest, and gently drawing out the stopple to let in the outward Air, we perceived that access to have a manifest effect upon the Mercury. (Boyle, 1675, p. 467)

I took the Leaden Balls A and B (Fig. I.), the first weighing one Pound, and the other two Pounds; and having from each of them cut off a Segment of about 1/4 Inch in Diameter, I press'd them together with my Hand, with a little Twist, to bring the flat Parts to touch as well as I cou'd. The Balls stuck so fast, that when the Hand H, by means of a String, sustain'd the upper Ball A, the lower one B (by reason of its Contact at C) was sustain'd, tho' loaded with the Scale S, and Weights E, which amounted to 16 Pounds. (Desaguliers, 1725, pp. 345–346)

The greater emphasis on quantitative measurement in 1725, as well as the prominence of physical phenomena as objects of study, is almost certainly related to the influence of Newtonian models of scientific research in this period.

In the next volume of the *PTRS* studied, 1775, 12 experimental reports appear. This larger number gives a better empirical basis on which to generalize regarding the experimental report in this period. At the same time, fully half these articles cluster around just two topics: Four concern the physiological responses of humans in superheated environments, and two involve the abilities of different fish species to generate electric shocks.

Of these 12 experimental articles, half begin with introductory paragraphs or paragraph parts. Four of these have mildly honoring/conventional epistolary introductions, while one begins with a physical description of a substance to be identified chemically, and the other begins by relating itself to the immediately preceding article by the same author. Of the remaining six experimental articles, four begin by jumping directly into narrative accounts of either experiments themselves or events leading up to experiments, as in the Huygens–Papin reports of 1675.

Two further observations can be made about experimental reports in 1775: (a) that they vary in the extent to which the experiments are reported discretely; and relatedly, (b) that they vary in the amount of detail in which individual experiments are described. Regarding the first point, 5 of the 12 reports are comprised of experimental narratives that are either numbered or clearly divided off from one another by various typographical conventions. An account of experiments on the effects of enclosure in a superheated room is representative:

> III. Another gentleman went through the same experiment [i.e., staying in a room heated to 202° for 10 minutes] in the same circumstances, and with the same effects.
>   IV. One of the porters to the Hospital, a healthy young man, with the pulse 75, was inclosed in the stove when the quicksilver stood at 210°; and he remained there, with little inconvenience, for 20 minutes. The pulse, now 164, and the animal heat, determined by another thermometer as in the former experiments, was 101½.
>   V. A young gentleman of a delicate and irritable habit, whose natural pulse is about 80, remained in the stove ten minutes when heated to 224° . . .
>   VI. Two small tin vessels, containing each the white of an egg, were put into the stove heated to 224° . . . (M. Dobson, "Experiments in an heated Room," 1775, pp. 464–465)

In contrast to articles like the above reporting discrete experiments in narrative form, four others organically combine accounts of experiments with theoretical observations, or merely summarize experimental results for theoretical purposes. However, even articles that report discrete experiments *seriatim* in this period usually follow them with discussions of their theoretical significance; where these articles also have introductions, at least an implicit *introduction* → *experiments* → *theoretical implications* discourse structure therefore exists. In only two cases, however, is this structure clearly and fully marked typographically.

The second phenomenon mentioned above—that experimental accounts vary in the detail in which they are reported—is more straightforward to describe. The passage on physiological changes in a superheated environment given just previously is located toward the less detailed end of the continuum, as are most reports in this period; a smaller number of reports describe experiments in more detail, with accounts of single experiments being in a few cases over a page long. Much of this added length is due to highly circumstantial descriptions of methods, as evidenced in the two passages by Hunter quoted earlier.

By 1825, the next period, experimental reports have undergone substantial development and change. Of the 12 experimental articles, 10 feature a new way of doing and certainly reporting experiments, and about half concern themselves centrally with the methodological aspects of experimental trials.[19] Regarding the first of these points, the narrative parts of these articles are locally organized according to the pattern: *short experimental narrative/report of results* → *notice of incremental adjustment of experimental conditions* → *short experimental narrative/report of results.* This approach is seen in an investigation of the actions of metals exposed to rotating magnets:

> 20. A thin disc of copper suspended at a given distance over the revolving magnet, performed 6 revolutions from rest in $54^3.8$. It was then cut in 8 places in the direction of radii nearly up to the centre and $45°$ asunder, by which operation its magnetic virtue was so weakened, that it now required $121^3.3$ to execute the same number of revolutions. The cuts were now soldered up *with tin,* and the magnetic action was now found to be so far restored as to enable it to perform its six revolutions in 57.3, that is to say, very nearly in the same time as when entire. This is the more remarkable, since tin, as we have seen, is not above half so energetic as copper when acting directly. This indirect mode of action therefore affords us a means of magnifying small magnetic susceptibilities which may hereafter prove very valuable.
>
> 21. To illustrate this more strongly, we suspended a brass disc of $2^{in}.25$ in diameter, and $0^{in}.15$ in thickness, as in the last case, and noted the time of its performing successive revolutions. . . . (Babbage & Herschel, 1825, pp. 481–482)

This article reports individual experiments in less detail than some in this period. But the way in which experiments are explicitly linked, leading from one to another in a relatively deductive way, and the way in which systematic manipulation of single variables per experiment is reported, indicate development in this period in the direction of experimental controls.[20]

The second innovation mentioned previously, a comparative emphasis on methods, is doubtlessly related to the first. By showing careful concern for describing the experimental setup, authors indicate a shared desire to eliminate potentially confounding variability from experimental trials. Although experimental narratives—as in the passage above—commonly include methodological details in this period, several reports also have sections near the beginnings of papers that are wholly devoted to describing experimental setups or apparatus. Another article on magnetism, for example, has a four-page description of a device used to position and measure deviations on a compass near a rotating bar of iron.

Due largely perhaps to such specificity in experimental techniques, replication of both one's own and others' experiments is reported commonly for the first time in 1825. Other developments include: (a) the first appearance of a *theory* → *experimental account* → *discussion format*, although articles frequently begin by citing earlier experimental anomalies which lead to an initial set of experiments, in the course of which theories are derived that are then tested through further experimentation; (b) experimental articles that go on for the first time to corroborate results mathematically, according to a mathematical model or theory; and (c) the first extensive use of tables to report experimental results. A final point concerns explicit top-level discourse structure: A few experimental articles feature it, but it still does not represent the norm. On the other hand, reports are generally better organized via advance organizers, local transition statements, and the like.[21]

As indicated previously, the small number of experimental articles in the next sampling period, 1875, appears to be an anomaly given statistics from adjoining years; only 4 of the 23 reports (17%) in this volume feature accounts of experiments. At the same time, these 4 reports occupy 30% of the volume's pages, so what is lacking in numbers is partly made up for in length.

As described further under "Orientation to Discourse Community," articles of all kinds in 1875 appear to provide comprehensive and even exhaustive treatment of their objects of study; this is equally true for experimental reports. Three of the four experimental articles report large numbers of experiments, three also have tables of contents, and two have extensive reviews of previous literature. Tables are again used extensively to report results, and graphs are used for the first time to digest and display large amounts of data.

Besides their exhaustiveness, the most notable characteristic of experimental articles in 1875 is the continuing development of methods descriptions. Demonstrably more than in 1825 even, articles focus on carefully delineating the techniques and devices on which experiments depend, prior to demonstrating in experimental narratives how these "tools" were actually used. Approximately half of a report entitled "On Repulsion resulting from Radiation," for example, describes various experimental devices, accompanied by 12 line drawings of these apparatus. Also for the first time, experimental articles report the use of *standard methods.*

Top-level discourse structure also shows continued development in this period: All four experimental articles are explicitly sectioned, although in one case individual sections, given subtitles in the article's table of contents, are simply numbered in the text itself. Finally, experimental narratives themselves are once again in evidence, resembling those that occurred in the 1825 volume.

By 1925, the next period sampled, experiments are reported in 63% of all articles. At the same time, they are deemphasized in this period as the only, or even primary, means of investigation—articles that do report experiments often supplement them with well-developed observational or mathematical/theoretical accounts.[22] Experimental narratives in particular are presented in reduced form, and methodological information is the focus of only a minority of experimental reports.[23]

A 49-page article entitled "Resin Canals in the Canadian Spruce—an Anatomical Study, especially in Relation to Traumatic Effects and their Bearing on Phylogeny" is a good representative of the less prominent place experiments occupy in 1925. This article has an extensive literature review, which is followed by a long and detailed description of the plant structures under investigation as they appear in different parts of the Canadian spruce's anatomy. Simple experiments involving injuring these parts are then related in a five-page section, while most of the rest of the article describes corroborating evidence from naturalistic, in situ observations. Other articles—particularly in physics—are so theory-oriented that only the barest description is given of experimental methods and results where they appear at all.

This lack of emphasis on the conduct of experiments is also seen in the way experimental narratives are downplayed. Individual experiments are often reported in summary or list form; in several instances, experimental details are restricted wholly to tables. The following excerpt from an article on the chemical effects of heating precious metals in the presence of oxygen and hydrogen (where "W" denotes "the readings of the ammeter at which combination of the gases started at the specified rate") is representative:

> The effect of heating the metal in a high vacuum was next investigated, and it was observed that after such treatment the filament was always in an active condition, irrespective of whether it had been previously heated in hydrogen or oxygen.

No. of experiment	Initial heating of—	W.
24	30 mins. in H_2; 83 mins. *in vacuo*	53
25	30 mins. in O_2; 40 mins. *in vacuo*	55
26	80 mins. *in vacuo*	53
27	30 mins. in oxygen	70
29 [*sic*]	40 mins. in O_2; 1 hr. 50 mins. *in vacuo*	55
30	30 mins. in oxygen	70
31	30 mins. in O_2; 90 mins. *in vacuo*	55

> In Experiment 31 evidence was sought for the emission of oxygen when the metal was heated in a vacuum, and it was found that a definite increase of pressure (which, however, was not large enough to measure accurately) occurred. A smaller apparatus was constructed later in order to make it possible to determine the pressure of this desorbed gas. (Chapman, Ramsbottom, & Trotman, *Proceedings* A, 1925, p. 96)

The authors then go on to discuss the implications of both these experiments and an earlier experimental series in summary form. Such truncated presentations of experimental doings and results have the effect of substantially decreasing the amount of narrative used in experimental descriptions in this volume, even as the actual number of experiments reported per article increases, in many cases substantially.

Accounts of experimental methods are also deemphasized in the 1925 volume. This is in sharp contrast to articles in the preceding period, where methods were foregrounded in the extreme. Instead, the focus is on theorizing and theoretical model building, particularly in physics articles. These articles sometimes concern themselves with methods-like issues, however, in that they discuss how best to go about theorizing or mathematically predicting abstract phenomena.

In terms of discourse organization, virtually all experimental articles in 1925 have explicit top-level discourse structures showing conventionalization in the direction of contemporary norms. Thus, introduction sections are pervasive, and methods sections are relatively common, despite the previously noted backgrounding of experimental concerns. At the same time, the conventionalization of sections is still under development: Introduction sections are comparatively long and rambling, although less so than in 1875; reviews of literature are frequently diffused throughout articles; and discussion sections, where they exist, are poorly developed. Instead of the latter, discursive remarks are usually localized within individual parts of the overall investigations, and virtually all articles have "conclusion" sections in which major findings and their implications are stated, usually in an enumerated-list style.

In the final period sampled in this study, 1975, experimental articles continue to develop in many of the same directions noted for 1925. Accounts of experimental methods are still further downplayed: In most cases methods sections, regardless of article length, are limited to one or two pages. Experimental results are also reported in more highly digested form than before (cf. Berkenkotter & Huckin, 1995, p. 38); where tables were a popular means of presenting such results in 1925 and earlier, line graphs, scatterplots, and other forms of visual representation are now more commonly employed. Thus, experimental articles in 1975 contain an average of 19 visual items, whereas those from 1925 had just 6.1 per article. This increase over time is partly offset by the lesser number of tables in 1975 experimental articles—3.4 per article versus 9 in 1925.[24]

In a separate development, the IMRD format has now become rigidly conventionalized: Nine of the 10 experimental articles from 1975 contain at least three of these article sections.[25] As suggested just previously, strong conventional expectations have also developed regarding amounts of page space to be given over to the contents of certain sections; thus, aside from methods sections being limited to one or two pages, introductions are typically given approximately one page.

More generally, it should be remarked that only a few articles in the 1975 *PTRS* and *Proceedings* volumes devoted to physical sciences and mathematics (i.e., the *A* volumes) have more than passing experimental concerns; even the minority of articles reporting experiments usually focus on developing theories and models. Although a much greater proportion of experimental articles appear in the volumes concerned with the biological sciences, the experiments themselves are also frequently deemphasized in favor of theoretical discussions. This deemphasis of experimental concerns continues a trend first seen in the 1925 volumes of the *PTRS* and *Proceedings*.

ORIENTATION TO DISCOURSE COMMUNITY

Research articles contain important information about the communities of researchers, readers, and writers in which they are embedded (Latour, 1987; MacDonald, 1994; Myers, 1989). In this section, I describe the changing nature of the discourse communities surrounding the *PTRS* across time, as indexed by various textual features found in the journal.

There was a strong tendency in the 17th and 18th centuries for *PTRS* articles to exist in a cooperative dialogic relationship with one another.[26] As evidenced especially in 1675, this approach fits in organically with the Baconian program for empirical science: cooperative activity in constructing a strong base of empirical knowledge from which generalizations could eventually be derived, in order to increase human utilization of nature.

These programmatic concerns are signaled in several ways. First, articles, and epistolary articles in particular, frequently either present or answer lists of "queries"—questions sent out by the Royal Society to obtain information about the natural world. Such lists are sometimes included at the ends of articles, but part of the miscellaneity of whole articles in this period results from the fact that they are on occasion composed simply of answers to lists of queries.

A second indicator of discourse community dialogue and cooperation in 1675 is the large number of articles written in direct response to other reports in the journal. This is often evident in article titles and openings:

An extract of a Letter, written by a Friend to the Publisher out of the Country, July 24. 1675; relating to the Contents of the Tract next foregoing.
I am very much obliged for the last pacquet which came safe, and I am not a little transported with Joy in the perusal of Honourable *Mr. Boyles Essay Instrument,* as he hath expressed the five principal uses of it, which obliges Mankind (that hath any regard for Honesty or Justice; or hath any concernment for *Coins,* or Mettals) to return him grateful Acknowledgments. Few of us are not sometimes cheated with counterfeit money . . . (Anonymous, 1675, p. 353)

This example indicates two further phenomena that also reveal discourse community characteristics in this period: (a) the relatively common appearance of anonymously authored articles, which Kronick (1988) has partly attributed to an ideal of communistic, self-abnegating science; and (b) the close personal relationships that then obtained in and around the Royal Society. Only the first of these characteristics can be related directly to the Baconian program. A third phenomenon relating to the discourse community is that around 20% of articles in 1675 (and this is true as well for 1725, the next period) were written in Latin, the international language of learned communication.

Finally in 1675, the active role taken by the journal's editor, Henry Oldenburg, in promoting Baconian cooperative science must be noted. Oldenburg frequently inserted his own remarks into articles, either by means of footnotes or via comments marked off in the text proper.[27] The thrust of these intrusions is often to remind the reader of other work done on a topic, or to encourage cooperative research, as here at the end of a short article in Latin:

> *So far these Assertions;* which we thought fit to insert here, to give the Curious and Learned amongst us the opportunity to consider them, and to give-in their thoughts upon them; which we are perswaded will be very welcom to the Author. (Linus, 1675, p. 387)

In the next period sampled, 1725, the dialogic nature of *PTRS* articles is also apparent; the dialogue, however, is no longer necessarily a friendly or cooperative one. Due largely to the fact that Newton had by then been president of the Royal Society for 20 years, the Society was fully under the sway of a Newtonian research agenda. As explained in chapter 2, the Newtonian program involved attacking competitors and their theories, especially those from the Continent. In keeping with this tradition, authors in the 1725 *PTRS* relate their work to that of others more polemically than had earlier been the norm.

This "oppositional" approach is manifested in articles in various ways, as when titles and openings take an immediate polemical stance:

> *An Enquiry into a Discovery, said to have been made by Signor* Valsalva *of* Bologna, *of an Excretory Duct from the Glandula Renalis to the Epididymis.*
> The late learned Signor Valsalva having some Time ago discover'd a Vessel, which he took to be an Excretory Duct going from the Glandula Renalis, to the Epididymus in men, and in the Ovarium in Women; . . . I lately procur'd a human Body, in order to search for it, which I did with all the Diligence I was capable of. I was not so happy as to discover any Duct of this Kind . . . (Ranby, 1725, p. 270)

A second marker of oppositional discourse in 1725 is the manner in which writers anticipate arguments against points they are making. This is the approach taken in a long article defending Newton's account of the shape of the earth:[28]

But here it may be objected, that tho' the Latitude was not taken with the ten Foot Sector, in the intermediate Places between Paris and Collioure, yet the Latitude was taken with that Instrument at Dunkerque, Paris, and Collioure, and therefore the southern Part of the Meridian, containing 6° 18′ 56″ may be compar'd with the northern Part of it, which contains 2° 12′ 16″; . . . To this it may be answer'd, that, even in this Case, the Observations made cannot be nice enough to determine the Difference of the Length of Degrees; but there is another Error, which might considerably mislead the French Gentlemen . . . (Desaguliers, 1725, pp. 209–210)

"Manners in dispute" (Shapin, 1984), that is, showing decorum toward one's argumentative adversaries, was another feature of oppositional discourse as it appeared especially in 1725. It is indexed in the preceding quotation via the use of the term "Gentlemen," and more substantially by the attribution "*learned* Signor Valsalva" in the quoted passage immediately preceding that one. Despite the more polemical nature of scientific research writing in this period, however, it would be misleading to portray this characteristic as an absolute difference between articles in this and the preceding period. Various indexes of oppositional discourse also existed in 1675, as indeed did markers of cooperative concerns in 1725. The difference is therefore one of degree.

In the next period, 1775, the dialogic nature of articles, having now recovered a more cooperative tone, is again well represented. At the same time, authors commonly take two other stances in relation to their readers. The first and more popular is one in which the author portrays himself as simply presenting or conveying information to the Royal Society in general, sometimes by way of its president. This less personalized approach is exemplified in the following article opening, in which the addressee is an important member of the Royal Society:

Dear Sir,
    I take the liberty to remit to you an account of the delivery of a very curious acephalous monster, accompanied with a short description of its anatomical structure. If, after a perusal of it, you should apprehend it may be acceptable to the Royal Society, I beg that you will do me the honour to lay it before them. (Cooper, 1775, p. 311)

Such openings may reflect the conventionalization in this period of a neo-Baconian stance (i.e., of seeking to add to the general store of natural knowledge) while at the same time avoiding a more personal dialogic orientation. In this sense, it may represent a transitional step toward the basically abstract approach to discourse community orientation that developed in the 19th century, as discussed below.

The second new discourse community orientation appearing in 1775 can be described as a comparatively *self-focused* approach. Authors taking this approach cast their work more as an inner quest for meaning in the face of nature's puzzles than as part of a friendly or agonistic dialogue. It is sometimes seen at the beginnings of articles, as in the following by a French cleric:

> I was concluding my essay on the sea anemonies inserted in the LXIId volume of the *PTRS*, when I discovered a fourth species of that animal; of which I could not at that time take a drawing; and I have reason to think, that I have since observed a fifth species. New observations have encreased the number of my experiments: my ideas have been enlarged, my views extended; and the phaenomena crowd in so fast upon me that I dare not flatter myself with the hopes of ever arriving at the end of this pursuit. (Dicquemare, 1775, pp. 207–208)[29]

Interestingly, this rhetorical approach seems to conflict with the very idea of scientific journalism—inasmuch, at least, as the latter represents an outgrowth of cooperative Baconian fact collection. Although reasons for its appearance are not clear, the phenomenon has also been noted by other commentators on the Royal Society of this period (e.g., Bazerman, 1988, chap. 3). As already suggested, however, articles foregrounding a primarily cooperative dialogic purpose were also common in the 1775 volume, as were reports taking a less personal "informative" stance.

By the next period, 1825, there is evidence of a revolutionary new dynamic forming in the discourse community. Research problem-statements and statements that certain topics are "important" or "interesting" commonly enter the discourse (cf. Valle, 1993, pp. 107–108):

> (I.) The nature of the heating effect emanating from *luminous* hot bodies has been distinctly shown to be, in many particulars, very different from that evolved from *non-luminous* sources; but the ideas commonly entertained on the subject are far from being precise and distinct. To gain if possible some ground for establishing more clear views, is the object of the following enquiries. (Powell, 1825, p. 187)

There are even occasional, albeit tentative, calls for further research:

> It was my intention to commence a series of such observations at the beginning of the present year, and to continue them for as long a period as I was able; but circumstances prevented my commencing at the time I proposed, and ill health has since put it out of my power to engage in such continued observations as would be required: but I trust the task will be undertaken by others who feel interested in investigating the phaenomena connected with terrestrial magnetism. (Christie, 1825, p. 27)

Such features suggest that a core of aficionados existed for at least some scientific research problems, and that authors now expected their own work to be followed up by others. A few articles even have what amount to proto-literature review sections mentioning typically small numbers of related investigations.

A second feature indexing discourse community orientation in 1825 is a concern with correct scientific methods. Far more than in earlier periods, but less than in the following period, texts of all kinds emphasize the important place of methods in scientific research. Several articles even focus wholly on methods, and two articles have what appear to be incipient "methods sections," although methods-centered discourse is generally spread across the articles that have it.

By the next period, 1875, there has been extreme development in the direction of research becoming contextualized in communities of reseachers working on similar problems. Literature reviews are relatively common and typically exhaustive. Problem-statements and attempts to link projects to more general concerns are also prominent:

A. INTRODUCTORY HISTORY
The investigations which form the subject of this memoir have occupied our attention for a considerable time, having been commenced in 1868. They have been made collaterally with a series of experiments carried on by a Committee appointed by the Secretary of State for War, with the view, among other objects, of determining the most suitable description of powder for use in heavy ordnance, which is still increasing in size; indeed our main object has been to endeavour to throw additional light on the intricate and difficult subject under investigation by that committee.

There are perhaps few questions upon which, till within quite a recent date, such discordant opinions have been entertained as upon the phenomena and results which attend the combustion of gunpowder. (Noble & Abel, 1875, pp. 49–50)

A 10-page literature review summarizing 21 earlier investigations directly follows this opening. Important developments in the organization of British science are also foreshadowed in the above-quoted passage—the coordination of research with a government committee suggests movement in the direction of an institutionalized and professionalized "big science," versus the long-lived tradition of high-level scientific amateurism that still survived in later 19th-century Britain.[30]

Without a doubt, however, the most notable aspect of *PTRS* articles in 1875 is their apparent exhaustiveness and definitiveness as reports of research. Thus, the article quoted just previously is 104 pages long and has 26 discrete sections, lettered from A to Z. Furthermore, it includes an 18-page appendix giving narrative accounts of each of 86 experiments, as well as 24 tables and a great number of charts. Although marking an extreme even in the 1875 volume, this article clearly represents the will to report research exhaustively which pervaded this period. Other indicators of this trend are the large average number of pages devoted to each article (35.5 as opposed to 24.4 in 1825 and 31.3 in 1925[31]), the occasional appearance of articles with their own tables of contents, and the extremely large numbers of results which quantitative articles report. For the first time in this period the majority of articles have explicit top-level discourse structures, which must result at least partly from having to organize the enormous amounts of information they contain in some fairly comprehensible way.

In the next period, 1925, there has been discourse community development and innovation in several areas. First, as described previously for experimental reports, articles have become substantially more theoretical: Especially in physics a number of articles focus only on theoretical model-building, but even those in other areas are more theoretically oriented. Articles sometimes begin with direct expressions of these concerns:

> The co-ordination theory of Werner ('Ann.' vol. 322, p. 261 (1902)) has led to a great advance in our knowledge of complex metallic compounds; as applied to such compounds as hexaminocobaltic chloride $[Co(NH_3)_6]Cl_3$, it involves the assumption that the six component ammonia groups are situate at the apices of a regular octrahedron of which the cobalt atom occupies the centre, and that the complex so constituted—the co-ordinated group—acts as a tribasic ion which combines as a whole with three equivalents of an acid radicle. (Mann & Pope, *Proceedings* A, 1925, p. 80)

Probably related to this more theoretical emphasis is a second development: Articles in 1925 show less attention to the close delineation of research methods. This is particularly true in the case of experimental reports, as mentioned previously, but holds across all types of articles. A sign that divergent research methods may be less of a problem in this period due to the regularization of community knowledge—and therefore less in need of detailed explication—is the very common citation of standard methods. In the initial paragraph of the "Experimental" section of the previously quoted article, for instance, three different standard methods for synthesizing parts of a particular compound, "Jerdan's method," "the method of von Pechmann and Wehsarg," and "Kalischer's method," are cited.

A third way in which discourse community concerns are indexed in 1925 is through the continued development of rhetorical conventions for embedding research in contextual "webs of relevance" (Knorr-Cetina, 1981). First noted at the beginnings of articles in 1825, the use of such contextualizing devices as importance-statements and centrality claims has developed to the extent that they appear conventionally across all kinds of articles, sometimes complexly sequenced. One such sequence appears commonly in article introduction sections, as represented in the following:

I. INTRODUCTION

Although the very remarkable mitochondria of the male germ cells of scorpions have attracted in the past a number of workers (12 and 13), no work had so far been undertaken on the female germs cells.

In the present work two different groups of scorpions, with and without ordinary yolk in their oocytes, were selected for study in the hope that some light might be thrown on the relationship between the nucleus and yolk formation. (Nath, *Proceedings* B, 1925, p. 4)

This author contextualizes his research within a discourse–community setting in three ways, resembling the rhetorical "move sequence" that Swales (1981, 1990) has identified for contemporary research articles. The first is a weak *centrality statement*—that a number of researchers have worked on male germ-cell mitochondria in scorpions, indicating that there is interest in the topic. This statement is "weak" because it implicates the subject of the article—the mitochrondia in *female* germ cells—only indirectly. The citation of past work on the subject is also integral to this first move. The second move is represented in the "no work . . ." clause of the first sentence: Swales calls this a "gap statement," a statement identifying a lacuna in the area of research under consideration. The third move—Swale's "gap-filling" move—is then made in the second paragraph, when the author presents his own research as the solution to the problem introduced in the gap statement. Although, as seen here, the rhetorical system of locating one's work within a research tradition is still actively under development, its relative conventionalization is an unmistakable sign of its growing importance in this period.

Finally, there are various indications in 1925 that British science is moving toward an institutionalized "big science" model. Although this phenomenon was a relatively late development in Britain (Ben-David, 1960), article bylines now include institutional affiliations for nearly all authors, a substantial number of whom are for the first time associated with nonuniversity (including commercial) research institutions.[32] In addition, many authors identify other institutional benefactors in article-ending acknowledgments, and less often in the texts themselves.

In the last period covered in the present analysis, 1975, nearly all developments described for 1925 have progressed further. All types of articles show greater concern for theoretical than empirical matters, with this phenomenon being particularly true for the physical sciences and mathematics. Articles in these areas give comparatively little attention to contextualizing the work they report within a larger discourse community, at least by the methods used in 1925 and earlier. Instead, theoretical articles tend to start off by simply describing the topic under consideration:

The differences $\partial<r^2>$ between the mean square radii of the nuclear charge distributions of the isotopes of an element can be determined from measurements of the isotope shifts in the atomic spectrum. It is the purpose of this paper to draw attention to systematic behaviour in the variations of $\partial<r^2>$ derived from measurements of shifts in the spectra of elements of even Z in the range $40 < Z < 56$. (Kuhn, Baird, Brimicombe, Stacey, & Stacey, *Proceedings A*, 1975, p. 51)[33]

Where such articles do mention previous work or a recognized "research problem," it is usually in a cursory way. Even physical science articles reporting experimental results evince little concern for building the contextual "webs of relevance" around projects that are evident in many articles from 1925, and virtually all 1975 articles in the biological sciences.

There is likewise a further downplaying of research methods and procedures across all types of articles in 1975, with standard methods being cited at approximately the same level as in 1925. As mentioned previously for experimental reports, methods sections are conventionally limited to a maximum of 2 pages in 1975 articles, even where the articles themselves are 50 or more pages long. The progressive deemphasis of methods in 20th-century scientific research writing has been generally noted by Berkenkotter and Huckin (1995, chap. 2), who attribute it to a greater desire among researchers and journal editors to foreground the new information generated by the research. This lesser attention to methods may also indicate a lesser concern among researchers with replicating others' work, which might itself suggest the triumph of standard methods, or simply the realization that replication studies are hard to get published.

A third area in which developments noted in 1925 have progressed further concerns the conventionalization of the IMRD format for certain types of articles. The more or less rigid use of IMRD in 1975 experimental reports was described previously; the single *nonexperimental* empirical article in the 1975 *PTRS* and *Proceedings* B (i.e., biological sciences) volumes studied here also adopted this format. Theoretical articles in the physical sciences and mathematics, on the other hand, are divided into essentially idiosyncratic sections. In other developments, abstracts are added to all articles in 1975, and all *PTRS* articles feature tables of contents.[34]

Finally, the use of article-beginning "rhetorical moves" (Swales, 1981, 1990) to contextualize scientific work in terms of specialist–community research problems has also undergone development in 1975. Even though by no means absolute, the three-part rhetorical move sequence already described for texts in 1925 (cf. Swales, 1990) is adhered to substantially in articles that are not purely theoretical. At the same time, there is considerable variability regarding how these moves are realized in discourse.[35]

SUMMARY: RHETORICAL CHANGE IN THE *PTRS*, 1675–1975

The major rhetorical findings of this study are summarized in Fig. 4.1. It should be noted that most of the developments displayed there are assumed to be continuous; that is, although this study is based on textual data sampled at 50-year intervals, Fig. 4.1 assumes that textual developments *between* these intervals were essentially linear and unbroken. Where exceptions to these patterns exist, or continuous development was unlikely, they are specially marked. General limitations of the form of representation employed in the figure should also be noted: It gives only a crude idea of developments in some areas, and is incapable of portraying others. Important points made in the present chapter are therefore not always represented.

In Fig. 4.1, timelines 1a and 1b portray the shift from an early *author-centered* to a later *object-centered* rhetoric. Both types of approaches have existed throughout the history of the *PTRS*, but a shift in preference at the whole-text level is patent when comparing articles up to and including 1825 with later articles. Articles from 1725, however, when comparatively impersonal mathematical discourse on a Newtonian model was common, represent something of an exception to the early author-centered rhetorical norm.

Timeline 2 displays the history of the *epistolary article* in the *PTRS*. The letter was a major genre for reporting research throughout the first four sampling periods; by 1875, however, the letter had disappeared altogether from the pages of the journal.

Timeline 3 shows that *experimental articles* were only occasionally found in the *PTRS* through 1775; starting in 1825, however, they became a major type of text. The one known exception to this pattern was 1875, when only 17% of articles reported experimental research. Evidence, however, that this low number is an anomaly was given earlier in this chapter.

The six timelines under item 4 characterize the period-by-period *orientation of PTRS authors to their discourse communities*. Texts from the 17th and 18th centuries evinced a dialogic approach to discourse community, one that was further either cooperative or oppositional. Two new approaches also appeared in 1775—an "informative" approach, and a "self-focused" approach. From 1825 onward, there is a strong tendency to frame research topics in terms of problems shared within relatively small groups of researchers. Contemporaneously, a strong emphasis on explicit accounts of

1675	1725	1775	1825	1875	1925	1975

1. Place of author

a) Author-centered rhetoric

_____| | |_____???_ _

b) Object-centered rhetoric

_ ??? _____

2. Letters as significant reporting genre

_____ ???

3. Experimental reports

_ _ _ _ _ _ _ _ _ _ _ _ _ _ _ ??? _____| | |_____
$\quad$?

4. Orientation to discourse community

a) Dialogic orientation

_____???_ _ _ _ _
cooperative oppositional cooperative

b) Informative orientation

$\quad\quad\quad\quad$???_ _ _ ???

c) Self-focused orientation

$\quad\quad\quad\quad$???_ _ _ ???

c) Problem-based orientation

$\quad\quad\quad\quad\quad\quad\quad\quad$ _____
$\quad\quad\quad\quad\quad\quad\quad\quad\quad\quad\quad\quad$ (except for theory-
$\quad\quad\quad\quad\quad\quad\quad\quad\quad\quad\quad\quad$ based articles)

d) Emphasis on research methods

$\quad\quad\quad\quad\quad\quad\quad\quad$ _____? _ _ _ _ _ _ _ _ _ _ _ _ _ _

e) Emphasis on theoretical concerns

$\quad\quad\quad\quad\quad\quad\quad\quad\quad\quad\quad\quad$ _____

FIG. 4.1. *Solid line* = phenomenon in evidence as main approach; *dashed line* = phenomenon in evidence but minor approach; *vertical stripes* = apparently temporary interruption or diminution of approach; *question mark* = exact sequence of development or nature of transition unknown.

research methods begins to be seen, and this phenomenon continues into the next period. By the 20th century, however, methods are no longer typically a rhetorical focus-point. Finally, explicit theoretical concerns are foregrounded for the first time in the two 20th-century sampling periods, in what appears to be an ongoing trend.

ENDNOTES

[1]The very concept of the "author" has been heavily critiqued by poststructuralists such as Foucault (1977) and Derrida (1977), as well as by Barthes (1977) and Bakhtin (1981). Although the overall critique is a complex one, many of these writers make the point that authorship is a changeable notion according to the type of writing and the period in which the work was written, and that readers change according to these variables as well. As a result, the heavy emphasis that modern Western cultures put on the author (especially in regard to "high" literature, where individual authors are frequently lionized for their inspired, self-contained "genius") is unproductive—and even systematically misleading—for an understanding of written texts. Rather, from this theoretical perspective texts must be looked at according to how readers are socially conditioned to read texts, and according to how texts relate to other texts that precede them in time.

Although I have sympathy for these concerns, I do not aim to critique the notion of author in the present context. Rather, I am interested in a narrower and more prosaic question: how the author—or more accurately the authorial persona—figures rhetorically in the activity or processes described in the text.

[2]The term "effaced" as used in this paragraph and elsewhere is meant to account for the norm in contemporary scientific research writing of excluding many or all overt indexes of the author, while at the same time acknowledging the use of language (e.g., Adams Smith, 1984; Myers, 1989; see Ochs, 1992, for nonscientific examples of indirect indexing) to subtly indicate the positions of authors vis-à-vis other members of their discourse communities. Examples of both effaced and distanced author norms are given further along in this section.

Although I generalize pronoun usage here and elsewhere to include both sexes, I do not mean to downplay an unfortunate historical fact—that authors were only very rarely women across the 300-year history of the *PTRS* studied. In fact, there are no female authors in my corpus up to the present century. The earliest female contributor to the journal I am aware of was Ann Whitfield, whose "Effects of a thunderstorm at Rickmansworth, Herts." was published around 1760. Caroline Herschel and Mary Somerville were two other well-known scientists who published in the *PTRS* in the later 18th and early 19th centuries (Royal Society, 1995). It was not until 1945, however, that women were admitted to the Society as regular members. Haraway (1997) theorizes about the exclusion of women from the Royal Society, and, more generally, from the social activity of science in the 17th century.

[3]Early articles in the *PTRS* have printing conventions that differ noticeably from those of today. I have tried to remain faithful to the text whenever possible, although I have been unable to reproduce all such conventions. Where typographical mistakes appear to have been made—or the text is not legible—I have added a bracketed *sic*, but in the more usual cases of variant spellings (e.g., the lack of final *-e* on words like *engin* or *troublesom*), word boundaries (e.g., *my self*), and punctuation conventions (e.g., the lack of possessive-marking apostrophes on nouns) I have left them as I found them.

[4]Michael Hunter, a leading authority on the early Royal Society (Hunter, 1982, 1989, 1995), informs me that this article is in fact known to be the work of Robert Boyle.

[5]If not their actual inventor, Robert Boyle was at least the foremost institutionalizer of "modesty" strategies in empirical scientific writing (cf. Shapin, 1984). As Boyle explained his use of such strategies in his *Proemial Essay:*

> [I]n almost every one of the following [experimental] essays I . . . speak so doubtingly, and use so often, *perhaps, it seems, it is not improbable,* and such other expressions as argue a diffidence of the truth of the opinions I incline to, and that I should be so shy of laying down principles, and sometimes of so much as venturing explications. (Quoted in Shapin, 1984, p. 495)

"Stance markers" (e.g., Biber & Finegan, 1989) mentioned in earlier studies of scientific writing include possibility modals (e.g., *may, could*), adjectives and adverbs expressing degrees of probability (e.g., *likely, perhaps*) and "distancing" verbs (e.g., *suggest, seem*), although these markers are in fact rarely referred to in such studies as stance markers. Myers (1989) categorizes many of these same features as "hedging" devices.

[6]Mathematical writings were, from 1675 forward, in evidence in the *PTRS*, and tended to contain relatively fewer of the features of author-centered discourse I have described here. At the same time, such writings did not exhibit any special or undue avoidance of author-centered features, as was generally evident in articles starting in 1875, and as described later in this section.

[7]The other apparent genre names occurring in 1775 *PTRS* titles were: *Abridged State, Bill of Mortality, Calculations, Comparison, Essay, Explanation, Extract, Inquiry, Investigation, Journal, Letter, Proposal,* and *Remarks.* It is also worth noting that titles in the 17th and 18th centuries functioned rather differently than they do today—they frequently combined the function of the abstract (i.e., a brief description of the contents) with that of the present-day title, which plays something more like the part of a one-line advertisement. Even into the 20th century, however, titles in the present corpus still retained traces of their older, more informative function (e.g., the experimental article from 1925 entitled, "Resin Canals in the Canadian Spruce—an Anatomical Study, especially in Relation to Traumatic Effects and their Bearing on Phylogeny"). Berkenkotter and Huckin (1995, chap. 2) discuss changes in research-article title conventions in the course of the 20th century.

It should also be mentioned in this connection that titles in the 17th- and 18th-century *PTRS* seem to have been assigned in many cases by the journal's editor, and that they appear in variable form in tables of contents and bibliographical citations.

[8]There were also some fairly well-defined but more *time-bound* article types that occurred in the *PTRS* in different periods. These include articles reporting observations of eclipses in 1675 and 1725, medical case reports (cf. D. Atkinson, 1992) from 1675 to 1775, and reports extracting observations from "meteorological journals" in 1775.

[9]For counting purposes, a "letter" was defined as an original article (see chap. 3, note 8) in the *PTRS* that included any of the conventional apparatus associated with the 20th-century letter form (e.g., salutations, closings, right-justified dates, ending signatures or printed versions thereof), as well as any mention in the title or body of the article that it was originally a letter. Any article that *contained* letters in either extracted or full form was also included in these counts.

Counts of letters for the 2 years directly preceding and following each of the first 4 years targeted in this study and averages across all 5 of these years for each period more or less confirm the statistical trends described here, although there is a large amount of year-to-year variation in most periods (target year counts are repeated for convenience in the following table):

1673:	57%	1723:	48%	1773:	73%	1823:	37%
1674:	49%	1724:	19%	1774:	67%	1824:	60%
1675:	51%	1725:	33%	1775:	48%	1825:	29%
1676:	55%	1726:	35%	1776:	54%	1826:	50%
1677:	45%	1727:	39%	1777:	56%	1827:	23%

5-year averages:

51%	35%	60%	40%

Five-year averages for the final two periods considered here suggest that letters were somewhat more heavily represented than target-year counts indicate for these years. However, the generalizations I make in this chapter regarding the prevalence of letters in each period are not greatly affected by this fact.

Katzen's (1980) impressionistic analysis also tends to confirm my findings for more-or-less comparable time periods: "[T]he letter was the predominant form of communication" (p. 195) in 1665; "the proportion of letters has decreased" (p. 198) in 1723; Katzen gives no information for 1792; and "there are no letters at all" in the 1845 volume.

[10]An article entitled "An Extract of a Letter, written to the Publisher by Mr. J. L. about the poisonous Fish in one of the Bahama Islands," for example, is a letter of transmittal containing a short account by a third party. It begins with a salutation and ends with a conventional epistolary closing, and because it functions simply to transmit a third party account, it is difficult to see what could have been left out so as to qualify this letter as an "extract."

[11]In fact, it is likely that substantially more of the articles in the 1675 volume of the *PTRS* had originally been sent to the publisher in letter form. Oldenburg's chief means of soliciting communications for the *PTRS* was certainly by letter (as attested by his 13-volume edited correspondence; Hall & Hall, 1965–1985), and the minutes of Society meetings show that letters sent in answer to Oldenburg's queries were often read there (and then often published, presumably).

[12]As explained in chapter 2, the period when Newton was president of the Royal Society—unlike any other in the 17th or 18th-century history of that body—appears to have been dominated by a single research agenda. This research agenda could be expected to have had a powerful restricting effect on both *what kinds of topics* were treated in the *PTRS,* and *the forms* in which they were treated. It should also be noted that John Jurin, the journal's editor from 1721 to 1728, was a committed Newtonian, and that topics in natural history—which many Newtonians considered beneath them—may have been more likely to be reported in letter form than were other types of scientific topics (see chap. 2, "The Newtonian Period," for negative attitudes of Newtonians toward natural history).

[13]These topic/location changes are introduced in ways such as the following:

> Having dwelt a little, in the course of this paper, on the physical geography, and particular vulcanic phaenomena of Auvergne, Velay, and the Veronese and Vincentine territories; I shall beg leave to add a few observations of the like nature relating to the Euganean hills. . . . (Strange, 1775, p. 33)

[14]A check of the companion *Proceedings* following its first 20 years—when it was used mostly to report paper abstracts and Society news—shows that articles in letter form sometimes appeared there. Thus, in the period 1850–1854, 22 of 143 articles (15%) were reported in letter form in the *Proceedings;* for the period 1857–1859, 16 out of 155 articles (10%) were in letter form.

[15]"Experimental report" is defined here as any article that has the rhetorical function of actually reporting original experimental research. This is substantially the same definition that

Bazerman (1988, chap. 3) used in his study of experimental articles in the *PTRS* from 1665 to 1800 (but see chap. 2, note 3 of the present work).

[16]It should be noted, however, that this feature also appears in experimental articles from later periods that are *not* extracted from larger works.

[17]Of theoretical interest here is the use of the first person singular personal pronoun in a clearly coauthored report. A likely explanation concerns the social relationship between Huygens, a bona fide gentleman, and Papin, his paid helper (Shapin, 1994, chap. 8, note 2). In his discussion of how paid technicians' work was subsumed and usually made invisible under the names of their genteel–scientific employers, Shapin (1994, chap. 8) describes a more-or-less similar case involving Papin and Boyle. Papin, however, like his associate Robert Hooke (cf. Shapin, 1989), was much more than a typical technician, and therefore had a somewhat ambiguous status vis-à-vis Boyle, Huygens, and their Royal Society peers. This may account for the fact that Papin's name appeared in the article under consideration's byline at all, although it apparently did not stop Huygens from using the first person pronoun in composing the article (if indeed he did compose it). See Pumfrey (1995) for more on the status in the Royal Society of paid experimenters such as Hooke, Papin, and later Hauksbee and Desaguliers.

[18]Thus, in the first article each experiment is marked off from the others by an italicized subtitle (i.e., *Experiment 1, Experiment 2,* etc.).

The second article is additionally of interest for what it indicates about the experimental narrative as a form in which experiments were conventionally reported in this period (Dear, 1985; Shapin, 1984). About a third of the way into the article, the author interrupts a more theoretical discussion with the following words, strongly suggesting normative audience expectations of an experimental narrative account:

> But you will, I suppose, expect from me rather Narratives than Conjectures. And indeed 'tis but reasonable, that, having but *mentioned* to you a Phaenomenon whose Credibility is by many denied, I should take notice of some Circumstances fit to *bring credit* to it. (Anonymous, 1675, pp. 521–522)

It is also significant in this respect that the author of this article is Robert Boyle (see note 4), as Boyle himself was a central innovator of the "experimental way of life" (Shapin, 1984) that was a vital part of the early Royal Society. Other evidence of the conventionality of experimental narratives in this period is given by Dear (1985) and Bazerman (1988, chap. 4), who report that Newton's famous 1672 *PTRS* article announcing the discovery that light was made up of different colors which were differentially refractible through a prism was actually a fabrication of sorts, because it put into experimental narrative form (and presented as a "crucial experiment" at that) discoveries that Newton had in fact made many years earlier, in a different order, and in a slow and incremental way. Other discussions of Newton's 1672 paper include Gross (1988).

[19]It should be mentioned that 5 of the 12 experimental articles in this period were on the subject of electromagnetism, with 3 of these being by a single author. Of the remaining 7 articles, only 3–2 by the same author—are life science oriented. Taken together, these articles thus represent a very different breakdown by subject than was evident in 1775, which makes it harder to compare experimental reports directly across the two periods. Regarding the large number of articles on electromagnetism, the 1820s was a notable period of activity by British physicists working on this topic, especially the group of mathematical physicists centered in Cambridge. At least 6 of the experimental articles in this volume emanated from members or associates of this group, who must have gotten a sympathetic reading from the Secretary of the Royal Society, John Herschel, the group's most illustrious member. Hershel himself is even represented in the 1825 *PTRS,* as coauthor with Charles Babbage of an article on electromag-

netism. The Cambridge physicists of this period are described in more detail in D. P. Miller (1986) and D. Atkinson (1993, Appendix 1, section VIII.A.2).

[20]It should be mentioned that a small number of articles in the 1775 volume (i.e., that from the period preceding this one) feature a form of experimental reportage resembling to some degree that described here. Bazerman (1988, p. 71) also notes the appearance of a comparable form in the *PTRS* as early as 1800. In a second study, Bazerman (1991) describes how Joseph Priestley, in his *History and Present State of Electricity* (1767), organized the work of his predecessors into a somewhat similar pattern (p. 24) while recommending this approach to experimental reporting more generally. At the same time, Priestley followed a variety of different approaches in reporting his own experiments (p. 36).

[21]That articles are better and more explicitly organized in this period holds as well for *nonexperimental* articles. At the same time, articles on life science topics still retain some of the digressive nature that they had in earlier times.

[22]Bazerman (1984) indicates that a new and highly theoretical paradigm in physics (i.e., quantum mechanics) was beginning to show itself around this time in the spectroscopic physics articles he analyzed, although this fact should not be taken as a comprehensive explanation of the increased theoreticality of articles in the 1925 *PTRS*, as they come from a much wider variety of scientific areas than physics. Crawford (1990, pp. 264–265), however, suggests that atomic physics—and quantum physics in particular—represented a kind of paradigm case for a new, substantially internationalized version of science in this period, one that appears to relate genetically to our current model (at least in some disciplines) of "big science."

[23]One possibility for the deemphasizing of methods in experimental articles in this period (see also Berkenkotter & Huckin, 1995, chap. 2) is that other kinds of journals took over this function. Thus, methods journals—journals devoted wholly to describing new or improved scientific methodologies and procedures—are currently a fixture in some fields of science (Charney, 1996). Although I have been unable to find information on the probable dates of origin of such journals, Swijtink (1987) dates the establishment of a closely related journal form, instrument journals, to the last quarter of the 19th century, and locates it in Germany.

[24]In fact, articles *of all kinds* feature large numbers of photographs, graphs, line drawings, and other kinds of visual apparatus in 1975, and they play major roles in presenting empirical information.

The counts of visuals in experimental articles given here are ad hoc: A more thorough approach would have to devise absolute rubrics for what counts as a single visual item (for example, six or more different drawings may be labeled as a single figure in the articles inspected, and table-like lists of numbers are not necessarily labeled as such). My approach has been rather to count large (i.e., more than about 2 inches square) drawings and graphs and all separate photographs as individual items, as well as to count as tables all lists of numbers in tabular form. In the counts of experimental article visuals for 1975, an outlier that contained 141 figures was excluded when individual counts were averaged. With this text included, the average was 31.2 visuals per article.

[25]Variants of the individual section names in the IMRD format also exist in 1975; for example, alternative names for methods sections include "Experimental," "Experimental Realization" (in a highly theoretical article), "Materials and Methods," and "Apparatus and Methods." It should also be noted here that some of the four major rhetorical sections are now commonly being divided into subsections, although the latter are largely unconventionalized. Results and discussions sections, however, are far more likely to be subdivided in this way than are introductions or methods sections.

[26]Bahktin (1981, 1986, 1990) argues that all language is essentially dialogic, in the sense that the meanings of utterances are ultimately determined in the interactions of their users, and within the dialectical relations among their heterogeneous environments and social histories of production and use. My own use of the term "dialogic" is much less radical and far-reaching—I

simply mean that early modern scientific authors often appear to produce their writing in direct response to the work of others, and, further, often frame these responses so that they resemble what amounts to one half of a dialogue in print.

Recent commentators (most notably Shapin, 1994, p. 352) have made the point that a "conversational" ideal marked the discourse norms of early modern British science, just as it did the wider norms of contemporary genteel discourse (see also Klein, 1994). This point is discussed further in chapter 6.

[27]Oldenburg's intrusion into a text is frequently signaled by an italicized "Thus far the author. . . ," following which Oldenburg's own comments are given. Others' comments are also on occasion inserted by using this frame. Paradis (1987) discusses Oldenburg's active/intrusive editorial role further.

[28]This is one of three articles constituting a larger "Dissertation" by a prominent Newtonian, J. T. Desaguliers, occupying between a quarter and a third of the total pages in the 1725 volume. These articles are also mentioned in the section of the present chapter entitled "Preferred Genres and Discourse Structures" as an example of the longer and more elaborate mathematically based articles that may have been favored in the *PTRS* when Newton was president.

[29]It should be noted, however, that the author goes on to place his research in a more social framework, suggesting that one aim in writing the article was "to communicate some of my ideas that have been suggested to me by my last experiments" (Dicquemare, 1775, p. 208). As often in discourse, the difference I am trying to highlight here is one of degree rather than kind—in this case of a tendency toward the expression of greater self-involvement on the parts of authors than can generally be found in other periods.

The excerpt from the 1775 article by Joseph Priestley quoted in the "Place of the Author" section of the present chapter evinces strikingly similar sentiments to those expressed in this opening, perhaps suggesting some degree of conventionalization (although the Priestley passage does not come from the article's opening).

Bazerman (1988) notes a similar tendency in the rhetoric of experimental articles in the *PTRS* from around 1740 forward. According to Bazerman:

> The experiment, no longer an end in itself, certainly no longer performed in public, becomes a private affair, an event in the individual intellectual journey of the investigator. In the volumes 40 [i.e., 1737–8] onward there is almost no direct conflict over results, but rather only over theories, and even the theories are presented more as the results of individual research programs rather than highly combative claims and counterclaims. (p. 74)

Historians of the Royal Society in this period (e.g., Lyons, 1944) suggest that there was a general lag in scientific activity in the 18th century, a phenomenon that may or may not relate to the inward turn of scientists being discussed here (but see chap. 2 of the present work, section entitled "Age of Stability," and D. P. Miller, 1989, for critiques of the claim that the 18th-century Royal Society was scientifically barren). Another possible explanation is that of Daston (1991b), who suggests that the origins of modern scientific objectivity were in the gradual estrangement and distancing of early modern scientists from one another, and eventually from themselves.

[30]"Big science" is the term popularized by Price (1986) for the large-scale, government-supported norm of scientific activity that has dominated Western Europe and North America in the 20th century, especially since World War II. According to Price (1986):

> Because the science we have now so vastly exceeds all that has gone before, we have obviously entered a new age that has been swept clear of all but the basic traditions of the old. Not only are the manifestations of modern scientific hardware so monumental

that they have been usefully compared with the pyramids of Egypt and the great cathedrals of medieval Europe, but the national expenditures of manpower and money on it have suddenly made science a major segment of our national economy. The large-scale character of modern science, new and shining and all-powerful, is so apparent that the happy term "Big Science" has been coined to describe it. (pp. 1–2)

[31]These numbers are based on page counts of the full first volumes of the *PTRS* from 1825 and 1875; the first A and B volumes of the *PTRS* for 1925; and the first A and B numbers (comprised of 11 and 7 articles, respectively) of the *Proceedings* from 1925. They may be less informative than they appear, however, because original research papers began to appear in the *Proceedings* prior to 1875, and these papers were often the shorter papers submitted to the Society. This division of labor between the two journals was not formalized, however, until the beginning of the 20th century (see chap. 2, note 32).

[32]An example of a byline containing a commercial affiliation is: "Irving Langmuir and K. H. Kingdon, of the Research Laboratory, General Electric Company." An example of a noncommercial/nonuniversity research affiliation is: "R. Frazer . . . , Aerodynamics Department, National Physics Laboratory."

[33]Paul and Charney (1995), in a study of how pioneering writers on chaos theory attempted to position themselves vis-à-vis their incipient discourse communities, found that the two authors they studied took different approaches in their early articles, with one taking a basically "low-context" approach (the article in question has no citations in its introductory section, for instance) like the one described here. However, both authors also began their articles by appealing to relatively well-known, paradigmatic issues in mathematical physics that chaos theory could account for in order to establish the relevance of their work. Unlike their early articles, later articles by these same authors were better embedded (using such standard devices as citations and Swalesian rhetorical move sequences) in their discourse communities.

[34]It may be noted here that individual *PTRS* articles were also being sold for the first time in 1975 as separate monographs. This, and the fact that these articles are sometimes quite long, may be the main reason that tables of contents are now supplied for all *PTRS* articles.

[35]The article introduction from which the following opening is excerpted shows both the highly patterned nature of these moves and some of the variability in the ways they are realized in this period (compare the example given previously for this same rhetorical move sequence in 1925):

> The relationship between organic matter, micro-organisms and inorganic nutrients in the sea is being increasingly recognized as a matter of ecological importance. It is also of great practical importance where the biological destruction of pollutants is involved. A particular case receiving much attention recently is the microbial degradation of crude and other oils. This subject has been reviewed extensively, for example by Floodgate (1972) and Zobell (1973). There is a great deal of qualitative work on the subject, but little data of significance for estimation of the rate of the process in nature. In general, experiments have been of short duration, or at temperatures higher than found in nature, or with nutrient concentrations orders of magnitude greater than those in the natural environment. To quote Zobell (1973): 'Conspicuous by its absence from the discussions in this workshop as well as in published papers is meaningful information on the absolute rates of biodegradation of oil pollutants.' (Gibbs, *Proceedings* B, 1975, p. 61)

Notable in this opening is the degree to which the "gap-statement" move dominates—three of the six sentences elaborate on the point that empirical work on the topic is problematic. Following this opening the article proceeds to review past literature on the topic in three paragraphs, and these are followed by a paragraph giving further details of the problems associated with quantitative studies on this subject, and another paragraph reviewing an earlier proposal by the present author of an initial solution to some of these problems. The next-to-last sentence in the latter paragraph constitutes the "gap-filling" statement or third rhetorical move:

The present work describes a modified form of this method, and measurements of oxygen and nutrient uptake during the degradative process. (Gibbs, 1975, p. 61)

Although a number of studies in this period follow the same general sequence of contextualizing "moves" seen here, none realizes it in a similar way.

5

Multidimensional Analysis

In this chapter, I present results from seven Multidimensional (MD) analyses of *PTRS* texts. Following this brief introduction, I first describe in detail an *overall analysis* of all *PTRS* articles in the corpus constructed for MD analysis (i.e., Corpus B). This analysis constitutes the main focus of the present chapter. The remaining six analyses are more exploratory in nature. They compare linguistic change across time in various smaller subgroupings of texts within the larger corpus: (a) all *epistolary articles* as compared to all *nonepistolary articles;* (b) all *experimental articles* versus all *nonexperimental articles*; and (c) all articles as categorized according to two domains of modern scientific activity—*physical sciences/mathematics* and *life sciences.* Finally, I briefly summarize the results of these analyses.

OVERALL MD ANALYSIS

Table 5.1 presents mean dimension scores resulting from MD analysis of all texts in Corpus B. Scores on the first two dimensions in particular show clear linear development over time, although various sorts of development are also evident on the latter three dimensions. In the following discussion, I treat each dimension individually.

Dimension 1. Biber (1988) interpreted this dimension as differentiating *involved versus informational production* of discourse. "Involved production" denotes the unplanned, or "online" production of language for primarily interactional purposes: Telephone and face-to-face conversations had the

TABLE 5.1

Mean Dimension Scores for All Scientific Research Articles From
the *Philosophical Transactions of the Royal Society of London* (Corpus B),
Collected at 50-Year Intervals From 1675 to 1975 ($N = 70$)[1]

Date	N	Dimension 1	Dimension 2	Dimension 3	Dimension 4	Dimension 5
1675	10	1.1	−0.8	2.3	−0.3	4.7
1725	10	−4.2	−1.0	2.4	−2.7	3.6
1775	10	−7.3	−1.3	4.3	−1.7	4.5
1825	10	−10.0	−2.1	6.5	−0.8	7.4
1875	10	−12.3	−2.7	4.5	−2.0	7.5
1925	10	−15.6	−2.8	3.4	−2.9	8.8
1975	10	−17.2	−3.3	4.4	−3.0	7.7
F		30.12	9.44	3.43	2.60	8.73
$p <$		.0001	.0001	.0054	.0259	.0001
R^2		74.1%	47.3%	24.6%	19.8%	45.4%

highest "involved" scores on this dimension in Biber (1988).[2] "Informational production," on the other hand, describes the carefully planned communication of highly integrated propositional content/information.[3] Modern-day expository genres such as official documents and general academic prose had high "informational" scores on Dimension 1 in Biber (1988).

A large number of linguistic features (see Fig. 3.1) including first and second person personal pronouns, present tense verbs, private verbs,[4] *be* as main verb, postverbal *that*-deletion (e.g., "I suspect [ø-*that*] he has not tried the Experiment"), and contractions tend to appear frequently in texts with high "involved" scores on this dimension. Texts with high "informational" scores tend to have frequent nouns, longer words, prepositions, attributive adjectives, and greater lexical variety.[5] An alternative but by no means contradictory characterization of Dimension 1 can be given in terms of *verbal versus nominal styles* (Wells, 1960; see also Biber, 1988). This is because unplanned, interactive language tends to have frequent verbs, while large numbers of nouns typically appear in planned language with an informational purpose, and all of the "informational" features on this dimension are associated with nominal components in texts.

Results of the overall MD analysis for Dimension 1 are displayed in Fig. 5.1, where parenthesized descriptors denote modern-day genres with comparable scores from Biber (1988).

As seen in Fig. 5.1, scientific research writing in the *PTRS* starts slightly above 0 (i.e., is slightly more "involved" than the mean for all genres analyzed by Biber, 1988, on Dimension 1) in 1675. It then grows steadily more "informational" over time without exception, reaching a value in 1975 of −17.2. This score rivals that of the single most "informational" genre identified by Biber (1988): official documents.

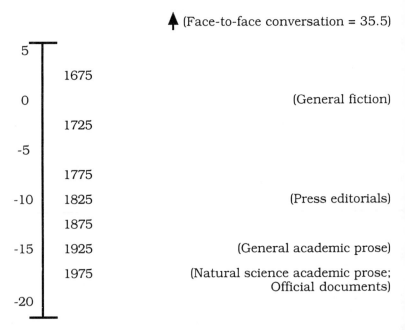

FIG. 5.1. Mean dimension scores for all *PTRS* research articles (Corpus B) by period on Dimension 1: *Involved versus informational production* (parenthetical descriptors indicate comparable factor scores for selected modern-day genres from Biber, 1988).

The pronounced evolution shown by the scientific research article on Dimension 1 can be illustrated by comparing text samples from articles at either end of the 300-year period of study (where italics mark "involved" features and bold type marks "informational" features):

1675:

After this **manner** *I* used to try the **Experiment**: *For I* have try'd *it* often; sometimes to *observe* the **circumstances of** *it*, sometimes in order to further **Experiments,** and sometimes to show *it* **to** others, and **in** all *my* **tryals** the **success** *was* the same. But whereas **Mr. Line** *thinks, [Ø-THAT]* I tried *it* **in** a **cloudy day**, and placed the **Prism at** a **distance from** the **hole of** the **window;** the **experiment** will not succeed well if the **day** *be* not clear, and the **prism** placed close **to** the **hole**, or so near at least, that all the **Sun's light** that *comes* **from** the **hole** *may* pass **through** the **Prism** also, so as to appear **in** a **round form** if intercepted **by** a **paper** immediately after *it* has past the **Prism.**

When **Mr. Line** has tryed *this, I could wish, [Ø-THAT]* he would proceed a little further to try *that* which *I* call'd the **Experimentum Crucis,** *seeing [Ø-THAT]* (if *I misremember* not) he denies *that* as well as the other. (Newton, 1675, pp. 500–501)

1975:

To account **for** the **maximum slope conductance-voltage curve** in the **nodal membrane** in **terms of Boltzmann's law** an **undetermined number of charged particles** transfering [*sic*] **3.5 electronic charges per channel** would have to move **from a blocking to** an **open position through** the **entire electric field within** the **membrane** (Fishman, Khodorov & Volkenshtein 1972). *Since* the **effective charge per particle** calculated **from** the **steady state distribution** (**item 3 in table 2**) *is* **1.65 electron charge** the **ratio**

$$3.5 / 1.65 = 2.1$$

represents the **number of charged particles** which would have to be displaced **from** a **blocking to** an **open position** to activate each **sodium channel.** The **coordination number of** 2 derived **from** the **properties of** the **asymmetrical displacement currents** *is* therefore **in good agreement with** the **results from kinetic data on activation of** the **sodium system** where the **variable** m was raised **to** the **power of two** (Frankenhaeuser 1960). The **data for** the **squid axon** *are* also **in agreement** but **for** a **coordination number of** 3. (Nonner, Rojas, & Stämpfli, 1975, pp. 491–492)

These samples show substantial differences in terms of Dimension 1 features. Perhaps the largest difference is in numbers of nouns: In virtually the same number of words, the 1975 sample has nearly twice as many nouns. Notable in this regard in the 1975 passage is the substantial number of noun compounds, an oft-noted feature of modern-day scientific research writing (Dubois, 1982; Salager, 1984); this feature is totally absent from the 1675 sample. There are also much larger numbers of attributive adjectives and prepositions in the modern-day sample, and its words are almost 25% longer on average than those in the 1675 passage. The 1675 passage, on the other hand, contains various "involved" features: Co-occurring first person personal pronouns, various types of verbs, and *that*-deletions indicate a somewhat interactive and possibly less planned character, but the passage also contains a moderate number of nouns and prepositions. In sum, register differences between these two samples relate to the extremely "informational"/nominal nature of the modern-day passage versus the relative balance of "involved" and "informational" features in the 1675 text.

A post hoc analysis of individual Dimension 1 feature counts in *PTRS* texts across periods supports the foregoing characterization.[6] Thus, the mean number of nouns per text per period rises virtually linearly across the 300-year period of study, with the average number of nouns per text in 1975 being 34.4% higher than in 1675.[7] Even more striking growth is seen in attributive adjectives, another common noun phrase element: They increase 120.5% between 1675 and 1975, again in a virtually linear pattern.[8] Word length also increases 16.3% across this period.[9]

Several features occurring relatively frequently in the early periods also show pronounced decreases across time; these features are invariably from the "involved" side of the dimension. Thus, first person personal pronouns decrease from a high of 24.7 per 1,000 words of text in 1675, to a low of 2.1 per text in 1925, the penultimate period studied. There is then a slight rise in the final period, 1975, to 5.1 per text, but the percentage decrease between the first and last periods is still 79.3%.[10] The pronoun *it* is another "involved" feature that shows a substantial decline across time, decreasing linearly from a high in 1675 of 17.2 occurrences per 1,000 words of text, to a low in 1975 of 6.3, a decrease of 63.4%.[11]

A third finding of post hoc analysis is that a number of features did not change substantially in frequency across time on Dimension 1. "Involved" features of this sort include two of the four verb types on this dimension.[12] The lack of change in another feature, prepositions, is at first glance more puzzling. As an "informational" feature and a sometime noun-phrase element, prepositions might logically be expected to increase in frequency in tandem with nouns and attributive adjectives. Closer analysis, however, reveals a more subtle shift—in terms of the specific syntactic functions that prepositional phrases perform. Thus, post hoc analysis of 10 randomly selected 100-word passages from articles (1 per article) at 100-year intervals from 1675 to 1975 reveals that the percentage of prepositional phrases modifying verbs in these samples has fallen in a fairly linear manner from 52.4% in 1675 to 37.6% in 1975, while noun-modifying prepositional phrases have increased from 33.3% in 1675 to 54.9% in 1975.[13] Although these numbers must be treated with caution,[14] they suggest yet another facet of the historical evolution of scientific research writing into one of the most highly nominal and "informational" types of contemporary English text.

Both the MD and post hoc analyses of Dimension 1 features demonstrate diachronic change in an area that has been relatively well studied in recent years (e.g., Halliday, 1988; Vande Kopple, 1994): the modern takeover of the written grammar of scientific research by the nominal group, or noun phrase. Thus, an analysis of the previously given text samples along the lines of Halliday (1988) would show that the 1975 sample was made up of "markedly long" (Vande Kopple, 1994) and complex noun phrases containing nouns, noun compounds, and "heavy" modification via prepositional phrases, attributive adjectives, and past participial reduced relative clauses. The first noun phrase in the 1975 sample, for instance—*the maximum slope conductance-voltage curve in the nodal membrane*—is 10 words long and contains both prehead and posthead noun modification, as well as a four-word noun compound; the average length of noun phrases in this passage is 6.9 words. Halliday (1988) further points out that such heavy nominal complexes are almost always connected to one another by semantically weak verbs. Thus, three of the four main clause verbs in the 1975 sample—two instances of the copula and *represents*—are, in Halliday's (1985, p. 112ff.) terms, "relational," describing "processes of being" rather than "processes of doing."[15]

In contrast, there is nothing even remotely resembling the complex nominal modification of the modern sample in the 1675 text. Instead, noun phrases have an average length of 1.7 words, with most being from one to three words long. Verbs are pervasive, and they carry a significant part of the content of the passage, which is manifestly a description of human action. Yet, although the growth of nominal elements is a crucial ingredient in the cross-time development of scientific research writing, it is by no means the whole story.

Dimension 2. Biber (1988) interpreted this dimension as differentiating *narrative versus non-narrative concerns* in discourse. Genres and subgenres with high "narrative" scores on this dimension from Biber (1988) include four types of fiction, whereas professional letters, general academic prose, and official documents have high "nonnarrative" scores (see Figs. 3.2 and 5.2). A single set of linguistic features underlies Dimension 2: Past tense, perfect aspect, and public verbs combine with third person personal pronouns to mark a text as "narrative."[16] Figure 5.2 presents a schematic view of change on Dimension 2 across the 300-year period of study.

Dimension 2 shows a pattern of evolution that is similar to Dimension 1's in terms of its steady progression in a single direction.[17] Scores start at a low level of "nonnarrativity" and become progressively more "nonnarrative" over time, until they approach extreme "nonnarrativity" in the modern period. In fact, of the modern-day genres and subgenres studied by Biber (1988), only radio broadcasts, telephone conversations among disparates, and technology/engineering academic prose have higher "non-narrative" scores on Dimension 2 than does scientific research writing from 1975 in the present study.

A comparison of text samples from 1725 and 1925 illustrates the overall pattern of development on Dimension 2 (bold print marks "narrative" features in these samples):

1725:

6. Food or Sustentation. For the first Year, as **has** been already **observ'd, they** all suck the Dam. After **they** are weaned, the right whales, as is generally supposed, live upon some ouzy Matter, which **they** suck up from the Bottom

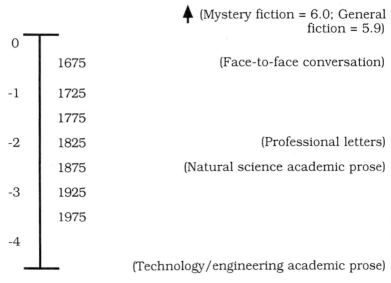

FIG. 5.2. Mean dimension scores for all *PTRS* research articles (Corpus B) on Dimension 2: *Narrative versus nonnarrative concerns* (parenthetical descriptors indicate comparable factor scores for selected modern-day genres from Biber, 1988).

of the Sea. The Triers, that open **them** when dead, **acquaint** me, that **they** never **observed** any Grass, Fish, or any other Sort of Food in the right or Whalebone Whale, but only a grayish soft Clay, which the People call Bole Armoniac; and yet an experienced Whale-man **tells** me, that **he has** seen this Whale in still Weather, skimming on the Surface of the Water, to take in some Sort of reddish Spawn or Brett, as some call it, that at some Times will lie upon the Top of the Water, for a Mile together. (Dudley, 1725, pp. 261–262)

1925:

We **have** not specially illustrated the details in the root, as in general the conditions are similar to those of the stem. A difference, however, that is quite in keeping with general root structure may be **mentioned.** Conifer roots, with exceptions in the case of those produced early by young seedlings, have a structure noticeably more lax and open than that of the stem. The tracheids have larger cavities and comparatively thinner walls, and the zones of summer wood in the growth rings are narrow and abrupt. The resin canals reflect this laxity in the greater breadth of **their** lumina, as compared with those of the stem. In addition the lumen of a horizontal canal in such a position is often found open in the cambial region, and connecting freely with the lumen of a vertical canal as well. (Thomson & Sifton, 1925, p. 75)

Neither sample contains great numbers of "narrative" features, but the 1725 passage still has about four times as many as the 1925 text. Although early scientific research articles sometimes contained substantial amounts of narrative, both of these samples are more in the way of "timeless" descriptions, although there is some reported narrative in the first sample. One "narrative" feature that does show substantial variation here is the third person personal pronoun. It appears commonly in the 1725 sample, usually referring to the discourse topic, *whales;* the more modern sample, on the other hand, uses full noun forms and demonstrative pronouns to specify and describe various structures of plant anatomy related to the roots of the conifer. There are also several public verbs in the earlier passage, which function substantially to introduce indirect speech (cf. Biber, 1988, Appendix II).

As noted previously, *PTRS* articles from the 17th and 18th centuries sometimes feature discourse that linguists would consider prototypically narrative, in the sense of Labov's (1972, p. 360) definition of the narrative unit as "two clauses which are temporally ordered." Texts of this type have already been excerpted in chapter 4, especially in the "Experimental reports" subsection of "Preferred Genres and Discourse Structures." Significantly, most of these texts include more-or-less detailed narrative descriptions of experiments being conducted. A somewhat different kind of narrative example, reprinted below, is from a short medical case report from 1725, a type of text appearing frequently only in the 18th century:

> James Bishop, an apprentice to a ship carpenter in Great Yarmouth, about 19 years of age, **had** violent pains in the lower part of the abdomen, for 6 or 7 months; it **did** not appear to be any species of colic; **he** sometimes **made** bloody urine, which **induced** me to believe it might be a stone in the bladder. **He was** very little relieved by physic; at length a hard tumor **appeared** in the left buttock, on or near the Gluteus Maximus, 2 or 3 inches from the verge of the anus, a little sloping upwards. A short time after **he voided** purulent matter by way of the anus, every day for some time; the tumor **broke**; I **suspected** a fistula in Ano, but **could** not get the probe, by the orifice of the sore, into the rectum. Shortly after the prongs of a fork **appeared** . . . (Payne, 1725, p. 408)

A variety of past tense verbs combines with third person personal pronouns in this passage, giving it a more prototypical narrative "texture." At the same time, in a comparable number of words it has about the same number of "narrative" features as the 1725 passage on whaling. Dimension scores for the full texts, however—.37 for the medical text versus −.70 for the report on whaling—differentiate them more clearly, although even the medical report does not receive a very high "narrative" score.

This last-mentioned fact can be explained by briefly considering the kinds of texts making up Biber's (1988) corpus, and thus influencing the baseline scale used in the present analysis on this dimension. Five separate categories of fiction (representing 74 texts in total) were included in Biber's corpus, and this appears to have pushed zero on the baseline scale in the "narrative" direction, since zero was set at the mean dimension score of all genres in Biber (1988) on a particular dimension. Although not affecting the relation of period scores to one another on this dimension, this phenomenon appears to cause the systematic downplaying of the narrative character of *PTRS* texts. That is, they are unavoidably if indirectly being measured against examples of fictional narrative, a type of text in which the linguistic features occurring on Dimension 2 are likely to appear very frequently.[18]

Post hoc analysis of the individual linguistic features making up Dimension 2 yields further information regarding the development of scientific research writing on this dimension. Interestingly, the decrease in the mean numbers of past tense verbs per text is in no sense linear across periods, although they generally drop across time. Thus, counts for the first three periods together average 27.7 past tense verbs per 1,000 words of text, while those in the last three periods average 18.1, a decrease of 35%.[19] Much more linear, and much more pronounced, is the drop in mean numbers of third person personal pronouns, which decrease by about 70%, from 35 per 1,000 words in the first three periods, to 12.4 in the last three.[20]

The large decrease across time in third person personal pronouns is almost certainly related to the increasing depersonalization of the research article. Early *PTRS* articles often include open and involved descriptions of the ideas and activities of humans. Thus, the article by Newton excerpted under "Dimension 1" above is partly a polemic against the English Jesuit Francis Line, who had earlier announced the nonrepeatability of Newton's famous refraction experiments. The article therefore contains numerous pronominal references to Line, as seen in the continuation of the passage (pronouns referring to Line are in bold print):

> When Mr. Line has tried this, I could wish, **he** would proceed a little further to try that which I called the Experimentum Crucis, seeing (if I misremember not) **he** denies that as well as the other. For when **he** has tried them (which by **his** denying them, I know **he** has not done yet as they should be tried) I presume **he** will rest satisfied. (Newton, 1675, p. 501)

In contrast, discussions of third persons and their activities are nowhere to be found in the modern-day *PTRS;* even literature reviews only rarely contain pronominal references to authors.

It is further the case that *all* pronouns seem to be dispreferred in the current instantiation of the research article. This may be partly because noun phrases now tend to represent whole processes rather than simple entities (see Halliday, 1988, and chap. 6), making pronominal reference to such noun phrases difficult or impossible. In addition, the information structure of modern scientific discourse—the tendency of early sentence or clause elements to summarize the content of whole previous clauses, sentences, or even paragraphs (Halliday, 1988)—also appears to contribute to a general dispreference for pronouns in favor of forms like nominalizations. There is one obvious exception, however: The "unattended" (Geisler, Kaufer, & Steinberg, 1985) demonstrative pronouns *this* and *these* sometimes play a sort of summarizing role in modern scientific research writing, as illustrated in the following from 1975:

> The wave number is not changed at all and the maximum amplitude increases only slowly with larger forcing, but is reached in a shorter distance from the nozzle, the growth rates being very similar. **This** suggests that there is an additional mechanism which limits the growth when waves reach a certain proportion. Indeed, **this** is confirmed by our photographs . . . (Crapper, Dombrowski, & Pyott, 1975, p. 219)

Demonstrative pronouns also play more typical roles in modern scientific discourse, substituting for distinct entities and concepts, as seen in the text sample from 1925 given for this dimension.

A final point regarding Dimension 2 involves the gradual lessening of internal variation within scores on this dimension across time. Dimension scores are mean scores (i.e., averages)—measures of central tendency that summarize individual dimension scores for each of 10 texts on each dimension. These individual dimension scores can fluctuate widely one from another or have the same or similar values, without, however, necessarily changing the overall (mean) dimension score in any way. The latter scores therefore do not provide information about the relative similarities or differences among the scores that make them up, information that can prove useful as a measure of progressive conventionalization in a particular style or register.

Two common statistical measures of variation among the individual components of any mean score are *range of variation* and *standard deviation* (Lauer & Asher, 1988, p. 70). Ranges of variation are simply the numerical result of subtracting the lowest component/unit score making up a mean score from the highest such score; such ranges of variation are given for the present study in Appendix B, part 1. Much more intuitive and useful, however, are visual displays of such ranges. These allow one to see at a glance how widely dispersed or tightly clustered individual-text dimension scores are around their overall, or mean, dimension score. This information is given in Appendix B, part 2.

Standard deviation, the second common measure of variation mentioned above, calculates the average deviation of all component/unit scores from the mean score. The higher the standard deviation, therefore, the more variability there exists in individual scores considered as a group in relation to the mean score (Welkowitz, Ewen, & Cohen, 1982, pp. 58–65). This measure of variation has a major advantage over the range of variation statistic mentioned above in that single very high or low scores are less likely to bias it. Standard deviations for the present study are given in Appendix C.

By both these measures, linguistic variation in *PTRS* articles on Dimension 2 decreases progressively from its 17th- and early 18th-century levels until it reaches a markedly low and stable level in the 20th century. Thus, standard deviations in 1675 and 1725 are 1.3 and 1.7, respectively, but by 1925 and 1975 have dropped to 0.5. Numerical ranges of variation on Dimension 2 likewise indicate the same trend: They decrease in a roughly linear pattern across the 300 years studied. Finally and perhaps most self-evidently, ranges of variation displayed visually (see Appendix B, part 2) show that individual-text dimension scores cluster progressively closer around their mean dimension scores from 1775 onward, to the point that by 1975 they are packed tightly together. This steady decrease in measures of variation clearly indicates the increasing conventionalization of *PTRS* articles across the 300 years studied on the basis of a highly nonnarrative norm.

Dimension 3. Biber (1988) interpreted the two sets of co-occurring features underlying Dimension 3 as representing *situation-dependent versus explicit reference.* "Situation-dependent reference" denotes linguistic reference to some aspect of the physical or temporal context of the language event (e.g., "And *now* the ball comes out just below us," reported by a soccer announcer): Place adverbials (e.g., *far, downstairs*), time adverbials (e.g., *now, tomorrow*), and a miscellaneous category of adverbs are the features underlying this part of the dimension.[21] "Explicit reference," on the other hand, refers to a referential strategy of elaboration for the sake of clarity, one that is common when the possibility of ambiguous reference must be avoided. Three kinds of WH-relative clauses, phrasal coordination, and nominalizations are the linguistic features underlying this part of the dimension.[22] Modern-day genres and subgenres from Biber (1988) showing the highest degrees of "explicit reference" include official documents, professional letters, press reviews, and technology/engineering academic prose; those showing pronounced "situation-dependent reference" are radio broadcasts, and telephone and face-to-face conversations (see Figs. 3.2 and 5.3).

As shown in Fig. 5.3, *PTRS* articles begin in 1675 at a moderate level of "explicit reference" on Dimension 3, and move generally farther in that

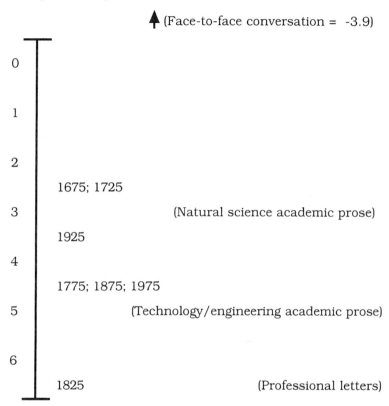

Situation-dependent Reference

↑ (Face-to-face conversation = -3.9)

0

1

2

1675; 1725

3   (Natural science academic prose)

1925

4

1775; 1875; 1975

5   (Technology/engineering academic prose)

6

1825   (Professional letters)

Explicit Reference

FIG. 5.3. Mean dimension scores for all *PTRS* research articles (Corpus B) on Dimension 3: *Explicit versus situation-dependent reference* (parenthetical descriptors indicate comparable factor scores for selected modern-day genres from Biber, 1988).

direction over time. Thus, scores averaged across the last three periods are about a point more "explicit" than those for the first three. Exceptions to this pattern occur, however, in: (a) 1825, when the period dimension score represents an extreme "explicit" value; and (b) 1925, when the dimension score falls a point further toward the "situation-dependent" pole than the scores in the two adjoining periods.

Post hoc analysis reveals that the interaction of two Dimension 3 features appear to account in part for the dimension scores from 1825 and 1925. In Fig. 5.4, mean frequencies of nominalizations (as always per 1,000 words) are graphed on the scale at left, while mean WH-relative clause frequencies

Nominalizations   Wh-Relative

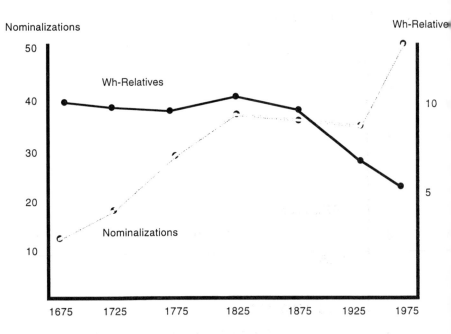

FIG. 5.4. Interaction of mean frequency counts of WH-relative clause types with nominalizations across periods on Dimension 3: *Explicit versus situation-dependent reference.*

(all three WH-relative types combined) are graphed on the scale at right.[23] In 1825, a relatively higher mean number of WH-relative clauses (10.8 vs. 8.9 in 1775 and 8.7 in 1875) can be seen to co-occur with a higher number of nominalizations (37.6 vs. 30.8 in 1775 and 32.7 in 1875), accounting for part of the high dimension score for that period. Most of the rest of the high score is attributable to a decrease in miscellaneous adverbs at the other end of the dimension (see note 34 for further analysis of the 1825 dimension score).

The same explanation holds true, but to a lesser degree, for the comparatively low 1925 score on this dimension. Mean numbers of WH-relatives have by this time declined in relation to the preceding period (to 5.7 from 8.7 in 1875), while nominalization counts are virtually unchanged. Without the large increase in nominalizations in the next period, 1975, the Dimension 3 score for that period would also have remained at approximately the 1925 level.

Although numbers of WH-relatives generally decline over time in the *PTRS*—with a correlative drop in dimension scores—a limiting factor in discussing these features is that they do not occur very commonly in *any* of the periods studied. Thus, all three WH-relative clause types combined vary from a high in 1825 of a mean of 10.8 per 1,000 words, to a low in 1975 of 5.3. When raw feature counts are this low in texts subjected to MD analysis, even small changes in their relative frequencies can substantially influence dimension scores since they are standardized (see chap. 3, "MD Analysis: Description and Procedures" and this chapter, note 6). On the other hand, it should be noted that WH-relatives are never a high-frequency linguistic feature in English, at least among the 23 modern-day genres of speech and writing analyzed by Biber (1988; cf. Huckin, Curtin, & Graham, 1986). There, the highest mean number of WH-relatives (three types combined) for any genre was 7.7 per 1,000 words for official documents—lower than for five of the seven periods in the present study.

Bazerman (1984) describes a reduction over time in relative clauses in the corpus of physics research articles he studied covering 1893–1980, although he does not give absolute numbers. This reduction correlated with an increase in other types of subordinate clauses. Bazerman's explanation of this shift is that relative clauses cannot express the complex relationships among physical objects that physics began to study in the early 20th century—other types of subordinate clauses allowed physicists to semantically relate concepts in more complex and precise ways.[24]

Unlike WH-relatives, nominalizations occur at relatively high levels of frequency in *PTRS* texts, at least from 1775 on. There are in fact two substantial increases in nominalizations across time: from 17.1 per 1,000 words in 1725 to 30.8 in 1775, an increase of 80%; and from 32 in 1925 to 51.2 in 1975, a 60% increase (see Fig. 5.4 for graphed frequencies across the full period of study). The development of nominalizations as a central feature of scientific English has been described by Halliday (1988; Halliday & Martin, 1993), who locates their proliferation particularly in the 20th century. Halliday views nominalizations as tools for linguistically reifying scientific processes and concepts (e.g., *the tissue culture was developed* → *the development of the tissue culture*) in order to "objectify," or concretize them for rhetorical purposes and to allow them to be discussed smoothly and efficiently.

Dimension 4. Dimension 4 was interpreted by Biber as indexing *overt expression of persuasion.* Suasive verbs (e.g., *propose, suggest*),[25] prediction (*will, would, shall*) and necessity (*ought to, should, must*) modals, conditional subordination (i.e., clauses beginning with *if* and *unless*), and split auxiliaries (e.g., "They *are* objectively shown"—Biber, 1988, p. 244) represent the features underlying this dimension. Modern-day genres from Biber (1988) that have the highest scores on this dimension are professional letters and editorials; press reviews and radio broadcasts have the lowest scores (see Figs. 3.2 and 5.5). As with Dimension 3, Dimension 4 scores show two exceptions to linear diachronic development: (a) the 1725 score, which jumps to a level approximating 20th-century scores on this dimension; and (b) the 1825 score, which is approximately one point less "overtly persuasive" than the scores for either 1775 or 1875.

Overt Expression of Persuasion

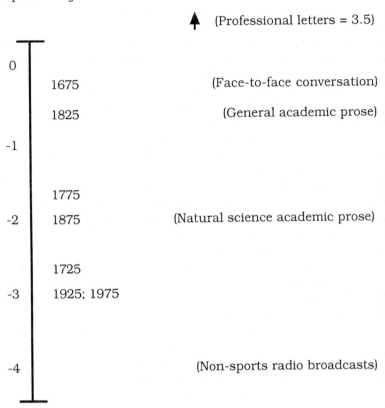

FIG. 5.5. Mean dimension scores for all *PTRS* research articles (Corpus B) on Dimension 4: *Overt expression of persuasion* (parenthetical descriptors indicate comparable factor scores for selected modern-day genres from Biber, 1988).

   In general, however, there is clear evolution toward a "nonpersuasive" norm on Dimension 4: Scores averaged over the first three periods are about a point more "overtly persuasive" than averaged scores for the last three periods. Marked decreases on measures of variation within mean dimension scores also confirm this trend, as discussed further later. A separate point is that dimension scores for the two most recent periods rival the least "persuasive" scores found by Biber (1988)—only contemporary radio broadcasts are less "overtly persuasive." Taken together, these findings suggest that the scientific research article has developed into a type of text having few if any signs of openly persuasive purposes in the present day.

A post hoc analysis focusing on cross-time frequencies of Dimension 4's linguistic features and their interactions was not very enlightening. The relatively high negative score for 1725 is largely attributable to lower numbers of necessity modals and split auxiliaries in the texts of this period, with the same being true to a lesser extent for the 1825 score. However, *none* of the features that occur on this dimension are common in *any* of the periods studied. Prediction modals, for example, range from a mean-score high of 8.6 occurrences per 1,000 words in 1675 to a low of 2.3 in 1925, and necessity modals range from a mean 2.5 occurrences in 1825 to 0.9 in 1925 (cf. Biber, 1988, and Collins, 1991, for comparable findings of low frequencies of necessity modals in other large text corpora).[26] Nor does the relationship between necessity modals and split auxiliaries appear to be a steady one: Except as noted previously, relatively higher frequencies of one of these two features in a period do not usually correlate with relatively higher frequencies of the other. However, some features on this dimension do show steady change across time, even if they do not occur commonly; thus prediction modals and conditional subordination decline fairly steadily across the 300 years studied.

Finally, regarding Dimension 4, measures of variation within mean dimension scores across periods reveal the progressive conventionalization of the scientific research article on this dimension. Thus, the visually displayed ranges of variation for individual-text dimension scores (Appendix B, part 2) indicate that, after 1725, texts varied little at the lower end of the scale, while texts became progressively *less* "overtly persuasive" at the upper end from 1825 forward. Standard deviations (Appendix C) reflect the same trend, falling from 2.3 and 2.8 in the first two periods to 0.9 and 0.7 in the final two.

Dimension 5. This dimension differentiates "informational discourse that is abstract, technical, and formal versus other types of discourse" (Biber, 1988, pp. 112–113), and is labeled *abstract versus nonabstract information.*[27] "Abstract" as used here is loosely synonymous with "passivized" (Biber, 1988, p. 112): Agentless passives, *by*-passives, and past participial reduced relative clauses (e.g., "the substance *submitted* to radiation") all co-occur on Dimension 5.[28] The other two features making up this dimension are conjuncts (e.g., *therefore, however*) and miscellaneous adverbial subordinators (e.g., *so that, whereas*). Conjuncts mark logical relations in highly informational and planned discourse, discourse that is often highly passivized (Biber, 1986; Ochs, 1979); miscellaneous adverbial subordinators are a subcategory of adverbial subordinators, which generally mark informational relations in discourse (Biber, 1988).[29] The presence of these two features on Dimension 5 thus functionally complements that of the three passives. Modern-day texts with the highest "abstract" scores on this dimension include general academic prose and official documents, while romantic fiction, face-to-face conversations, and telephone conversations have the highest "nonabstract" scores (Biber, 1988).

Dimension 5 is of particular interest in the study of modern-day scientific writing because such writing is frequently described as highly passivized (e.g., Bazerman, 1984; Ding, to appear; Halliday, 1988). Figure 5.6 presents the results of MD analysis on this dimension.

Figure 5.6 reveals a profound shift in the use of passives and associated features in *PTRS* texts over the last 300 years. Thus, texts in the 17th and 18th centuries cluster at a moderately "abstract" level, while texts in the 19th and 20th centuries are as highly "abstract," or passivized, as any studied by Biber (1988). This clustering at two different levels of "abstractness" represents a quite different pattern than those seen on the other dimensions, suggesting major developments in this area between 1775 and 1825, as described in chapter 6.

Post hoc analysis confirms the important role of passives in linguistic change on this dimension: Counts of passives (three types combined) show a 40% increase from 1775 to 1825, and they average 22.4 per 1,000 words for

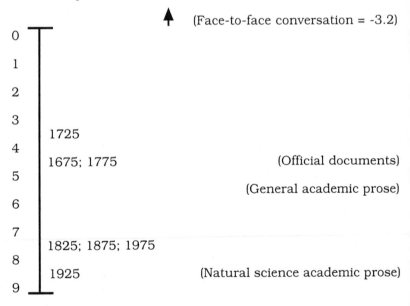

Non-abstract Information

0

1

2

3

    1725

4

    1675; 1775   (Official documents)

5

                                      (General academic prose)

6

7

    1825; 1875; 1975

8

    1925   (Natural science academic prose)

9

(Face-to-face conversation = -3.2)

Abstract Information

FIG. 5.6.   Mean dimension scores for all *PTRS* research articles on Dimension 5: *Abstract versus nonabstract information* (parenthetical descriptors indicate comparable factor scores for selected modern-day genres from Biber, 1988).

the first three periods against 35.7 for the latter four.[30] Of the three types of passive constructions analyzed here, by far the most common across time is the agentless passive.

Development on Dimension 5 can be illustrated by comparing text samples from 1675 and 1975, each giving accounts of experimental procedures (bold print marks "abstract" features):

1675:

All **being** well **evacuated,** I shook the Engine, **so as that** the little Receiver fell off from the Hail-shot, and stood everywhere close to the skin, **expanded** over the cover of the Glass-plate. Then I had no more to do but to suffer the Air to re-enter into the great Receiver, and this Air pressing upon the little one, kept it so closely fasten'd to its cover, that it was impossible for me to sever them. And I **am assured,** that the Air enters not into the small Receiver, when 'tis **thus applied** upon the skin; for I have often put Gages in them which alwaies kept at the same height, although the Air **was permitted** to repass into the great Receiver. You might also let alone the putting under of the Hail-shot to keep up the little Recipient, because the Air by its Spring would lift it up sufficiently; but then the vacuum would not **be** so perfectly **made** [Huygens & Papin, 1675, pp. 477–8].

1975:

Lobsters weighing about half a kilogram **were purchased** from a commercial supplier in Maine and **transported** by air express in ice-cooled containers. The animals **were kept** at 11°C in a tank of seawater which **was** continuously **circulated** through a filter of gravel, fibre glass and activated charcoal. The lobsters **were fed** raw fish approximately once per week but **otherwise** the conditions of their confinement complied with those **advised** by the Maine Department of Sea and Shore Fisheries (Goggins 1960).

(b) Anatomy

Observations on the muscles and nerves **were made** either from freshly dissected animals or from limbs **fixed** in Bouin's fixative and then **dissected** in 70% alcohol. The nerves **were studied** by immersing the preparations in solutions of 5% methylene blue **diluted** with seawater (Pantin 1946). Preparations **prepared** in this way **were kept** in a refrigerator at 5°C for several hours. The staining solution **was** then **replaced** with fresh seawater and the preparation **examined** under a binocular microscope [Macmillan, 1975, p. 4].

A major difference between these two texts resides in the fact that virtually all finite verbs in the 1975 sample are passivized, as compared to only about a third of the verbs in the earlier sample; the later passage also has frequent past participial reduced relative clauses. These samples well exemplify the main locus of variation on this dimension—various types of passive constructions of which the agentless passive is the most common. The results of this analysis therefore corroborate descriptions of the passive as a high-frequency feature of modern-day scientific research writing.

Finally in regard to Dimension 5, there is progressive lessening in measures of variation within dimension scores from the 17th through 19th centuries, indicating the increasing conventionalization of texts over time. Thus, period standard deviations (see Appendix C) decrease from an average of 2.2 in the 17th and 18th centuries, to 1.6 in the 19th century. The picture is more complicated in the 20th century: The standard deviation for 1925 is 3.0, while that for 1975 (1.8) is approximately the same as the 19th-century average. But the relatively large standard deviation for 1925—and the larger number of passives found there overall (see note 30)—can be accounted for by the almost unique appearance of a particular type of article in this period: descriptions of chemical syntheses of new and experimental materials. As these articles are heavily methods-oriented, they maintain highly passivized styles throughout.[31] Excluding these texts, the standard deviation for 1925 would be at about the same level as for 1975.

MD ANALYSIS OF EPISTOLARY ARTICLES

Six additional MD analyses were performed in this study, each treating a subcategory of the articles covered in the overall MD analysis. As these analyses are quite exploratory in nature—largely because the numbers of articles analyzed is small—they are described here only in summary form.

As mentioned in chapter 4, epistolary articles were the most common single article type appearing in the *PTRS* from 1675 to 1825, during which time they appear to have had, to some extent, their own rhetorical norms. An important question, therefore, is whether texts written in letter form pattern differently across time, linguistically speaking, than texts not appearing in that form. To the extent that they do, additional evidence that epistolary articles represented a more-or-less coherent text type in the *PTRS* can be said to exist.

Data are here presented from analyses of two groupings of *PTRS* B corpus articles: (a) all epistolary articles (Table 5.2); and (b) all nonepistolary articles (Table 5.3). Because articles ceased appearing in letter form between 1825 and 1875, this analysis covers only the period 1675–1825.

Disregarding the 1825 score for epistolary articles due to the existence of only two such texts in this period, moderately strong patterns emerge from this comparison. Epistolary articles are generally less "informational" across periods on Dimension 1 than nonepistolary articles, and consistently less "overtly persuasive" and "abstract" on Dimensions 4 and 5, respectively.

TABLE 5.2
Mean Dimension Scores for All Epistolary Research Articles From the
PTRS (Corpus B), Collected at 50-Year Intervals, 1675 to 1825 ($N = 18$)[32]

Date	N	Dimension 1	Dimension 2	Dimension 3	Dimension 4	Dimension 5
1675	6	0.8	−1.3	2.2	−1.0	4.5
1725	5	−2.8	0.1	0.5	−3.7	3.2
1775	5	−5.8	−1.3	4.3	−2.3	3.5
(1825	2	−11.2	−1.8	3.5	−1.0	8.5)
F		4.54	1.68	1.56	2.71	3.77
p <		.0201	ns	ns	.0849	.0356
R²		49.3%	26.5%	25.1%	36.7%	44.7%

Note. ns = not significant.

TABLE 5.3
Mean Dimension Scores for All Nonepistolary Research Articles From the
PTRS (Corpus B), Collected at 50-Year Intervals, 1675 to 1825 ($N = 22$)

Date	N	Dimension 1	Dimension 2	Dimension 3	Dimension 4	Dimension 5
1675	4	1.6	−0.1	2.4	−0.6	5.0
1725	5	−5.6	−2.1	4.2	−1.7	4.0
1775	5	−8.7	−1.4	4.3	−1.0	5.5
1825	8	−9.6	−2.2	7.3	−0.8	7.1
F		6.96	.54	4.08	.15	3.95
p <		.0026	ns	.0226	ns	.0251
R²		53.7%	8.3%	40.4%	2.4%	39.7%

Note. ns = not significant.

The basis for each of these generalizations is discussed in the following paragraphs.

On Dimension 1, epistolary articles are less "informational"/more "involved" in two of the three periods for which nonminimal sample sizes exist, 1725 and 1775. These scores are each approximately three points closer to the "involved" pole than their nonepistolary counterparts. The 1675 score, on the other hand, is 0.8 points closer to the "informational" pole for articles in letter form.

Dimensions 2 and 3 show mixed orientations for epistolary articles that are not straightforwardly interpretable. Thus, the 1675 score for Dimension 2 is less "narrative" than the comparable nonepistolary score; the 1725 score is more "narrative"; and the 1775 score is approximately the same. On Dimension 3, two of the three scores are substantially the same as scores for their nonepistolary counterparts, while the third (1725) is markedly less "referentially explicit."

On Dimension 4, scores for epistolary articles are consistently less "overtly persuasive" than their nonepistolary counterparts in all three periods considered. In the cases of 1725 and 1775, the comparable scores diverge substantially, while for 1675 the difference is relatively small. The 1825 score for epistolary articles, though based on only two texts, is also slightly less "overtly persuasive" than its counterpart for nonepistolary article types. Whether one considers the latter scores or not, however, the more general pattern is clear.

Finally, Dimension 5 shows epistolary articles to be consistently less "abstract" than other types of articles, though period-by-period differences are not generally large. Thus, the 1675 score for letters is half a point less "abstract" than the comparable nonepistolary score, while the 1725 score is 0.7 points below its nonepistolary counterpart. The 1775 score for epistolary articles, on the other hand, is two points less "abstract" than the comparable score for nonepistolary articles. Although none of these scores is in itself enough to indicate a substantial divergence between epistolary and other types of articles on this dimension, the emergence of a consistent cross-time pattern suggests that one is likely to exist.

These comparisons provide suggestive evidence that epistolary articles pattern differently than their nonepistolary counterparts on three of the five linguistic dimensions. To this degree, they provide support at the linguistic level for the finding made at the rhetorical level of analysis, that epistolary articles represented a more or less internally coherent (though evolving) text type during the period in which it appeared in the *PTRS*.

MD ANALYSIS OF EXPERIMENTAL ARTICLES

Tables 5.4 and 5.5 show the results of two further MD analyses: (a) of articles that contain reports of original scientific experiments, and (b) of all articles not containing such reports. For the same reasons given for epistolary articles in the preceding section, an important question to be asked is whether systematic linguistic differences can be found to exist between these two groupings of texts.

Setting aside the scores for experimental articles in 1725—for which only a single text was sampled—comparison of these tables reveals no systematic differences between experimental and nonexperimental articles on Dimensions 1, 3, and 4. Dimensions 2 and 5, however, show consistent differences between the two types of texts.[33]

Scores for Dimension 2, the "narrative versus nonnarrative concerns" dimension, show that experimental articles are consistently more "narrative" than nonexperimental articles across time, with the lone exception of the 1975 score. This finding corroborates results arrived at in the rhetorical

TABLE 5.4

Mean Dimension Scores for All Experimental Research Articles From the
PTRS (Corpus B), Collected at 50-Year Intervals, 1675 to 1975 ($N = 24$)

Date	N	Dimension 1	Dimension 2	Dimension 3	Dimension 4	Dimension 5
(1675	2	4.0	0.8	2.7	−0.7	5.2)
(1725	1	−5.6	−1.4	3.8	−1.7	3.4)
1775	3	−4.1	−0.7	5.7	−1.7	5.6
1825	4	−9.1	−1.7	4.7	−0.8	6.3
1875	3	−11.9	−2.1	3.8	−1.9	8.6
1925	5	−16.2	−2.5	4.0	−2.5	10.5
1975	6	−17.3	−3.5	3.9	−2.8	8.8
F		12.83	16.37	.35	1.10	3.92
$p <$		.0001	.0001	ns	ns	.0121
R^2		82.9%	85.2%	11.1%	27.9%	58.0%

Note. ns = not significant.

TABLE 5.5

Mean Dimension Scores for All Nonexperimental Research Articles From
the *PTRS* (Corpus B), Collected at 50-Year Intervals, 1675 to 1975 ($N = 46$)

Date	N	Dimension 1	Dimension 2	Dimension 3	Dimension 4	Dimension 5
1675	8	0.4	−1.2	2.2	−0.3	4.6
1725	9	−4.1	−0.9	2.2	−2.8	3.6
1775	7	−8.6	−1.6	3.7	−1.7	4.0
1825	6	−10.5	−2.4	7.7	−0.9	8.1
1875	7	−12.4	−3.0	4.8	−2.0	6.9
1925	5	−15.0	−3.1	2.8	−3.2	7.0
1975	4	−17.0	−2.9	5.1	−3.2	5.9
F		13.83	2.69	3.94	.84	5.28
$p <$		.0001	.0277	.0036	ns	.0005
R^2		68.0%	29.3%	37.7%	11.4%	44.8%

Note. ns = not significant.

analysis (chap. 4), where it was found that narrative accounts of experiments were part of experimental articles at least up to the present century.[34]

Scores for Dimension 5, the "abstract versus nonabstract information" dimension, again show a consistent pattern: Experimental articles have scores that, for all periods except one, are more "abstract," or passivized, than those for nonexperimental articles—the single exception is 1825. This finding may be related to the common inclusion of research methods descriptions in experimental articles; these descriptions are more-or-less passivized even in their embryonic form in the 17th and 18th centuries, as seen, for example, in the first passage by Hunter in the chapter 4 section entitled

"The Place of the Author." By the 20th century they are highly passivized, as are experimental reports throughout in this period.

MD ANALYSIS OF ARTICLES BY DOMAIN OF SCIENTIFIC ACTIVITY

As described in chapter 3, the sampling procedures employed in the MD analysis portion of this study involved placing selected texts into one of three categories of scientific activity: A, physical sciences and mathematics; B, biology/life sciences; or C, a miscellaneous/"other" category. In the final MD analyses performed in this study, articles from all periods were grouped and analyzed according to which of these categories they fell into. Category C texts, however, were subsequently excluded from further consideration due to the small number of texts (9) contained therein. The results of MD analysis for categories A and B are presented in Tables 5.6 and 5.7.

Comparisons of scores from these two tables show few systematic differences. For example, although four of the values on Dimension 1 for Category A texts are more "informational" than the corresponding values for Category B, three are more "involved"—and this nonsystematicity holds as well for Dimensions 2, 3, and 5. On Dimension 4, on the other hand, Category A texts are consistently closer across time to the "overt expression of persuasion" pole than Category B texts. The overall results of these final two MD analyses suggest that the modern-day categories of scientific activity into which the present corpus was divided represent only small differences at the linguistic level of discourse.

TABLE 5.6

Mean Dimension Scores for All Category A ("Physical Sciences and Mathematics") Research Articles From the *PTRS* (Corpus B), Collected at 50-Year Intervals From 1675 to 1975 ($N = 35$)

Date	N	Dimension 1	Dimension 2	Dimension 3	Dimension 4	Dimension 5
1675	4	2.4	−0.3	3.5	−0.2	4.0
1725	5	−4.5	−1.8	1.8	−2.2	4.2
1775	5	−6.7	−1.1	5.0	−1.6	4.4
1825	5	−8.5	−2.3	6.3	1.0	7.5
1875	6	−12.5	−2.8	4.3	−1.0	7.7
1925	5	−17.1	−2.7	4.5	−2.8	9.7
1975	5	−15.2	−3.3	3.1	−2.8	7.5
F		11.16	5.21	1.05	1.69	6.52
$p <$		.0001	.0011	ns	ns	.0002
R^2		71.3%	53.6%	18.8%	27.2%	59.1%

Note. ns = not significant.

TABLE 5.7

Mean Dimension Scores for All Category B ("Life Sciences")
Research Articles From the *PTRS* (Corpus B), Collected
at 50-Year Intervals, 1675 to 1975 ($N = 26$)

Date	N	Dimension 1	Dimension 2	Dimension 3	Dimension 4	Dimension 5
1675	3	1.7	−1.2	−0.2	−1.4	4.3
1725	4	−3.9	−0.9	2.6	−3.4	2.2
1775	3	−5.3	−1.8	3.1	−1.9	5.1
1825	3	−12.3	−2.1	8.8	−3.0	6.7
1875	3	−11.3	−2.5	4.0	−3.9	6.0
1925	5	−13.9	−2.9	2.2	−3.0	7.8
1975	5	−19.1	−3.2	5.7	−3.2	7.8
F		23.23	3.14	2.85	1.43	2.93
$p <$		.0001	.0262	.0377	ns	.0340
R^2		88.0%	49.7%	47.3%	31.1%	48.0%

Note. ns = not significant.

SUMMARY

MD analysis of all texts considered together across all periods yielded a number of interesting results. On Dimensions 1 ("involved vs. informational production") and 2 ("narrative vs. nonnarrative concerns") texts became steadily more "informational" and "nonnarrative," respectively, over time, until they reached extreme values on these dimensions in the present day. For their part, Dimensions 3 ("explicit vs. situation-dependent reference") and 4 ("overt expression of persuasion") exhibited moderate development in the "explicit reference" and "nonpersuasive" directions over time, until by 1975 *PTRS* articles showed extreme scores on these dimensions in comparison to the majority of modern-day genres in Biber (1988). Finally in regard to the overall MD analysis, Dimension 5 ("abstract vs. nonabstract information") showed marked development in the "abstract"/passivized direction with two minor exceptions—and the 1975 score rivals the highest scores found among the 23 modern-day genres Biber (1988) analyzed. Text samples from early and late periods were also given and compared to exemplify cross-time development of the scientific research article on Dimensions 1, 2, and 5, and a variety of post hoc analyses provided further details about scores.

In the next two MD analyses, articles appearing in the form of letters were analyzed in comparison to all other (i.e., nonepistolary) articles. In this comparison, the former were found to be generally less "informational," less "overtly persuasive," and less "abstract" than their nonepistolary counterparts. Such systematic differences suggest that the epistolary article represented a relatively coherent and well-formed text type during the periods in which it appeared in the *PTRS.*

Two further MD analyses compared experimental and nonexperimental research articles. Systematic differences occurred on two dimensions in this analysis: Dimension 2, where experimental articles were found to be consistently more "narrative," with a single exception; and Dimension 5, where experimental articles were found to be uniformly more "abstract"/passivized, again with one exception.

Finally, a comparative MD analysis of physical science/math and biology/life science research articles indicated that these two text groupings differed systematically only on Dimension 4, with physical science/math articles being consistently closer over time to the "overt expression of persuasion" pole.

ENDNOTES

[1]The tables in this chapter include measures of statistical significance (F and *p* values) and statistical importance (R^2 values) for each column of dimension scores. The *p* values indicate whether the individual values in each such group of dimension scores differ from each other at statistically significant levels—*p* values up to .1 are considered statistically significant in this study because it is exploratory in nature. R^2 values indicate how much of the variance among these scores is common, or covariance.

These statistics are reported partly for conventional reasons—in no case are the main generalizations of this chapter affected by these scores (cf. Biber & Finegan, 1989, note 9). It should also be mentioned that the F, *p*, and R^2 values apply only to comparisons *within* specific text groups—e.g., the group of 70 texts treated in the overall MD analysis; they do not figure into comparisons of score patterns *across* text groups, as in the six comparative analyses made in the latter part of the chapter.

[2]The modern-day genres and subgenres from Biber (1988) that I cite for comparative purposes throughout this chapter require further explanation. The two computerized corpora of modern English used in Biber (1988) and described in chapter 3 are organized according to "genres," defined by Biber (1988, p. 68) as "text categorizations made on the basis of external criteria relating to author/speaker purpose." A sampling of genre categories from the 23 genres Biber utilized in his study is: press reportage; spontaneous speeches; general fiction; general academic prose; face-to-face conversations; and radio broadcasts. Some of these genres were further broken down into subgenres—general academic prose, for instance, was made up of seven academic prose types, that is, natural science; technology/engineering; math; medicine; social and behavioral sciences; political science, law, and education; and humanities. Lists of the genres and subgenres from the corpora used by Biber and referred to in the present study are given in Biber (1988, pp. 67, 69).

[3]The dimension labels used throughout this chapter (e.g., "involved vs. informational production") are, strictly speaking, interpretive. That is, they are functional interpretations of empirically determined sets of co-occurring linguistic features across a wide variety of texts (see chap. 3, section entitled "MD Analysis: Description and Procedures" for a detailed description of the MD methodology). All dimension labels are for this reason placed in quotation marks in this chapter following their initial mention. At the same time, it must also be

emphasized that these dimension labels have strong claims to validity for two reasons: (a) they are based on a substantial literature on the sociolinguistic functionality of particular linguistic features and feature complexes (see Biber, 1988, Appendix II, and Atkinson & Biber, 1994); and (b) their accuracy is verified by reference to the genres or text groups analyzed by Biber (1988) that actually attain high or low scores on the dimensions. For example, when modern-day face-to-face and telephone conversations have the most "involved" and general academic prose and official documents the most "informational" scores on an empirically determined dimension labeled "involved versus informational production," as here on Dimension 1, this functional interpretation is strongly confirmed.

[4]Private verbs are verbs such as *understand* or *feel*, which express cognitive or emotional states. They are one of several specialized functional verb classes considered by Quirk, Greenbaum, Leech, and Svartvik (1985, especially pp. 1180–1182).

[5]"Longer words" are measured by automatically counting the number of letters per word. Lexical variety is calculated by the measurement of type/token ratios (see Biber, 1988, p. 238).

Dimension 1, like Dimension 3, has two sets of co-occurring linguistic features (see chap. 3, section entitled "MD Analysis: Linguistic Makeup of Dimensions"), whereas Dimensions 2, 4, and 5 have only one.

[6]All individual feature counts reported in this chapter are normalized to 1,000 words (see chap. 3, "MD Analysis: Description and Procedures"). These feature counts are the output of step 2 of the "target" MD analysis (see chap. 3, section entitled "MD Analysis: General Description"), and also represent part of the input to step 5, out of which comes the specific dimension/factor scores. Even if summed with individual frequency counts for all other features on a particular dimension for a particular period, however, they would not be directly equatable to the corresponding dimension scores, because the latter are standardized, that is, put on a common scale based on their relative frequencies of cross-genre occurrence. Standardization allows features like nouns, for example, which tend to occur hundreds of times per 1,000 words of text in this corpus, to be directly compared with (and summed with or subtracted from in producing dimension scores) features like contractions, which occur only rarely.

[7]Counts of mean numbers of nouns per 1,000 words of text for each period are:

1675:	208.6	1775:	226.4	1875:	241.7	1975:	280.4
1725:	227.6	1825:	228.7	1925:	265.7		

[8]Counts of mean numbers of attributive adjectives per 1,000 words of text for each period are:

1675:	34.6	1775:	52.4	1875:	56.8	1975:	76.3
1725:	34.6	1825:	53.6	1925:	65.2		

[9]Mean word lengths (see note 5) for each period are as follows:

1675:	4.3	1775:	4.5	1875:	4.6	1975:	5.0
1725:	4.3	1825:	4.6	1925:	4.7		

[10]Counts of mean numbers of first person personal pronouns per 1,000 words of text for each period are:

1675:	24.7	1775:	15.4	1875:	11.7	1975:	5.1
1725:	19.1	1825:	14.5	1925:	2.1		

[11]Counts of mean numbers of the third person pronoun *it* per 1,000 words of text for each period are:

1675:	17.2	1775:	15.2	1875:	10.3	1975:	6.3
1725:	15.8	1825:	10.8	1925:	8.1		

[12]The two verb types not exhibiting much change across the 300 years studied are private verbs and present tense verbs, although the latter did show one substantial decrease, from 62.6 per 1,000 words in 1675 to 47.3 in 1725. The other two verb types on Dimension 1, *be* as a main verb in its various forms and possibility modals (i.e., *may, might, can,* and *could*), occurred at such low levels across time that they were not considered for post hoc analysis.

However, although the verb types on Dimension 1 do not show clear and patterned variation, a rough calculation of active-voice verbs *across* dimensions does show such variation. This calculation was made by summing for each period all present tense verbs, past tense verbs, and past-participial WH-deletions—the three verb types that are wholly independent of one another in this study—and then subtracting the sum of all *by*-passives, agentless passives, and past-participial WH-deletions (the three passive verb types) from the first sum. The results of these calculations across periods are shown in the following table:

1675:	70.3	1775:	53.3	1875:	37.0	1975:	37.1
1725:	65.3	1825:	35.1	1925:	32.4		

The pattern exhibited here (in what can informally be called the "active-voice verb count") shows a 47.2% decrease in the mean numbers of active-voice verbs across the period under study. More interesting and meaningful than this simple decrease, however, is the period-to-period patterning of these numbers. Frequencies decrease linearly over the first four periods, articulating with movement from an "involved" to an "informational" norm (Dimension 1), but from 1825 on seem to follow the score pattern on Dimension 5, where there is a pronounced increase in "abstract–passivized" scores in 1825, which holds more or less steady from then on. Of course, the roughly inverse proportional relationship of active-voice verb counts and scores on Dimension 5, which is made up largely of passivized verb types, may not be very surprising.

[13]An example of a verb-modifying prepositional phrase (from 1675) is: "I passed *into the little hole* a sprig of a known plant"; an example of a noun-modifying prepositional phrase (from 1975) is: "small segments *of behavior.*"

Full counts and percentages for each period in the analysis of prepositional phrase functions are as follows (N = Noun-modifying prepositional phrases, V = Verb-modifying prepositional phrases, and O = Other, or any prepositional phrase not clearly fitting into the N or V categories)

Date	N	(%)	V	(%)	O	(%)
1675	35	(33.3)	55	(52.4)	15	(14.3)
1775	58	(44.6)	58	(44.6)	14	(10.8)
1875	80	(57.1)	44	(31.4)	16	(11.4)
1975	73	(54.9)	50	(37.6)	10	(7.5)

[14]This is true for two main reasons: (a) 10 individual 100-word samples give only a partial picture of what actual percentage of prepositional phrases modify nouns versus verbs in each text per period, because each sample represents a notably small part of the whole text in most cases, and there appears to be considerable text-internal variation in terms of the proportional frequency with which the different types of prepositional phrases occur, at least as texts approach the present day; and (b) the coding of prepositional phrases as either nominal, verbal, or "other" (see note 13) is not always unproblematic, especially given the complex adverbial functions of such features (see Quirk, Greenbaum, Leech, & Svartvik, 1985, pp. 657ff.)

[15]Halliday (1985, chap. 5) differentiates clause types by, among other criteria, the kinds of processes they describe. Verbs play the central role in expressing these processes, of which there are three main types: *material processes,* or processes of doing; *mental processes,* or processes of thinking, feeling, and perceiving; and *relational processes,* or processes of being.

On a scale of prototypical dynamic, contentful verbal activity (cf. Quirk, Greenbaum, Leech, & Svartvik, 1985, p. 74), relational processes have the lowest value of these three process types, as their basic function is simply to specify the relations of one noun or nominal group to another. It is in this sense that they are "semantically weak."

[16]Public verbs are verbs (e.g., *claim, report*) that express a publicly observable communicative act (Quirk, Greenbaum, Leech, & Svartvik, 1985, pp. 1180–1182).

Although third person personal pronouns and past tense and perfect aspect verbs have been widely accepted as prototypical markers of narrative—and especially *literary narrative* (e.g., Fleishmann, 1990 for the verb types; Labov, 1972)—public verbs are less commonly thought of as narrative markers. However, the latter frequently introduce indirect discourse, a common feature of at least certain kinds of narrative. It is important in this connection to note that the prototypically narrative genres considered by Biber (1988) were almost all literary/fictional, as discussed later in the description of Dimension 2.

[17]The difference in the *level* of change on Dimension 1 in comparison to Dimension 2 (with Dimension 1 seeming to show a comparatively dramatic level of change) is mostly apparent—it is largely due to the greater number of features occurring on Dimension 1. That is, the more features occurring on a particular dimension in the original factor analysis, the larger the range of scores that individual texts and texts grouped together by period will exhibit on that dimension.

It is useful here to consider the relative amounts of score variation shown on all dimensions in the present study versus the total amounts of such variation across the same dimensions shown by the 23 modern-day text genres studied by Biber (1988). The following table shows the maximum and minimum scores exhibited by scientific research articles in the present study, versus maximum and minimum scores across all genres on each dimension in Biber's study. In the far right (or fourth) column of this table, the amount of such variation in the present study (second column) is expressed as a percentage of the total amount of variation found in Biber's (1988) study (third column) on each dimension. Related measures of variation on each dimension for texts in each time period are given in Appendix B.

Dimension	*Ranges of variation covered in present study versus Biber (1988)*		*% of variation in Biber (1988) covered in present study*
	Present study	*Biber (1988)*	
Dimension 1	1.1 → −17.2	37.2 → −18.1	33%
Dimension 2	−0.8 → −3.3	7.2 → −3.3	24%
Dimension 3	6.5 → 2.3	7.3 → −9.0	26%
Dimension 4	3.0 → −0.3	3.5 → −4.4	42%
Dimension 5	8.8 → 4.7	5.5 → −3.7	44.5%

[18]Another reason why Dimension 2 scores may have been artificially lowered in the present analysis is that Biber's (1988) original MD analysis included two features that have since been excluded: synthetic negation and present participial clauses. Typically, the more features are on a dimension, the larger the dimension score. It should be pointed out, however, that these changes affect only the absolute dimension scores, not the relationships among scores themselves. The latter is what is being considered here, except where direct comparisons are made with scores on Dimension 2 from Biber (1988).

[19]Counts of mean numbers of past tense verbs per 1,000 words of text for each period are:

| 1675: | 21.9 | 1775: | 24.9 | 1875: | 17.1 | 1975: | 15.1 |
| 1725: | 36.3 | 1825: | 19.1 | 1925: | 22.1 | | |

[20]For the purposes of MD analysis, third person personal pronoun forms included: *he, his, him, himself, she, her, hers, herself, they, them, their, theirs,* and *themselves.* Counts of mean numbers of third person personal pronouns per 1,000 words of text for each period are:

1675:	36.3	1775:	30.5	1875:	14.7	1975:	11.0
1725:	38.4	1825:	20.3	1925:	11.6		

[21]Like Dimension 1, this dimension is made up of two sets of co-occurring linguistic features—sets which tend to occur in the relative absence of their counterpart set. I refer to these sets here and in what follows as each marking one "part" or "end" of the dimension.

Adverbials (Quirk, Greenbaum, Leech, & Svartvik, 1985, p. 440) are clause elements distinct from subject, verb, object, and complement which function by modifying either the verb or the whole clause. Adverbs (Quirk, et al., 1985, pp. 445ff.), on the other hand, modify verbs, adjectives, other adverbs, or whole clauses—thus, only some adverbs are also adverbials. The "miscellaneous" category of adverbs occurring on this dimension consisted of all adverbs in the online dictionary used in the text tagging process (see chap. 3, "MD Analysis: Description and Procedures") or which ended in -*ly* and were more than five letters in length. Features counted as time adverbials, place adverbials, hedges, amplifiers, or downtoners in the present study were excluded from this category (cf. Biber, 1988, Appendix II).

[22]The three WH-relative clause types found on this dimension are: WH-relatives on subject position, that is, where the relative pronoun replaces the subject in the relative clause (e.g., "A coextensive field of rods, *which* always exerts the same sign of control"); WH-relatives on object position (e.g., "I have seen this specimen, *which* I have measured."); and pied-piping constructions, that is, where a relative clause—final preposition is moved to the position preceding the relative clause—pronoun (e.g., "the Connexion of Triangles, by *which* our Author measur'd . . ."). It should be mentioned that *that*-relatives were also tagged and counted in Biber's (1988) original analysis, but they did not group with the Dimension 3 features in the factor analysis.

Other Dimension 3 features include: phrasal coordination, i.e., the use of *and* to coordinate two features of the same grammatical class below the level of the clause (e.g., "The base of the brain *and* the cranial nerves were intact."); and "nominalizations," here defined as abstract nouns ending in -*tion, -ment, -ity, -ess, -al, -dom, -tee, -er, -or, -ence, -ant, -ance, -lty, -ure, -ery, -cy* and their plural forms. Both phrasal coordination and nominalizations are considered markers of highly integrated informational language by linguists (e.g., Biber, 1988; Chafe, 1982, 1985; Halliday, 1988), suggesting that "referentially explicit discourse also tends to be integrated and informational" (Biber, 1988, p. 110).

[23]The fact that lines are used to connect period scores in Fig. 5.4 should not be taken to suggest that this graph accurately represents variation *between* sampling intervals in the present study. As elsewhere, the feature counts represented here were normalized to a text length of 1,000 words.

Counts of mean numbers of WH-relative clauses (three types combined) per 1,000 words of text for each period are:

1675:	9.6	1775:	8.9	1875:	8.7	1975:	5.3
1725:	9.6	1825:	10.8	1925:	5.8		

[24]Bazerman, however, considered only "two-clause sentences" in his analysis (1984, note 24). It should also be noted that neither Bazerman's nor the present study took into account the standard functional distinction between restrictive and nonrestrictive relative clauses (e.g., Quirk, Greenbaum, Leech, & Svartvik, 1985, p. 1239).

[25]Suasive verbs are verbs implying a desire or intention to effect future change (Quirk, Greenbaum, Leech, & Svartvik, 1985, pp. 1182–1183).

[26]Modal verbs, which also include the category of possibility modals that appears on Dimension 1, have been frequently discussed and studied as markers of an ethic of caution and precision in scientific research reporting (e.g., Butler, 1990; Hyland, 1996; Myers, 1989). Their low frequency in this corpus and elsewhere appears to contrast with their important rhetorical functions, especially in introduction and discussion sections of modern-day scientific research reports.

[27]Biber (e.g., Biber & Finegan, 1994b) currently prefers the interpretive label "nonimpersonal versus impersonal style" for Dimension 5, largely because of the wide range of meanings the term "abstract" seems to conjure up for readers. However, Biber's current preference also has its problems: "Impersonal style," for example, does not clearly account for nonagentive personalizing expressions such as the "by" phrase that accompanies agented passives. I have therefore retained Biber's older label for this dimension, accompanied now with the warning that "abstract" is used here as a rough synonym for "passivized," and that other senses of the former should be held in abeyance in this context.

[28]Past participial reduced relative clauses are considered passive forms by linguists because the reduction only takes place where the alternative full form would be passivized (e.g., "the substance [which *was* → ø] submitted to radiation").

[29]This adverbial subordinator category is "miscellaneous" in the sense that it is comprised of all adverbial subordinators that do not fit into one of Biber's (1988, pp. 235–236) other three adverbial subordinator categories—that is, causative, concessive, or conditional subordinators.

[30]Counts of mean numbers of passives (three types combined) per 1,000 words of text for each period are:

1675:	19.5	1775:	24.7	1875:	34.3	1975:	33.4
1725:	23.3	1825:	34.5	1925:	40.4		

[31]The unusual character of these texts can be clearly seen in the markedly large range of variation for 1925 on Dimension 5, shown in Appendix B, parts 1 and 2. This high value is wholly attributable to two such texts with high positive scores (13.1 and 14.5—the next highest score is 10.5); apart from these two exceptional texts, articles show markedly small and similar ranges of variation from 1825 onward, a finding that points toward the pronounced conventionalization of the large majority of articles on Dimension 5 throughout the 19th and 20th centuries.

In work on a related genre, modern-day medical research articles (see D. Atkinson, 1992 for the historical development of this genre), which are typically sectioned according to an Introduction–Methods–Results–Discussion format, Biber and Finegan (1994b) have shown that, although all four of these sections are marked in terms of passive voice and high scores on Dimension 5, methods sections are by far the most "abstract"/passivized sections.

[32]As mentioned above in note 1, the F, p, and R^2 statistics for Tables 5.2–5.7 measure significance and covariance only *within* the tables, not *across* them.

[33]The two texts representing 1675 were included in this analysis because their scores were consistent with the more general patterns evidenced on the dimensions. The general patterns themselves were also more robust than in the analysis of epistolary versus nonepistolary articles, because the experimental/nonexperimental comparison covered the full 300-year period of study rather than just the 150 years from 1675 to 1825.

[34]Although Dimension 3 does not serve to distinguish experimental from nonexperimental articles in this analysis, it sheds interesting light on the high Dimension 3 score for 1825 as found and discussed in the overall MD analysis. Thus, experimental articles show a moderate score of 4.7 for this period/dimension, which is midway between scores in the two adjoining periods. Nonexperimental articles, however, show an extreme score, 7.7, indicating that such texts are substantially responsible for the extreme score on this dimension for 1825 in the

overall analysis. Further analysis reveals that this score is the product of three very high scoring nonexperimental texts out of the six sampled—those by Home, Pond, and Kidd (cf. Appendix A for full citations and Appendix B, part 2, for graphed dimension scores of these texts). Large numbers of WH-relative clauses appear to be substantially responsible for the high scores of each of these texts: Home has 13.6 WH-relatives (summed across all three WH-relative types) per 1,000 words, while Kidd has 18 and Pond 15—a mean of 15.5. The mean number of WH-relatives per 1,000 words for the other seven (both experimental and nonexperimental) texts in this period is 8.6. Two nonexperimental texts in this period also have extremely large numbers of nominalizations: the text by Kidd mentioned above, with 71.9 per 1,000 words, and that by Woodhouse, with 67.8. The counts contrast with a mean of 37.6 nominalizations in texts overall on this dimension, and with means for nonexperimental and experimental articles of 41.6 and 31.6, respectively. It is therefore the case, as described in the discussion of Dimension 3 in the overall MD analysis, that nominalizations interact with relative clause markers to bring about the extreme dimension score for 1825—and it can now be added that nonexperimental texts play a disproportionally large role in raising this score.

CHAPTER

6

Synthesis and Discussion: Scientific Discourse and Scientific Forms of Life

From the results reported so far, it is clear that scientific research writing in the *PTRS* has evolved dramatically, if for the most part incrementally, over the past 300 years. In this chapter, I first attempt to synthesize these findings, considering both long-term, continuous development in the journal's rhetoric and language as well as cross-time discontinuities revealed therein. I then discuss these synthesized results in relation to their larger sociohistorical contexts: the Discourse histories of British science, generally, and to some degree the Royal Society and its *PTRS*. It is only in accomplishing the latter that the model of discourse analysis laid out in chapter 1 will be brought to bear, and the data presented in chapter 4 and 5 be seen to make sense.

SYNTHESIS OF RHETORICAL AND LINGUISTIC FINDINGS

Cross-Time Linear Development and Continuities

The rhetorical and linguistic findings of this study can be synthesized in terms of three sets: (a) the decline of an "author-centered" rhetoric and the extreme linguistic shift on Dimension 1 from low-level "involved" to highly "informational" discourse; (b) the rise of an "object-centered" rhetoric and the development on Dimension 5 of a highly "abstract"/passivized form of language; and (c) the gradual loss of narrative elements in *PTRS* texts over time, as indicated at both the rhetorical and linguistic (Dimension 2) levels.

(a) Decline of Author-Centered Rhetoric and Linguistic Change on Dimension 1. At least in terms of its dominant rhetoric and ideology, scientific research involves human beings carrying out actions on aspects of the natural world. These may be direct physical actions, such as manipulating experimental conditions, or mental/perceptual actions, such as observing natural phenomena or theorizing about their causes. Viewed in this way, then, scientific activity can be described in a standard three-part formula: *human(s)* → *acting on* → *nature.*[1] Which elements of this formula a group of scientists living in a particular time and place chooses to emphasize will depend on various factors, many of which can be classified as social and historical.

As part of a larger sociohistorically conditioned view of reality (to be discussed later), early modern British scientists chose to place comparatively strong emphasis on the first two elements of the above-mentioned formula, *the human actor/author* and *his or her actions.* Thus, an active author–researcher and that individual's activities played a central rhetorical role in the 17th- and 18th-century *PTRS:* The researcher was typically characterized as a full participant in the events related. At the same time, God-ordained (and thus God-demonstrating) nature was itself by no means neglected in early modern British science, given its central position as the focus of scientific research.

This early modern author-centered rhetoric has clear correlates at the linguistic level of analysis on Dimension 1. Thus, indexes of the author-centered approach or the closely associated epistolary article included first person personal pronouns, stance markers such as hedges and possibility modals, active-voice verbs of various types, and second person personal pronouns, as described in chapter 4. It is notable that *each of these features is also represented on the "involved production" end of Dimension 1 in the MD analysis.* Although only some of the features actually decrease individually across time in tandem with the author-centered rhetoric, as part of the larger feature set underlying Dimension 1—which *does* show definite movement away from an "involved" norm for *PTRS* texts—they strongly suggest the linkage of author-centered rhetoric with an early low-level "involved production."

The connectedness of these specific rhetorical and linguistic findings is also signaled in a second way, and one that highlights their complementarity rather than their strict congruency. The rhetorical analysis performed here documents the gradual decline of the author-centered approach—that much is clear; but it tells us substantially less about *what took the place of the author-centered rhetoric.* That is, although the notion of an object-centered replacement rhetoric is introduced, the rhetorical analysis focuses on the continuing erosion of a strong authorial presence, as expressed in such relatively negative terms as "distanced" and "effaced" authorial norms.

Considered in contrast to these rhetorical findings, the MD analysis appears to tell us more about *what replaced* the author-centered rhetoric—about the increasing "object-centeredness" of *PTRS* texts. Thus, whereas *some* individual linguistic features underlying the "involved production" side of Dimension 1 decreased in frequency over time, almost all "informational production" features *increased,* in most cases dramatically.

As indicated in chapter 5, all five of the linguistic features representing "informational production" on Dimension 1 are either major noun phrase elements (i.e., nouns and attributive adjectives) or features strongly associated with noun phrases (i.e., prepositions, word length, and lexical variety). Thus, the increasing object-centeredness identified but not extensively described at the rhetorical level closely parallels at the linguistic level the gradual takeover of scientific clause structure by the noun phrase.

What was the nature of noun phrases in scientific discourse at this time, and why did they gradually take over? As Halliday (1988; Halliday & Martin, 1993) in particular has made clear, scientific "objects" or "things" assumed increased prominence in scientific writing across the period under study, but they were often objects or things of a decidedly odd nature. Rather than referring to common person/place/thing/idea type referents, nouns were used increasingly to represent *nominalized reifications of scientific activity,* such as "the resolution of the experimental difficulties associated with producing and probing exotic atomic nuclei" (Halliday, 1988, p. 175).[2] By being converted into nouns and noun phrases in this way, scientific processes and activities were thus reconfigured as scientific objects and products, through an operation Halliday characterizes linguistically as *grammatical metaphor,* and semiotically as *objectification:*

> Where the everyday 'mother tongue' of commonsense knowledge construes reality as a balanced tension between things [prototypically represented by nouns] and processes [prototypically represented by verbs], the elaborated register of scientific knowledge reconstrues it as an edifice of things. It holds reality still, to be kept under observation and experimented with; and in so doing, interprets it not as changing with time (as the [everyday] grammar of clauses interprets it) but rather as persisting—or rather, persistence—through time, which is the mode of being of a noun. (Halliday & Martin, 1993, p. 15)

Noun phrases were thus a central resource, and their growth into formidable constructions a direct result, of the process by which modern scientific discourse's "thingish" (Killingsworth & Gilbertson, 1992) style was innovated. Rather than scientific people and their agentively controlled scientific activities being emphasized as before, the static, "thingish"—and therefore object-like and (at least in this sense) "objective"—nature of scientific processes and phenomena was brought to the fore. It is in large part the movement, then, from something substantially closer to an "everyday 'mother tongue' of commonsense knowledge" to a highly object-centered/objectified form of language and rhetoric, which is accounted for in synthesizing this first set of findings.

(b) The Growth of Object-Centered Rhetoric and the Rise of "Abstract" Language on Dimension 5. The developments described so far are also implicated in a second convergent set of linguistic and rhetorical findings. This is the parallel innovation of a highly "abstract"/passivized linguistic norm for scientific writing with the object-centered rhetoric delineated previously.

As shown in Fig. 5.6, texts clustered at a moderately "abstract"/passivized level on Dimension 5 in the 17th and 18th centuries, but rose to an extreme level in the 19th and 20th. Thus, it can be said that scientific research writing has always been a moderately passivized genre in the *PTRS*, but only in the last two centuries has it been highly so.

Interpreting these data vis-à-vis the rhetorical development of *PTRS* texts from an author-centered to an object-centered norm, one finds clear and direct relationships. As mentioned previously in introducing the *human(s) → acting on → nature* formula, the natural phenomena being investigated in science were always particularly important. Thus, science is centrally—at least from a rhetorical and ideological point of view—the attempt to acquire knowledge about such phenomena. But even into the 19th century, the individual taking an active role in investigating nature was also given textual prominence, as were that individual's actions. The result was therefore a mixture of emphases—on the individual as agent/actor and on his or her actions as dynamic operations, but also on the ultimate subjects or foci of science: the natural phenomena themselves. The latter emphasis explains the moderately "abstract" or passivized nature of scientific research writing even in the earliest periods studied here. That is, no matter how author-centered, scientific texts attempt to tell their users ultimately about the object of study, and that object (or its stand-ins—see note 1) will thus frequently occupy a grammatically/information-structurally central place in clauses, represented prototypically by a noun or pronoun in subject/topic position. There thus obtained a certain figurative competition between the active author and the natural object of study for subject/topic position—a competition that led to a relative balance between active and passive clauses in the 17th and 18th centuries.

As the author-centered rhetoric began to wane, however, the natural objects of study—and increasingly both those nominalized and "objectified" processes described by Halliday (1988) and various kinds of scientific instruments and procedures—came further to the fore. And the increased prominence of these "objects" was reflected in their much more common appearance as grammatical subjects/information-structural topics of clauses.

These objects were still, of course, often portrayed as being acted upon, but who was doing the acting—and even the fact that someone *was* still acting—became less important.[3]

(c) The Decline of Narrative Elements. The third area of development in which rhetorical and linguistic findings appear to agree involves the presence of narrative elements in texts. Narrative was never a major discourse type in the writing sampled in this study, although it was more prominently represented in the earlier periods, and in certain types of texts. Reports of experiments, in particular, frequently included narrative accounts of how they were performed, as indicated at the rhetorical level of analysis. Over time, however, actual accounts of experiments were given less and less prominence and space, so that by 1975 what experimental narrative remained was usually highly circumscribed.

The gradual deemphasis over time of narrative elements in the *PTRS* is also indicated at the linguistic level of analysis. Results of the overall MD analysis (Fig. 5.2) show that, although the group of features underlying Dimension 2 has never been heavily represented, articles in the 17th and 18th centuries were comparatively less "nonnarrative" than those in the 19th and 20th centuries. Results of MD analysis of two subsets of *PTRS* articles, experimental versus nonexperimental texts, also confirms that the former were consistently more "narrative," linguistically speaking, than the latter in all periods but one. These findings—that scores on Dimension 2, never "narrative,"[4] show a steady and linear trend in the "nonnarrative" direction, while experimental articles were almost always more "narrative" than nonexperimental articles—dovetail well with the rhetorical-level findings mentioned previously.

Diachronic Discontinuities Across Analytical Levels

Two sampling periods in the present corpus, 1725 and 1825, feature notable discontinuities in patterns of textual development at both the rhetorical and linguistic levels of analysis. In this subsection, I undertake to relate these discontinuous developments to each other across analytical levels.

As described in chapter 4, articles in the 1725 *PTRS* differed rhetorically from those of 1675 in several important ways. First, a gap in the dominance of the author-centered rhetoric was indicated: Articles in 1725 were less likely to portray the author as an active participant in textual events. Likewise, articles in letter form appeared much less frequently than in either of the adjoining periods. A third development specific to 1725 was the use of a significantly oppositional rhetoric—although authors retained the dialogic character of their discourse community orientation from the preceding period, they tended to replace the typically cooperative tone found there with one which emphasized disagreement and opposition. In chapter 4, each of these developments was attributed to Isaac Newton's dominant influence over the Royal Society in the early 18th century.

There are also numerous idiosyncrasies for 1725 at the linguistic level of analysis. Thus, in the overall MD analysis (Table 5.1), there is a large score increase in the "informational" direction on Dimension 1 ("involved vs. informational production") as well as a sizable jump in the "nonpersuasive" direction on Dimension 4 ("overt expression of persuasion"). Texts in this period furthermore show the lowest level of "abstractness" seen in the overall analysis for *any* period on Dimension 5 ("nonabstract vs. abstract information"). Some of these linguistic discontinuities appear to complement the rhetorical discontinuities mentioned so far.

Specifically, it is possible to correlate the first rhetorical discontinuity mentioned here—the clear (if temporary) decrease in author-centeredness—with the pronounced drop in the level of "involved production" at the linguistic level for 1725. As suggested previously, a textworld in which the author played a highly visible and active role would be expected to be realized linguistically in comparatively "involved" terms. Although this picture is complicated to some extent in the case of scientific writing—wherein the focus of attention is necessarily at least in part on the natural phenomena under study (see previous discussion)—a rough correlation still appears to hold. Thus, a notable decrease in author-centered rhetoric in 1725 is mirrored in a precipitous drop in the "involved" scores of texts. What is not explainable by means of this interpretation, however, and what makes it less than fully convincing, is that the scores *keep* dropping on Dimension 1 in the succeeding periods, even as author-centered rhetoric appears to be making a substantial comeback.

Tentative relationships can also be posited among the remaining rhetorical and linguistic discontinuities mentioned previously for 1725. First, a notable score increase in the "nonpersuasive" direction on Dimension 4 at the linguistic level might be taken to suggest that the oppositional rhetoric favored by Newtonians represented something other than an "argumentative" or persuasive norm—that the latter had some other rhetorical purpose. This interpretation is unlikely, however, as those individual texts featuring a highly oppositional rhetoric that *were* subjected to MD analysis in fact have high "persuasive" scores. Rather, it appears that the methods used to select texts for MD analysis resulted in a sample for 1825 in which "oppositional" rhetoric was not heavily represented—most texts in the sample do not exhibit this characteristic, and they also have scores that are "nonpersuasive" to varying degrees. Taking the latter point as a finding in its own right, the dearth of articles featuring a strong oppositional rhetoric among the 10 texts sampled for MD analysis appears to suggest the existence of a sort of "style schizophrenia" in the 1725 volume. That is, it may be that the "oppositional" norm described in chapter 4 actually characterizes only a *subset* of articles, whereas another subset—from which the sample chosen for MD analysis was largely though unintentionally taken—represents a quite different approach.

Indeed, other findings at the linguistic level of analysis appear to corroborate the existence of "style schizophrenia" in 1725. Thus, the texts sampled in the overall MD analysis for this period show more variation among themselves (as represented by range of variation and standard deviation statistics—see Appendixes B and C) on three of the five dimensions than those from any other single period. In addition, there are broad differences (see Tables 5.2 and 5.3) between epistolary and nonepistolary articles for this period on four of the five dimensions studied—epistolary articles from 1725 are conspicuously less "informational" (Dimension 1), more "narrative" (Dimension 2), less "referentially explicit" (Dimension 3), and less "overtly persuasive" (Dimension 4) than their nonepistolary counterparts. If, as suggested in chapter 2, there was movement in 1725 away from the types of research commonly featured in epistolary articles and toward a more elaborate Newtonian norm, the fact that the former were still included in the *PTRS* may account for the style differences exhibited therein.

The year 1825 is the second sampling period exhibiting multiple discontinuities at both levels of analysis vis-à-vis earlier periods. Unlike 1725, however, there appears to be only one development at the rhetorical level in 1825 that correlates with notable change at the linguistic level: the new prominence of descriptions of research methods, whether in experimental or nonexperimental texts. This rhetorical innovation may be reflected linguistically in a sudden increase in the level of "abstractness"/passiveness on Dimension 5. The latter change was related previously to the gradual decrease in a predominantly author-centered rhetoric, and a corresponding increase in object-centeredness; together they appear to mark a major shift in the means of scientific persuasion. This evolutionary pattern is more fully discussed in the following section.

DISCUSSION: RHETORICAL–LINGUISTIC CHANGE IN THE *PTRS* AND SCIENTIFIC FORMS OF LIFE

Having so far delineated synthetic relationships between the rhetorical and linguistic results of this study, it is now possible to locate these combined results—along with findings that do not appear to correlate across analytical levels—within a larger sociohistorical/discursive frame. The two layers of discursive context primarily referred to here are: (a) that of British (and in a few cases European) empirical science between the late 17th and late 20th centuries as a developing cultural "form of life"; and (b) that of the Royal Society of London itself over this same period. In a few cases, explanatory recourse will also be had to larger historical trends, such as the move toward centralized government and the innovation of political democracy in 19th-century Europe.

The Genteel-Scientific Worldview
and 17th- and 18th-Century Scientific Discourse

Recent historical research (e.g., Daston, 1991a, 1991b, 1995; Golinski, 1987, 1989; Iliffe, 1992; Johns, 1991; to appear; Nye, 1989; R. Porter, 1977, 1978; T. Porter, 1995; Shapin, 1988, 1989, 1991, 1994) paints an unambiguous picture of social conditions accompanying the development of empirical science in 17th- and 18th-century Britain. As briefly described in chapter 2, the empirical study of nature was substantially parasitic on a larger preexisting cultural form of life—that of the British gentleman—adopting many of its modes of social conduct, epistemological conventions, and favored means of communication. In the following paragraphs, I lay out the connections between early modern science and genteel culture in more detail, with an intermittent focus on the Royal Society.

To start at the beginning, the early British empiricists *were* predominantly gentlemen, and in a society where professional identities had not yet been extensively developed in contradistinction to social roles and status, they fashioned and pursued their science according to gentlemanly norms and conventions. There is even good evidence to suggest that gentlemanly culture continued to influence the Royal Society—and to some degree British science as a whole—right into the present century (see chap. 2, section entitled "Modernity"; cf. Berman, 1975).

Shapin (1988) has shown how the gentlemanly nature of 17th-century empiricism determined many of the conventions by which experiments, loosely defined, were conducted and verified by Boyle, Hooke, and their followers in the Royal Society. Experimental demonstrations were most frequently undertaken in the private residences of gentlemen like Boyle, locations in which a highly formalized code of genteel conduct obtained. Such conduct thereby substantially attached itself to the nascent activity of scientific experimentation. On a more general level, similar social rules were in force wherever gentlemen gathered (Klein, 1994), whether in the London coffeehouses—an important venue for scientific teaching and discussion—or in the quasi-societies prefiguring the Royal Society, described in chapter 2. By the founding of the Royal Society in 1660, genteel precedents therefore already existed for determining the proper conduct of scientific activity.

Nor is their reason to doubt the common early description of the Royal Society as "a society of gentlemen" (e.g., Harwood, 1989, note 35; Hunter, 1982, 1989).[5] Few besides men of independent means could have found the leisure or money requisite for cultivating even dilletantish scientific pursuits. Neither, as is sometimes thought, does the occasional appearance in the early Society of individuals with only marginal gentlemanly status call into question its dominantly genteel character. Robert Hooke, Henry Oldenburg, and Denis Papin, for example, were all functionaries of their patron, Robert Boyle. In the cases of Hooke and Papin, duties included actually performing the experiments designed and financed by that patron (e.g., Shapin, 1989; Shapin, 1994, chap. 8; chap. 4, note 17 of the present study). Analogous roles were still being played over 100 years later by, among others, Jonas Dryander and Daniel Solander for Joseph Banks (Carter, 1988).[6]

Considering these realities, it should not be very surprising to find frequent signs of genteel social practice in the scientific rhetoric of the 17th and 18th centuries. But this is the beginning—not the end—of the story. Early modern British science was also an *oppositional Discourse* (in the sense of Gee, 1990; see chap. 1, note 3), that is, it had developed and was sustained partly out of a profound dissatisfaction with the then-prevailing mode of intellectual inquiry, late scholasticism. A major thrust of Bacon's work was to attack scholastic approaches to learning, which pervaded contemporary education and scholarship. In this critique, developed further by later 17th-century empiricists, scholasticism was widely associated with intellectual servitude: To be a "schoolman" was to follow the closed philosophical system of a "school" (Dear, 1985; Shapin, 1991; Shapin, 1994, chap. 4).[7] In opposition to these intellectual indentured servants, the early empiricists portrayed themselves as freely pursuing the study of divinely created nature, unfettered by philosophical predispositions or the need to support themselves as professional scholars. In adopting this stance, they traded on the conventional social image of the gentleman for rhetorical purposes.

Preindustrial British society constituted a social hierarchy in which power flowed from the landed aristocracy and gentry downward. The British gentleman therefore represented the moral and social ideal in this system, all other social categories being defined relative to this one. The ideal gentleman had his own conventionalized set of ideal qualities: He was self-reliant and individualistic, being at the top of the social structure and independently wealthy; at the same time he was modest and polite, due to a code of civility that strictly defined relations with other gentlemen. But above all else, he was "free" and independent, a disinterested social actor "owned" by and beholden to no one, and honest and honorable to a fault for this very reason. In short, he was incorruptible because he had nothing to gain by lying. Of course, realizations of this ideal type were often its inferiors by far, but this hardly affected the power and influence of the ideal image.[8]

The early identity of the empirical scientist was therefore intimately bound up with the social position of the gentleman. In fact, genteel independence and disinterestedness were in this important sense almost absolute preconditions for full and unfettered insight into nature's secrets. It was thus no accident that when the Royal Society adopted a motto, "Nullius in verba"—"In the words of no man"—it emblematized this position perfectly.[9]

Within the context of a scientific form of life so strongly influenced by genteel norms of thought and conduct, the present study's findings start to make sense. From this perspective, the author-centered, relatively "involved" discourse of the early *PTRS* represented a self-evident expression of a way of life in which author-researchers really did stand at the center of, and were significantly in control of, events. It further depended for its rhetorical effectiveness on the trust conventionally accorded gentlemen by other gentlemen (and of necessity by all lower classes in British society, because they were, in nontrivial ways, dependent on the good will of gentlemen–patrons or others in their control). This was a crucial aspect of early modern scientific rhetoric, as made clear by Shapin (1984, 1994): If scientific reports in this period described "a definite occurrence happening to a particular person" (Dear, 1985, p. 152), that person's credibility substantially determined the credibility of the account. And gentlemen in this society, viewed as self-reliant, free, and beholden to no one, had the market cornered on credibility.[10]

In a similar vein, Daston (1991a, note 41; cf. T. Porter, 1992) has described how 17th-century British science was based on "a moral economy of . . . proximity and trust." In Daston's view, this was in some senses the exact opposite of our current model of science with its "technology of distance and distrust"—for example, objective and explicit research methods and procedures. Borrowing from and extending Daston's argument, I would like to claim that, as part of this larger "moral economy," or Discourse, 17th- and 18th-century scientific writing was itself a *discourse of proximity and trust.* Here, "trust" denotes the genteel basis of credibility just delineated, and "proximity"—itself intimately bound up with trust—signifies the direct acquaintanceship and face-to-face contact that were the primary conditions of sociability among gentlemen in 17th- and 18th-century London.[11]

Proximity and trust were represented at the level of written discourse in multiple ways. As already mentioned, an author-centered, "involved" stance was a crucial element: In a world where who (or at the least *what*) you were centrally mattered, the author did well to make himself conspicuous in his text. And the *way* he did so was equally important:

> Early modern gentlemen were highly skilled in decoding and manipulating manners and gestures in order to assess and enhance the veracity of communication. When communication was in written form, attention might be focused on the rhetoric and style in which relations and the authorial self were presented, and, when communication took place orally in a face-to-face forum, fine details of gesture, posture, manner of speech, and auditors' response were also available for inspection and exploitation. Here the relevant maxim, pervasive in the civil conversations of early modern gentlemanly society, was 'believe those whose manner inspires confidence.' (Shapin, 1994, p. 221)[12]

A genteel persona was therefore critical to the rhetorical success of a scientific text. An unmistakably genteel style was the best warrant of credibility, especially where the author was not in fact personally known. Beyond the active textual presence of the author, ways in which a genteel persona was indexed in this period included the use of elaborate politeness and "modesty," aspects of early scientific writing that were associated in chapter 4 with an author-centered rhetoric. They were elements of a worldview wherein gentlemen were to conduct themselves with great decorum and civility, a social ideal transformed in 17th- and 18th-century Britain into a cult centered on the concept of "politeness" (Klein, 1986, 1994; McIntosh, 1986). Klein (1994) delineates the contemporary meaning of this notion as regards the use of language:

> At its most elaborate, "politeness" could be used to evoke a vision of social life and culture, appropriate to modern times. This vision, linking moral improvement and cultural refinement, was epitomized in urbane and gentlemanly conversation. . . . "Politeness" was in general a condition of refined social interaction, but social "politeness" was paradigmatically conversational. When writers defined "politeness" as a dextrous management of words and actions in company, words had pride of place. . . . The social disciplines aimed to enhance social interaction, making it more pleasurable and agreeable and sometimes also more useful and instructive. Such social disciplines demanded the ability to locate oneself in a complex social situation, recognizing one's own desires and interests while comprehending the legitimate desires and interests of others. Contemporary exhortations to modesty, discretion, decorum, propriety and politeness were demands that the moral agent recognize the social context of his or her actions. (pp. 33–34)

The encomia appearing at the beginnings of articles from 1675, as well as textual references to "ingenious" ideas and "intelligent" and "honourable" individuals, were as much markers of genteel politeness as the rules by which discussion was conducted at Royal Society meetings. Modesty, as advocated by Boyle (Shapin, 1984, 1994, chap. 4; Golinski, 1987; Harwood, 1989) and as indexed by linguistic stance markers, the reporting of unsuccessful experiments, and unwillingness to engage in explicit theorizing, was employed frequently in the early *PTRS* to enhance credibility. Such displays of modesty comported well with the moral positions widely held to accrue to genteel status, including self-deprecation, disinterestedness, humility before God, and, ultimately, veracity. To the early empiricists, such modesty contrasted directly with the egoism and grand theorizing of their adversaries the scholastics, who, as the polar opposites of urbane and open-minded "polite gentlemen," were widely characterized as argumentative, pedantic, vain, close-minded, and intellectually constrained.

In describing early modern scientific discourse as a discourse of trust and proximity, I have so far focused on textual markers of trust. Proximity, the direct corollary of trust in the early modern moral economy, was also indexed in manifold ways. Thus, the relatively "involved" language of the early *PTRS*–language in this respect substantially closer to conversation (Klein, 1994), or to Halliday and Martin's (1993, p. 15) "everyday 'mother tongue' of commonsense knowledge"–recapitulated the interactive nature of social systems based largely on face-to-face relations. Likewise, the dialogic approach taken by 17th- and 18th-century *PTRS* authors to their discourse communities directly indicated an economy of proximity.

As noted in chapter 4, there was certainly a Baconian element at work in the interactive, usually cooperative nature of early research writing, but gentlemanly norms of conduct may well have been what allowed such communication to take place at all. Thus, Shapin and Schaffer (1985) have argued that the constant emphasis in later 17th-century writings on the rational, consensual character of natural philosophical knowledge reflected the ideals of genteel culture. These ideals, all the more valued after the violent upheavals of the Civil War, were thought to permit discussion without the constant threat of disagreeable or even disasterous conflict.[13] Once again, this was in stark contrast to what was at least portrayed (usually by gentlemen, it should be noted) as the case among the scholastics.

Finally, the epistolary article itself can be viewed as a major emblem of genteel culture and proximity in the early *PTRS*. Polite letter writing was cultivated among the 17th- and 18th-century gentry as a quintessentially genteel pursuit (Klein, 1994; McIntosh, 1986), as evidenced by the great numbers of their private letters still surviving from this period. If, as Klein (1994) avers, conversation was the speech event in which politeness was paradigmatically expressed, then the letter was its written equivalent:

> The conversational ideal operated to validate certain [written] genres and stylistic modes. For instance, Shaftesbury [the aristocratic 18th-century champion of polite culture and learning] assigned centrality to the genre of the letter. Since the letter, he thought, was a continuation of conversation at one remove from conversation itself, it was the literary form best able to carry the particular burdens of conversation. . . . This endorsement of the epistolary genre was widely shared in the eighteenth century and an obvious foundation of many characteristic literary practices during the era. (Klein, 1994, p. 35)

It can therefore be argued that the letter's role as the single most common written genre for reporting scientific research in the early *PTRS*–as well as its continued use into the 19th century–was no coincidence. Part and parcel of the form of life shared by most members of the Royal Society, the letter was therefore in this sense *preselected for* as the main genre in which scientific research was initially to be reported. And like other "adopted genres" (cf. Clanchy, 1979; Ferguson, 1994; Street, 1984; Yates & Orlikowski, 1992), it remained in use side-by-side with newer, more "functional" (because purpose-built) alternatives. There may even have been disagreement in the early 18th-century Royal Society over which genres were appropriate for reporting scientific research, as there was regarding what properly constituted "scientific research" itself. Such conflict may go some way toward explaining the sudden proportional drop in letters in the 1725 *PTRS,* and may relate to the "style schizophrenia" already noted therein.[14]

"Conservative Change" and "the Second Scientific Revolution": Discourse, Science, and the Royal Society in 19th-Century Britain

As described by recent historians of British science, the 19th century (including, for present purposes, the last quarter or so of the 18th century as well) presents something of a paradox: It was a time of profound change in science and society, to the degree that the period has sometimes been called, though by no means in reference only to Britain, "the second scientific revolution." At the same time—and this was especially true in Britain—there were substantial continuities with the past, and the changes that took place were mostly of a gradual and continuity-preserving kind.

Considering the latter point first, Morrell and Thackray (1981) provide a useful overview of the social context of 19th-century British science in their extensive work on the British Association for the Advancement of Science (BAAS) from 1830 to 1850:

> The alterations in social organization and cultural mode which accompanied the Industrial Revolution may thus be seen as parts of one especially striking episode in the long, slow change in economic, demographic, and technological realities. On this level of analysis, the significant features of British experience in the past three centuries have been these: the unbroken continuity of the monarchy and the hereditary principle; the strength of the Established Church, the common law, and prevailing political forms; the endurance of deference and those traditional values associated with a landed aristocracy; the inability of peripheral groups of any kind to capture the commanding centres of power in London or those of socialization in Oxford and Cambridge; and always and everywere as an underlying theme the integration of the new with the old. The persistence of these patterns renders 'revolution' a curious term. (p. 5)

Along with many other scholars (e.g., Berman, 1975; Geison, 1972; Heyck, 1982; Morrell, 1990; R. Porter, 1977, 1978; Rudwick, 1963; 1985), Morrell and Thackray (1981) describe how genteel culture substantially maintained its influence on scientific activity in Britain well into the 19th century. If this was true of the BAAS, a group ostensibly formed to bring science to the rising middle classes, it was all the more so for the Royal Society, an organization still solidly devoted at century's beginning to genteel, amateur science. The political ferment that preoccupied the Society from 1820 to around 1850, although it led to no cataclysmic change, was even instigated largely by well-heeled gentlemen. The difference was that Babbage, Hershel, and their compatriots envisioned an ideal of scientific activity that was quite opposed to 17th- and 18th-century norms.

Some of the discrete sciences that emerged in the 19th century clung to their genteel heritage more closely than others, with the natural history subjects, the nascent life sciences, and geology especially prone to do so. The 19th-century development of geology in particular has been extensively documented, revealing the continued influence of gentlemanly norms. Thus, R. Porter (1977, 1978) and Rudwick (1963, 1985) show how virtually all the top-ranking British geologists up to 1850 had genteel origins, and that the study of geology itself was closely associated with proprietary interest in land, the romantic notion of the individual collecting in the field, and a "muscular Christianity" that celebrated exploration and physical effort. That quintessential 19th-century genteel–amateur scientist himself, Charles Darwin, began his scientific life as a geologist, following in his 18th-century grandfather's footsteps.

In an atmosphere like this, it is not surprising to find research writing in the *PTRS* maintaining significant continuities with the past. Thus, author-centered rhetoric, a paradigmatic feature of the genteel–scientific form of life and its moral economy of proximity and trust, still appears to have operated as a dominant norm in the 1825 *PTRS*. Likewise, epistolary articles still made up roughly 30% of the volume in that year. This is not to say, however, that no change whatsoever was taking place in these areas: If, as I have tried to show earlier in this chapter, author-centered rhetoric and the linguistic-feature complex underlying Dimension 1 of the MD analysis are indeed parts of a larger gestalt, then gradual development on Dimension 1 toward a more "informational" norm shows that change was indeed occurring. Further supporting this interpretation, rhetorical analysis of letters in the *PTRS* indicates that change was also taking place in that genre by 1825, the last period in which it appeared in the journal: Letters were much longer than earlier, tended to be less honoring and more "to the point," and less often concerned natural history topics. Yet, although other developments in this period clearly distinguish the *PTRS* from its 17th- and 18th-century ancestors, the relative maintenance of genteel norms points to substantial continuities leading back to the beginnings of modern empirical science in Britain.

Turning now to the sociocognitive *differences* that divided 19th-century British science from its forerunners, three are especially noteworthy in the present context. The first concerns the advent of standardized quantitative measurement procedures in the later 18th and 19th centuries; the second, the growth of scientific disciplines and specialties; and the third, the slow and incomplete professionalization of British science. These changes combined to have a profound effect on the shape of scientific discourse in 19th-century Britain.

T. Porter (1995) describes the development of standardized measurement systems in many areas of endeavor that accompanied attempts to centralize political and economic power in the European nation–states from around 1775 to 1850. Measurement conventions varied widely from locale to locale in preindustrial Europe: Local ways of measuring grain, for instance, represented obstacles to interregional trade and capitalism, much as local approaches to measuring property and inhabitants bedeviled the establishment of national systems of taxation and military conscription. Democratic movements, widely evidenced starting around this time, also favored standardized quantitative measurement over more qualitative local alternatives, because the subjectivity of the latter favored higher-ups in the social hierarchy.

While scientists were often directly involved in developing these new systems of bureaucratic and economic control, parallel efforts to standardize measurements and procedures also proceeded along a more purely scientific track. Up to this point the scientific uses of quantification had been substantially limited by the idiosyncrasies of measurements and measurers, making it impossible to realize the ideals of large-scale, cooperative endeavor that Bacon had envisioned (e.g., Feldman, 1990). From this (partly retrospective) viewpoint, the technologies of proximity and trust mentioned previously were necessary evils: They existed in part because there were no more objective or stable means of warranting scientific knowledge. And in a world where scientific contacts and observers were starting to proliferate both nationally and internationally, such means were increasingly desired and sought after.

Porter thus identifies in this period a common underlying impulse among scientists and bureaucrats to develop standardized quantitative measuring systems. To serve their purposes, such systems needed to be: (a) *portable,* because they often had to be employed far away from the centers of knowledge and power from which they emanated (cf. Latour, 1987); (b) *objective,* because high levels of skill and discipline could not automatically be assumed of their appliers; and (c) *communicable* (Daston, 1992), because to be widely used and their uses defended in more-or-less democratic contexts, they had to be able to be described in explicit terms.

The result of this impulse, according to Porter (1995), was the development of complex, quantitative "technologies of distrust and distance":

[Q]uantification is a technology of distance . . . It exacts a severe discipline from its users, a discipline that is very nearly uniform over most of the globe.

. . . Since the rules for collecting and manipulating numbers are widely shared, they can easily be transported across oceans and continents and used to coordinate activities or settle disputes. Perhaps most crucially, reliance on numbers and quantitative manipulation minimized the need for intimate knowledge and personal trust. Quantification is well suited for communication that goes beyond the boundaries of locality and community. A highly disciplined discourse helps to produce knowledge independent of the particular people who make it. (p. ix)

However, lest these words be taken to suggest that the new norms of scientific conduct simply occurred as faits accomplis, Porter adds that they had actively and arduously to be innovated, argued for, modified, and defended. The outcome was as much a natural world refashioned to fit the new methods of science—partly in the sense that phenomena unable to be so investigated were de facto ruled out of court—as science refashioned to better fit nature. Daston (1992) develops a similar argument, granting the name "communicative science" only to the eventual outcome of this refashioning process:

> There is nothing inevitable about communicative science; it required hard work at every juncture: new instruments and new methods of data analysis were a precondition for amalgamating measurements made by far-flung observers; international commissions met and wrangled over the standards and definitions that would make the result of, say, statistical or electrical research comparable; scientific labour had to be divided and disciplined to equalize differences of skills and training. The very phenomena had to be pruned and filtered, for some were too variable or capricious to travel well. Already in the 18th century, scientists had begun to edit their facts in the name of scientific sociability; by the mid-19th century the contraction of nature to the communicable had become standard practice among scientists. It would be an exaggeration, but not a distortion, to claim that it was scientific communication that was the precondition for the uniformity of nature rather than the reverse. (pp. 608–609)

This 19th-century development of what Porter calls "technologies of distance and distrust," and Daston calls "communicative science," had direct implications for the shape of scientific discourse. As described here and in chapter 4, scientific writing was becoming more "objective" in this period—in the sense of becoming more "object-focused." That is, in terms of the *human(s)* → *acting on* → *nature* formulation, there was rhetorical movement away from a relative emphasis on the first and second elements toward a relative emphasis on the third.

The most obvious textual realizations in the *PTRS* of the "technologies of distance and distrust" described by Porter and Daston must be the elaborate methodological descriptions first found there in 1825. As seen previously, such descriptions were a prominent new feature of *all types* of articles in this period, with some even focusing solely on methods. Fully half of all experimental articles, as well, were centrally concerned with the methods and procedures by which the experiments reported were carried out, and much attention was given to describing complex measuring devices and instruments. Replication of one's own or others' research was also commonly reported for the first time, and the closely related development of experimental controls was also underway. These innovations point un-ambiguously to a model of scientific activity that grounded rhetorical authority in more-or-less explicit, rule-governed accounts of what was done to produce or observe certain results, such that a scientifically able reader could, in principle, reproduce them.[15]

Equally indicative of the growth of a "distance-and-distrust" rhetoric is the pronounced "abstract"/passivized score increase on Dimension 5 in 1825, and the extreme "abstract" scores *PTRS* texts thereafter exhibit. It was argued earlier that this finding indicates in part the displacement of gram-matical subjects and information–structural topics of clauses focusing on the author, in favor of those representing natural phenomena and their stand-ins.

It is not the case, however, that a rhetoric of distance and distrust simply replaced the formerly dominant author-centered rhetoric in this period; as described here and in chapter 4, author-centered rhetoric was still strongly represented in the 1825 *PTRS*. It rather appears that the two rhetorics were working side by side at this time. That is, a "distance-and-distrust" rhetoric, in which nonpersonal subject/topics and passive verbs were clausally domi-nant, seems to have co-occurred with a "trust-and-proximity" rhetoric, wherein first person personal pronouns and active-voice verbs were cen-tral.[16] Thus, passages like the following, in which the author is intermittently foregrounded even as procedures and methods are described, appear com-monly in 1825:

In order to determine the distance between the points which I ought to con-sider as the poles of the needle, I fixed it at right angles to the meridian; and bringing another needle, freely suspended, near to it, I moved the center of this needle along a line parallel to the axis of the first, and noted the points opposite to which the axis of the second was exactly in the magentic meridian; these points I considered as the poles of the first needle. The distance between the points thus determined was 4.28 inches.

In my former paper I have stated the length of each of the magnets to be 12 inches; more accurately, the length of the two joined together was 23.84 inches; so that the length of each might be taken to be very accurately 11.92 inches: they are .95 inch wide, and .375 inch thick. In all my other observations the same magnet was always placed on the same side of the centre of the needle; so that in ascertaining the situations of their poles I distinguish one as the north, the other as the south magnet. The distances of the poles of the magnets from their ends, determined in the same manner as for the needle, were measured on each side, and a mean of the whole taken to obtain the distances between the pole; they were these: [table omitted]. Taking half the sum of these, 1.64 inches, from the length of each magnet, we have 10.28 inches for the distance between the poles.

A meridian line being drawn on a firm table, standing on a stone floor, the compass was accurately adjusted on it, so that the needle pointed to zero on the graduated circle. The magnets were fixed at the bottoms of earthen pans, secured in such a way to rectangular pieces of board that their positions could not be accidently changed, and projecting from these boards were small pieces of brass, on each of which a line was drawn to indicate the position of the axis of the magnet . . . (Christie, 1825, pp. 8–9)

In this passage, the author-centered approach seems to slide gradually and almost seamlessly into the object-centered one, until it is largely, if not completely, submerged in an object-centered rhetoric of methods; and there are many such passages in this volume. The year 1825 can thus be thought of as a transitional period, one in which an author-centered rhetoric was still a vital part of the discourse, but in which a passivized, nonpersonal norm also had an important—indeed central—place. And the latter, as we have seen, was a direct correlate of the new rhetoric of communicative science.

A second confluent contributor to the shaping of scientific discourse in this period—and one obviously closely related to that just described—was the innovation of scientific specialties and disciplines. In the case of British science, such developments were signaled or prefigured by the establishment of specialist scientific societies starting in 1788, as described in chapter 2. A few of these societies, like the Society for Animal Chemistry (established 1809), were built directly into the structure of the Royal Society, while others, such as the Geological (1807) and Astronomical Societies (1820), were wholly independent.

In the case of the independent societies, their founding members saw their own scientific interests as diverging markedly from the amateur, eclectic, and essentially unified version of science dominating the Royal Society at this time, although they typically held membership also in the larger society. This eventually proved to be the death of natural philosophy in Britain, with its vision of science as at base a unified whole, and the foundation of the modern, self-sustaining sciences.[17] The birth of more-or-less discrete scientific disciplines (e.g., physics—see D. P. Miller, 1986) seems often to have followed this initial branching-out, although their full institutionalization, at least in Britain, had to await the reorganization of university science teaching later in the century (e.g., Geison, 1978).

Whatever the exact sequential relations between the birth of specialist societies and the establishment of scientific disciplines in Britain (and they were bound to vary according to the individual science), these phenomena had clear consequences socially, cognitively, and textually. Thus, by 1825, the bulk of articles in even the ostensibly antispecialist *PTRS* show scientific research being organized around rather specific, depersonalized research problems, with these problems sometimes themselves being contextualized within burgeoning specialist literatures. Such developments were in pronounced opposition to the earlier, often personalized approaches taken by authors to their discourse communities. In fact, the development of this new discourse–community orientation may even signal the appearance of research-based discourse communities as we know them today.[18]

Direct relationships between "distance-and-distrust"/"communicative science" technologies and the growth of scientific specialties and disciplines should also be noted. As indicated by T. Porter (1995) and Daston (1992), developing regular and objective measurement systems in science meant schooling individuals in the rigorous discipline of using them. Specialist technologies therefore brought with them specialist people—or, more accurately, an integral part of the development and success of such technologies was the development of cadres of individuals who could make them work. Thus, Feldman (1990) describes the beginnings of a discrete meteorological science in the late 18th century as a function of specialized, standardized quantification:

> [W]e can see the first hints of a discipline of climatology: a standard and consistent practice in the gathering and analysis of weather data. This practice is reflected in the emergence of a standard set of climatological variables calculated by meteorologists such as Bégulin, König, and Horsley. Their work marks the beginning of a quantitative climatology. (p. 171)

In the growth of scientific specialties and disciplines, we once again see movement away from a science based on personal qualities like social status and interpersonal ones like face-to-face relationships, toward a science based on impersonal norms and objective, standardized measurement systems.[19]

The third area of significant change in 19th-century British science, again closely related to the foregoing, was the rise of career positions in the sciences, and the subsequent development of professional cadres of scientists to meet this demand. Although these changes represent the clearest conceptual break with gentlemanly science, the seeming paradox exists that the earliest professional scientists in Britain, the geologists, came almost exclusively from the ruling classes.[20] The still semigenteel Royal Society was also instrumental in lobbying for institutionalized government funding of scientific research (the so-called "Government Grant"—see chap. 2) around midcentury; and it was given the task of managing the system once it was established. This was seen largely as a continuation of roles the Society had frequently played in the 18th century—of both consultant to the government and beneficiary of its largesse.

It is harder to find direct textual correlations with the professionalization of British science in the 19th-century *PTRS*. The concern for precise and objective methods of investigation discussed previously—and the concomitant need for expert specialists in those methods—obviously relates to it. At the same time, the notion that gentlemanly norms continued to inform scientific practice throughout the 19th century may partly account for why textual development therein was largely gradual and continuous, despite the growth of science as a profession.[21]

Scientific Modernity: Theoretical Versus Methodological Concerns in the 20th-Century *PTRS*

Little historical literature taking a social view of the 20th-century Royal Society has in fact been produced, nor have the overall contours of 20th-century British science, to my knowledge, been extensively sketched. The discussion here will therefore be both brief and speculative.

Historians have pointed out that by the end of the 19th century a revised attitude toward the importance of scientific methods was finding expression in Britain. Whereas earlier in the century methodology itself had been viewed as the ultimate source of scientific authority, by the 1890s a more reflective view can be seen forming. Yeo (1981) relates this less sanguine approach in part to debates over the methodology of Darwin's research.[22]

Whatever the exact status of methods in British science at this time, the findings of the present study—that explicit descriptions of methods are deemphasized starting in 1925—are loosely corroborated in two studies of 20th-century *non*-British scientific writing. Thus, Bazerman (1984), in his analysis of spectroscopic articles from the American *Physical Review* from 1893 to 1980, found a distinctly reduced emphasis on methods descriptions starting around 1920. In a second study, Berkenkotter and Huckin (1995, chap. 2) found that articles from a number of scientific disciplines showed a steady reduction in the proportion of space allotted methods starting in 1944, the beginning of the period they studied. Although Berkenkotter and Huckin's is somewhat later than the period when methods first appear as deemphasized in the present study, their progressive reduction had likely been underway for some time.

These results suggest that carefully delineated research methods no longer represented the dominant basis of scientific persuasion in the second quarter of the 20th century. Their place, at least at a gross textual level, seems to have been taken by expanded theoretical descriptions and discussions. Less clear, however, are the reasons behind the gradual deemphasis of methods. Did methodological descriptions really lose their effectiveness as rhetorical tools in the 20th century, as might be inferred from debates over Darwin's own methods at the end of the 19th? Or, is it rather that methodologies have become so standardized and unproblematic, and journal page space so expensive and precious, that there is little practical reason to describe methods in any detail, as suggested by the increased citation of standard methods in the *PTRS* starting in 1925?[23]

The growth of explicit theorizing in all types of research articles starting in 1925 is in itself an interesting result of the present study. It is neither possible to relate this development to an exact set of contextual events—as in the case of the physics articles studied by Bazerman (1984)—nor to give at this point a broader explanation. It seems clear that this development must have its own reasons, but further investigation of the socio-epistemological conditions of 20th-century British science is required before they can be accurately described.

CONCLUSION

In sum, it can be suggested that the new emphasis on precise research methods in the early 19th century signaled a larger reform in the rhetorical strategies underwriting British science. A rhetoric based on ideals of genteel character and conduct dominated early modern British science, as reflected in the presence of a strong author-centeredness and its various linguistic correlates. In the 18th century, however, some movement away from these norms may have been in progress, although the gentlemanly approach was again the dominant one. Although the precise nature of 18th-century influences on scientific rhetoric and language is unknown—and large-scale changes are not indicated in the main findings of this study—they may have emanated from alternative models of persuasion developed by Newton and his followers. Whatever their origins, by the beginning of the 19th century substantially different norms of scientific rhetoric—based on a rhetoric of objective methods—were being innovated and put in place. I do not mean to suggest, however, that there was a radical break: The development of new rhetorical norms in the *PTRS* was for the most part gradual, and occurred in tandem with substantial continuities in the evolution of British science. The genteel worldview continued to persist in some areas well into the 19th century, although it may no longer have been as often or as clearly manifested in the dominant rhetorical conventions of British science. Then, by the first quarter of the 20th century, the rhetoric of methods itself had been substantially replaced, by a focus on theoretical issues and discussions.

ENDNOTES

[1]Philosophers and sociologists of science (e.g., Hacking, 1983; Latour, 1987; Latour & Woolgar, 1986) have seriously questioned the notion that scientists usually (or ever) actually work on unmediated natural phenomena—or, to put it more strongly, on any recognizably "natural"

nature at all. Latour and Woolgar (1986, pp. 58–60), for example, delineate at least 14 kinds of highly constructed laboratory activity that need to be accomplished before a new hormone-releasing factor in the brain of a rat can be "discovered." Therefore, in my formulation of *human(s)* → *acting on* → *nature*, I mean only to suggest a general conceptual framework in which modern scientific rhetoric and ideology have functioned—in which scientists, that is, have conceptualized themselves as working—over the past 300 years. How this system corresponds to some "deeper reality" is not my concern here.

At the same time, I recognize the insufficiency of this characterization at anything more than a very gross level, even when talking about scientific rhetoric and ideology. Where, for instance, I refer later in this chapter to an increasing focus on the third element of "human(s) → acting on → nature" as leading to the more frequent placement of natural objects in the subject/topic position of clauses, I recognize that these "natural objects" are as likely to be some element of a technology of investigation (e.g., "In addition, the *interaction terms* used . . . do not have a direct meaning."), an objectified process ("The *interpretation* of the Rydberg states . . . depends . . . on a knowledge of the states of the molecular ion. . . ."), or some component of the "natural object" under study (e.g., "Each ommatidium . . . consists of the following elements . . ." in a paper entitled "The Eye of Anoplognathus"). In some cases, it is even difficult to tell if there *is* a natural object under study at all in a particular paper, as science is such a highly constructed human activity.

[2]Indeed, individual frequencies of nominalizations (though they occur on Dimension 3 instead of Dimension 1 in Biber's MD analysis) increase strikingly over the full period of study (see Fig. 5.4), and the progressive development of nominalization strategies is an important part of the story (Halliday, 1988), though not one I focus on directly here.

[3]It should be added that this synthesis does not attempt to explain everything. Thus, change at the rhetorical level appears to occur relatively evenly and gradually from an author-centered to an object-centered norm—and this is also true when rhetorical and linguistic results are synthesized, as here. Linguistic change on the "abstract"/passivized dimension (Dimension 5), on the other hand, occurs all at once; that is, moderately passivized norms appear to completely give way to highly passivized ones in the 50-year period between 1775 and 1825. Beyond restating the (unfortunate) fact that I devoted relatively slight attention at the rhetorical level to a close analysis of the "object-centered" rhetoric under innovation in the 19th century (as I was more concerned at the time with the demise of its author-centered predecessor), I can only account for the apparent discrepancy here by suggesting that full agreement between the two analyses, given their divergent origins and their differing strengths and sensitivities, is probably not a realistic goal.

[4]As already described in chapter 5, the fact that *PTRS* texts were never "narrative" on Dimension 2 is likely to have more to do with the corpus Biber (1988) used in the baseline analysis than with any real absence of narrativity from (especially early) texts. Biber's (1988) corpus included seven types of fiction, which are likely to have pulled the overall mean score of all dimension scores—which represented zero on the dimension scale and therefore determined the dividing line between "narrative" and "nonnarrative" dimension scores in the present analysis—toward the "narrative" end of Dimension 2.

[5]This description largely contradicts the claim, made by at least some Royal Society apologists (e.g., Sprat, 1667/1959) and borrowed from them by later authors (e.g., Hall, 1991; Sorrenson, 1996; Stimson, 1968), that the Society's membership was socially diverse. In a detailed statistical study, however, Hunter (1982) has shown this claim to be false (see chap. 2, note 16) for the period 1660–1699, and his statistics are corroborated by both Carter's (1988) and Sorrenson's (1996; see also present work, chap. 2, note 16) for much of the 18th century as well, although the latter's own interpretation of his findings shows a lack of appreciation of this fact.

[6]Dryander, however, appears never to have attained membership in the Royal Society.

[7]Not surprisingly, this association was also a reflection, in many instances, of economic and class differences. Shapin (1991), for example, notes the reproduction of the distinction between "scholars" and "gentlemen" in the 17th-century British universities:

'Scholars' and 'fellows' on the college establishment were generally of plebeian origin while aristocratic 'commoners' and 'gentlemen-commoners' paid their way and used their inferiors as 'battlers' and 'servitors.' Thus, the contours of social standing very roughly followed the boundaries between those who were professionally committed to a scholarly life and those who were not. (p. 286)

[8]There was also, of course, a contrasting version of the "English gentleman"—and especially the *country* gentleman, it should be noted—as drunken, dissolute, boorish, profane, and prone to violence. The popularity of this type in 18th-century English literature may have been based on its exceptional nature, as explicitly contradicting the social norms and expectations of ideal gentlemen that I have laid out here. Shapin (1994, p. 52) also points out that the pursuit of unmitigated pleasure by some English gentlemen in the 17th century was directly related to their social independence and lack of beholdenness to others, as described here.

[9]Shapin (1994, chap. 5) discusses seven approaches to gaining assent available to the British natural philosopher in the 17th century, and the practical shortcomings of each approach. He comes to the conclusion that:

There is . . . one inducement to assent to which I cannot find, nor indeed have I been able to imagine, a counter: this is the maxim which counseled assent to testimony from people characterized by their integrity and disinterestedness. To say that people were disinterested was to identify the adequate grounds of their truthfulness; there was nothing that worked on such people to induce them to represent matters otherwise than there were. . . . Truth-speaking then emerged unmotivated, simply as an attribute of persons so circumstanced that the passions and the interests could not wreak their distorting effects. (p. 237)

[10]At the same time there could never be *too much* credibility—and this is where the notion of "witnessing" as an aspect of author-centered rhetoric (for which see chap. 4) fits in. If a number of gentlemen could be named as having been present at and witnessed a scientific event, even more credibility accrued to its description. It was perhaps for a similar reason, some have suggested, that the Royal Society's membership rolls originally included large numbers of aristocrats with little or no seeming interest in science—simply the *names* of well-born individuals would have added further legitimacy to the Society's endeavors.

[11]Personal intimacy or acquaintanceship based on longstanding familial and social relationships was certainly the most common form of proximity in genteel society (e.g., see Galton's, 1874/1970, statistics, already mentioned in chap. 2, showing that just 13 old-line genteel families dominated Royal Society membership as late as 1874). In lieu of such connections, genteel trust was warranted by either nonhistorical personal acquaintanceship and the complex social evaluation procedures that accompanied it (Shapin, 1994), or the testimony of intimates to the genteel character and thus inherent trustworthiness, unless otherwise indicated, of a hitherto unknown individual.

[12]Klein (1994) describes further how the "polite" reputation of gentlemen and their characteristic prose style became confused and conflated:

"[P]olite writing" not only was the product of "polite gentlemen" but also shared the traits of "polite gentlemen." Thus, "politeness" bestowed gentlemanly attributes on literary expression: "polite" writing was free from pedantic stiffness and uncleanliness; it enjoyed "a free Air and genteel Motion"; it gained the love of others. . . . the same vocabulary came to characterize the "polite" writer and his product. (p. 39)

[13]For example, Golinski (1987) describes and quotes from the opening pages of Boyles' *Sceptical Chymist* (published in 1661), widely considered to have been composed as a model for the conduct of empirical science:

A smooth and civil language was said to be suitable to the *Sceptical Chymist*, 'a book written by a Gentleman, and wherein only Gentlemen are introduced as speakers'. 'A man may be a Champion of Truth, without being an Enemy to Civility', Boyle insisted, and accordingly the characters in the dialogues exchanged elaborate expressions of courtesy. They also, being 'Gentlemen, and very far from the litigious humour of loving to wrangle about words or terms or notions as empty', adopted without dispute the definition of an element which set the terms of the debate. (pp. 66–67)

[14]It should be remarked here that there were notable scientific precedents for reporting research in letters in the 17th century and probably before: Voluminous correspondence survives, for example, for both Kepler and Galileo. This fact, however, does not lessen the likelihood of the point I am trying to make; that is, that the adoption of the letter genre as the Royal Society's preferred genre for reporting research, and especially that genre's durability in this role, make good sense as part of the Society's genteel orientation.

The case for conflict over appropriate text forms and genres in which to report scientific research in the Newtonian Royal Society is circumstantial and retrospective at this point. It is known, for example, that in the second half of the century, Priestley condemned the nonnarrative strategies used by Newton in his major works as unnecessarily obfuscating the actual processes by which Newton came to his most revolutionary realizations (Bazerman, 1991). Priestley further championed both circumstantial miscellaneity and cooperative dialogue—two major features of non-Newtonian science, including scientific writing, in this period—as crucial to scientific progress (Golinski, 1992). That miscellaneity at least was more than simply an artifact of the free-wheeling nature of early modern science is persuasively argued by Daston (1991a), who locates it clearly within the Baconian program, and that miscellaneity as practiced by non-Newtonians/natural historians was roundly and frequently condemned by Newtonians is clear from historical evidence (e.g., Jurin's quotation cited in chap. 2, "The Newtonian Period and Its Aftermath").

[15]Yeo (1981) has also noted the programmatic concern for methods that appeared in British works on the general philosophy and aims of science in the first half of the 19th century. One highly influential statement of this concern was Hershel's *Preliminary Discourse on the Study of Natural Philosophy,* which appeared in 1830. In it, Hershel describes scientific method as the bond that united all areas of scientific endeavor. Other scientists in this period began to use the explicitness of methodological descriptions as a major criterion for differentiating sound and unsound scientific research.

Along with other historians, Yeo (1981) also notes the coincidence of widespread agitation for democratic reform in Britain during the first half of the 19th century, and a more general belief that, through the inculcation of correct rules or principles of thought, people from the lower levels of society might be able to better their lot. Proper methods of conduct and inquiry therefore had implications for the democraticization of British society, as well as for the division of the sciences in Britain.

[16]This scenario does not provide a complete explanation. It leaves aside important clause types, such as those featuring the copula, and impersonal/nonanimate subjects with active verbs (Master, 1991).

[17]In fact, the division of empirical natural philosophy into separate sciences starting around the beginning of the 19th century was a much more complicated process than I have described here. In particular, my characterization leaves out important developments taking place in continental Europe, where science and the sciences were more highly organized, and also frequently government-supported. Some—perhaps much—of the impetus for constructing autonomous scientific research specialties therefore came from the Continent.

[18]Stichweh (1992) makes essentially this same point in his discussion of scientific "disciplines"—by which he means entities somewhat different that those I signify by the same term:

> Modern scientific disciplines constitute relatively precariously constructed networks dependent on communications (conceptually) linked to other communications, and on third parties observing this process. In turn, if these third parties want to convey messages, they must be prepared to provide communications that also use such (conceptual) links. As complexes of communications, scientific disciplines are based on events. They change from one moment to the next, from one event to the next, and they also may . . . cease at any moment to exist. This happens not because something said is falsified, but because nobody has felt the need to establish connections to a previous communication. (p. 8)

Stichweh's description seems to hold more perhaps for "scientific specialties" as I conceptualize them than for the relatively more stable scientific disciplines (e.g., physics, chemistry). But it certainly covers a large part of what modern composition scholars and applied linguists refer to by the term "discourse community."

[19]As suggested above, the growth of specialties and disciplines, causing as it did divisions both within the Royal Society and more widely, encountered strong opposition based on the then-current ideology of science. Strenuous efforts were made on a number of fronts—for example, at the annual BAAS meetings—to demonstrate the essential unity of science (Yeo, 1981). On a more personal level, scientific specialists (initially by and large themselves gentlemen) were characterized within genteel scientific circles as narrow-minded or poorly rounded individuals—as often no more than mere technicians. And although the association of negative virtues with specialism in Britain seemed gradually to diminish in relation to the physical sciences, it held on in other areas, such as physiology and medically oriented research, even into the 20th century.

Lawrence (1985) describes antispecialist sentiment among a related group—the late 19th-century medical elite—as based on several convergent lines of thinking:

> First . . . specialism was a form of narrow-mindedness in the doctor himself. Specialism ran counter to culture, it was a sort of cerebral lop-sidedness. Gentlemen did not specialize, for it prevented breadth of vision. The related argument was the appeal to nature: the body did not specialize either. Special diseases were always part of a more general disturbance. The distrust of specialism had, of course, more tangible origins. Many specialists were perceived of as quacks, and therefore competitors. The quack was the very antithesis of the gentleman. (p. 512)

This quotation is particularly telling in the way it associates the gentlemanly epistemological repertoire with "ideological" purposes such as legitimating one form of medical practice over another. Smith and Nicholson (1989) show how a similar ideological nexus in early 20th-century physiology was used to promote conservative upper-class interests in Scotland.

[20]It is widely known that British geology professionalized largely on the initiative of a gentleman geologist, Henry de la Beche. As described by Rudwick (1985), de la Beche was

frantic to find a means of carrying on his geological research after his family lost its large holdings in the West Indies. The geologist therefore developed a scheme to geologically survey the whole of Britain, successfully lobbied the government to support it, and in this way established the first scientific entity to be fully dependent on government funds in Britain, the Geological Survey. Not surprisingly given this history, the conventions of genteel culture were dominant in the Survey (for which see Porter 1977, 1978), wherein many of the leading British geologists received their training through the turn of the century.

[21]It is not hard to find signs of continued adherence to at least weaker versions of basically nonprofessionalized, amateur–genteel science in the Royal Society in the late 19th century. For example, T. H. Huxley—a professional himself—accepted the presidency of the Society in 1883 only reluctantly, partly in order to prevent "the noble old Society [from being] exploited by enterprising commercial gents who make their profit out of the application of science" (Hall, 1984b, p. 158). Geison (1972), Morrell (1990), and especially Berman (1975) persuasively argue on behalf of the continued influence of genteel norms in late 19th-century British science.

[22]Related to debates over Darwin's methods was the role that explicit theorizing should properly take in British science. Amazing as it may seem in relation to current views of science, in which building theories and confirming hypotheses are taken to be integral parts of scientific activity, British empirical science has had a powerful antitheoretical bias throughout much of the last three centuries (see, e.g., Yeo, 1985). Thus, Newton constantly proclaimed that his notions of attraction of objects via long-range forces were nothing more than a necessary consequence of certain generally observable facts, and Priestley (Bazerman 1991, p. 28) believed that theory had, at most, a heuristic function.

[23]Berkenkotter and Huckin (1995, chap. 2) argue that pressure on scientists to deal with the vast amount of published scientific work currently available has caused increased interest in scientific "news"—that is, results and conclusions—leading to the gradual eclipse of methods. Another possible influence is the advent of "methods journals," described in chapter 4, note 23. Such journals might have worked in combination with some of the other forces mentioned here and previously.

Sociologists of scientific knowledge (e.g., Collins, 1985; Knorr-Cetina, 1981; Latour & Woolgar, 1986; cf. also Gilbert & Mulkay, 1984) have thrown real doubt on the possibility of replicating experimental research from the information found in article methods sections, if at all. This of course would suggest that the second alternative posited here—that using methods descriptions for such purposes became unproblematic in the 20th century—is not a possible one.

Work on methods in anthropology suggests yet another possibility, which could work independently or in combination with others among the alternatives mentioned here. According to Myerhoff and Ruby (1982, cited in Watson, 1987):

> The more the ethnographer [reports] on methods, the more he or she must acknowledge that his or her own behavior and presence in the field are data. Statements and methods then begin to appear to be more personal, subjective, biased, involved and culture bound . . . [so] . . . it is not too difficult to see why most anthropologists have been less than candid about their methods. (p. 33)

That is, the less one reports one's methods, the less one leaves oneself open to attacks on that front (see Latour, 1987). This could be especially the case where methods are being called into question for other reasons, in a climate where they no longer function self-evidently to warrant research findings.

CHAPTER

7

Implications and Conclusions

In the much described and frequently mythicized history of the early Royal Society and its *PTRS,* any number of scholars have found the "missing link" or well-preserved residue of a critical moment in Western modernity, if not the whole history of humankind. Let me illustrate with two examples.

In a widely influential article, Olson (1977) describes the process by which language and literacy developed in the West as a technology of abstract thought, moving from highly context-dependent oral forms to highly context-independent written forms. For Olson, this evolutionary process is crucial to a clear understanding of the West's distinctive epistemological traditions, including logic, reason, objectivity, and science.

For Olson, the development by the early Royal Society of a prose tradition which, in Sprat's (1667/1959, p. 113) words, represented "a close, naked, natural way of speaking . . . bringing all things as near the Mathematical plainness as they can" is a watershed moment in the history of the West. It marks the moment when meaning was freed from the bonds of language, society, and intuition, thereby becoming autonomous:

> The process of formulating statements, deriving their implications, testing the truth of those implications, and using the results to revise or generalize from the original statement characterized not only empiricist philosophy but also the development of deductive empirical science. . . . No longer did general premises necessarily rest on the data of common experience, that is on commonsense intuition. . . . It is just this mode of using language—the deduction of counterintuitive models of reality—which distinguishes modern from ancient science. (Olsen, 1977, p. 269)

Olson's account has had enormous influence in the study of language and literacy since its publication—Cazden (1992),[1] Farr (1993), Scollon and Scollon (1995), and Trimbur (1990) are just a few of the better known scholars who appear to have based their accounts of the origins and development of "essayist literacy" substantially on the work of Olson.

In more recent work, the feminist science critic Donna Haraway (1997) also assigns to the early Royal Society and its members broad responsibility for shaping the modern world. Interpreting Shapin and Schaffer (1985), she sees the various technologies of "fact production" described there, and particularly the roles of scientific modesty and witnessing within them, as both determinative and diagnostic of a quintessentially modern worldview:

> In order for the modesty . . . to be visible, the man—the witness whose accounts mirror reality—must be invisible, that is, an inhabitant of the potent "unmarked category," which is constructed by the extraordinary conventions of self-invisibility. . . . . This is the culture within which contingent facts—the real case about the world—can be established with all the authority, but none of the considerable problems, of transcendent truth. This self-invisibility is the specifically modern, European, masculine, scientific form of the virtue of modesty. This is the form of modesty that pays off its practitioners in the coin of epistemological and social power. This kind of modesty is one of the founding virtues of what we call modernity. (pp. 23–24)

Haraway is arguing here that the unique epistemological status of empirical science is based on a kind of sociorhetorical trick: the making invisible of the producers and conditions of production of scientific "facts" by such strategies as genteel modesty, that is, an unwillingness to assert oneself overstrongly, or to insist dogmatically on a narrow version of "truth." This argument fits in with Haraway's larger concern regarding ways in which innovators of the modern scientific worldview chose not simply to ignore women (and other "marked" social groups), but in fact fashioned their distinctive form of life *in opposition to them.*

I mention these two widely differing treatments of the Royal Society and its rhetorical–linguistic traditions for several reasons. My first is to suggest a broader commonality—a certain "master myth" (Gee, 1992)—regarding the foundational influence of the Royal Society on modern, scientific–rational knowledge. To some extent, the appeal to the Royal Society as a prime instigator of modernity recapitulates early rhetorical work done by the Society itself—in the person of Thomas Sprat, commissioned to write the Society's history less than 3 years after its founding. Sprat's description of a distinctive set of language-using practices, though recently problematized by scholars (see chap. 2, note 4), has apparently become embedded in our own master-narrative of modernity.

A second reason for mentioning Olson's and Haraway's accounts is to point to a different part of their somewhat mythic character. As such, they appear to satisfy the need of scholars to discover defining historical moments—compressed bursts of radical, revolutionary change. Appadurai (1996) has noted this phenomenon in the modern social sciences in particular:

> One of the most problematic legacies of grand Western social science . . . is that it has steadily reinforced the sense of some single moment—call it the modern moment—that by its appearance creates a dramatic and unprecedented break between past and present. Reincarnated as the break between tradition and modernity and typologized as the difference between ostensibly traditional and modern societies, this view has been shown repeatedly to distort the meanings of change and the politics of pastness. (pp. 2–3)

By the account given in the present work, the evolution of the Royal Society and its literate practices was characterized most notably by slow and gradual development based on current and past "forms of life," rather than sudden, apocalyptic change. I therefore consider Olson and Haraway's propensity to find radical and far-reaching change at variance with a close account of the literacy history of the Royal Society, and therefore in need of revision and emendation.

But, ultimately and most basically, I mention the work of Olson and Haraway for the acontextuality of their treatments of the Royal Society—or at least their lack of understanding of the context or contexts in which the Society actually developed its literate practices. Without a doubt, the Royal Society and the *PTRS* figure significantly in the historical career of science and scientific knowledge—and to that large degree modernity itself: I have tried to indicate some of these significances in chapters 2 and 6 of the present study, occasionally describing them in terms of forms of life, or Discourses. But these Discourses are the result of several centuries of gradual, incremental, and organic development and change: To attribute a sudden, magical social-transformative quality to the linguistic and rhetorical strategies of the early Society can only be affected, it seems to me, in a situation where these strategies are considered largely if not wholly out of context. If the present study has succeeded in placing these strategies in their sociohistorical context—or larger Discourses—even partially, then it should act as a "passive constraint" (Bazerman, 1988), or at least an antidote, to such broad and abstract views.

The other implications of the present study, at least to my mind, I have already described in the introduction and chapters 1 and 3. Let me conclude by restating them.

First, discourse, including cross-historical scientific discourse, is a complex, reticulated phenomenon (Kaplan, 1987). Complex phenomena are best engaged by approaching them from a number of methodological directions—basically the more the better. The historical study of scientific discourse, and to a lesser degree the study of scientific discourse in general, has depended heavily on a single variety of methodological approach: rhetorical analysis. By bringing a substantially different way of looking at scientific texts to the endeavor, I hope I have contributed nontrivially to it.

Multiple perspectives in themselves, however, may not be enough: They may also benefit substantially from integration. I have therefore tried to show how the two discourse–analytic methods used here can work together, and, especially in conjunction with a third level of discourse analysis that to this point is imperfectly realized—that of sociohistorical forms of life or Discourses—can yield results that are mutually informative and synthetic. I do not want to suggest, however, that multiple viewpoints must always undergo synthesis and (often therefore) reduction. This in itself is a "modern's disease," and one that should be treated accordingly. I hope I have not fallen too much a victim to it here.

Second, studies in the modern history of scientific discourse have focused overwhelmingly on restricted periods of scientific activity, and restricted notions (usually involving scientific experiment) of such activity. This fact, in itself, may well be an effect of the modern desire to find the revolutionary, defining moments and features described by Appadurai, but it is certainly a result of wanting to read history backwards (i.e., retrospectively). I am hopeful that my broad account provides a necessary balance to such readings, but also that it complements studies which, through their narrower foci, provide finer details and descriptions than I have given.

Third and finally, the study of discourse, and I refer here particularly to work done in that part of the field in which I am located—linguistically oriented discourse analysis—is badly in need of historicization, as I indicated in chapter 1. To quote Appadurai (1996) again:

> All major social forces have precursors, precedents, analogs, and sources in the past. It is these deep and multiple genealogies that have frustrated the aspirations of modernizers in very different societies to synchronize their historical watches. (p. 2)

If discourse is truly language-in-the-world—language in all its dizzying array of contexts and uses—then history must be given a much greater role in accounting for, and even subsuming under a larger theory of discourse, the breathtaking variation and situatedness that human language displays.

ENDNOTE

[1]This is true of Cazden (1992) even though the express purpose of her article is to refute Olson's view of the "autonomous text."

Appendix A:
Contents of "Corpus B"

Period I: *Philosophical Transactions*, vol. 10, 1675

A Conjecture concerning the Bladders of Air that are found in Fishes, communicated by A.I.; and illustrated by an Experiment suggested by the Honorable Robert Boyle.

An Extract of a Letter of the Learned Dr. Gothofredus Guil. Leibnitz, concerning the Principle of exactness in the portable Watches of his invention.

Extracts of several Letters sent to the Publisher from Edinburg, by the Learn'd Mr. James Gregory to whom they were written by the intelligent Knight Sir George Mackenzy from Tarbut.

A Letter written to the Publisher by the Learned Mr. Ray, containing some Considerations on the Conjecture in Numb. 114. of these Tracts, about the swimming Bladders in Fishes.

A summary of what hath been hitherto discovered in the matter of the North-East passage; communicated by a good Hand.

A particular account, given by an anonymous French Author in his book of the Origin of Fountains, printed 1674 at Paris; to shew, that the Rain and Snow-waters are sufficient to make Fountains and Rivers run perpetually.

Some Experiments made in the Air pump upon Plants, together with a way of taking exhausted Receivers away from off the said Engin: Tryed by the same Persons mention'd in Numb. 119. viz. Monsieur Hugens and M. Papin.

Mr. Isaac Newton's Consideratons on the former Reply; together with further Directions, how to make the Experiments controverted aright: Written to the Publisher from Cambridge, Novemb. 13. 1675.

An Experimental Discourse of Quicksilver growing hot with Gold; by B.R.

Advertisements, occasioned by the Remarks printed in Numb. 114 upon Frosts in some parts of Scotland, differing in their Anniversary Seasons and Force from our ordinary Frosts in England; Of Black Winds and Tempests; Of the warm or fertilizing Temperature and Steams of the surface of the Earth, Stones. . . By the Reverend and Learned Dr. J. Beal, F.R.S.; who by way of Letter imparted them to the Publisher.

Period 2: *Philosophical Transactions,* vol. 33, 1725

Some Observations made in an Ostrich, dissected by Order of Sir Hans Sloane, Bart. By Mr. John Ranby, Surgeon. F.R.S.

An Essay upon the Natural History of Whales, with a particular Account of the Ambergris found in the Sperma Ceti Whale, In a Letter to the Publisher, from the Honourable Paul Dudley, Esq.; F.R.S.

A Dissertation concerning the Figure of the Earth. Part the Second. By the Reverend J. T. Desaguliers, LL.D., F.R.S.

Observations concerning the Height of the Barometer, at different Elevations above the Surface of the Earth, in a Letter to the Publisher from the Learned Dr. Nettleton.

Remarks upon the Observations made upon a Chronological Index of Sir Isaac Newton, translated into French by the Observator, and publish'd at Paris. By Isaac Newton.

Observations of the Dipping Needle, made at London, in the Beginning of the Year 1723. By Mr George Graham, Watchmaker, F.R.S.

Two Letters on the Effects of Lightning, from the Reverend Mr. Jos. Waffe, Rector of Aynho in Northamptonshire, to Dr. Mead.

A Short Account of the anomalous Epidemic Small-Pox, beginning at Plymouth in August 1724, and continuing to the Month of June 1725. By the Learned and Ingenious Dr. Huxham, Physician at Plymouth.

An Account of the Strata in Coal-Mines, etc. By John Strachey, Esq; F.R.S.

An Account of a Fork put up the Anus, that was afterwards drawn out through the Buttocks; communicated in a Letter to the Publisher, by Mr. Robert Payne, Surgeon at Lowestofft.

Period 3: *Philosophical Transactions,* vol. 65, 1775

An Account of the Gymnotus Electricus, or Electrical Eel. In a Letter from Alexander Garden, M.D. F.R.S. to John Ellis, Esq, F.R.S.

The Supposed Effect of boiling upon Water, in disposing it to freeze more readily, ascertained by Experiments. By Joseph Black, M.D. Professor of Chemistry at Edinburgh, in a Letter to Sir John Pringle, Bart. P.R.S.

An abridged State of the Weather at London in the Year 1774, collected from the meteorological Journal of the Royal Society. By S. Horsley, LL.D., Sec. R.S.

The Process of making Ice in the East Indies. By Sir Robert Barker, F.R.S., in a Letter to Dr. Brocklesby.

Observations on the State of Population in Manchester, and other adjacent Places, concluded. By Thomas Percival, M.D., F.R.S. and S.A. Communicated by the Rev. Dr. Price. F.R.S.

An Account of the Effect of Lightning on a House, which was furnished with a pointed Conductor, at Tenterden, in Kent. In Two Letters from Richard Haffenden, Esquire, the Proprietor of the House, to Mr. Henley. To which are added some Remarks by Mr. Henley.

An Account of Further Discoveries in Air. By the Rev. Joseph Priestley, LL.D., F.R.S. in Letter to Sir John Pringle, Bart. P.R.S. and the Rev. Dr. Price, F.R.S.

Experiments on Animals and Vegetables, with respect to the Power of producing Heat. By John Hunter, F.R.S.

A Proposal for measuring the Attraction of some Hill in this Kingdom by Astronomical Observations. By the Rev. Nevil Maskelyne, B.D. F.R.S. and Astonomer Royal.

Of the House-Swallow, Swift, and Sand-Martin. By the Rev. Gilbert Whilte, in Three Letters to the Hon. Daines Barrington, F.R.S.

Period 4: *Philosophical Transactions,* vol. 115, 1825

Observations on the changes the Ovum of the Frog undergoes during the formation of the Tadpole. By Sir Everard Home, Bart. V.P.R.S.

The description of a floating Collimator. By Captain Henry Kater, F.R.S.

On the Anatomy of the Mole-cricket. By J. Kidd, M.D. and F.R.S. Reg. Prof. of Medicine in the University of Oxford.

Further observations on Planariae. By J. R. Johnson. M.D. F.R.S.

On the temporary magnetic effect induced in iron bodies by rotation. In a Letter to J. F. W. Herschel, Esq. Sec. R.S. by Peter Barlow, Esq. F.R.S. Communicated April 14th, 1825.

Further researches on the preservation of metals by electrochemical means. By Sir Humphry Davy, Bart. Pres. R.S.

Some account of the transit instrument made by Mr. Dollond, and lately put up at the Cambridge Observatory. Communicated April 13, 1825. By Robert Woodhouse, Esq. A.M. F.R.S.

On the fossil Elk of Ireland. By Thomas Weaver, Esq. Member of the Royal Irish Academy, of the Royal Dublin Society, and of the Wernerian and Geological Societies.

On the annual varations of some of the principal fixed Stars. By J. Pond, Esq. F.R.S. Astron. Royal.

On the magnetism developed in copper and other substances during rotation. In a Letter from Samuel Hunter Christie, Esq. M.A. &c. to J. F. W. Herschel, Esq. Sec. R.S. Communicated by J. F. W. Herschel, Esq.

Period 5: *Philosophical Transactions,* vol. 165, 1875

Researches on Explosives—Fired Gunpowder. By Captain Noble (late R.A.), F.R.S., F.R.A.S., F.C.S., &c., and F. A. Abel, F.R.S., President, C.S., &c.

On the Atmospheric Lines of the Solar Spectrum, illustrated by a Map drawn on the same scale as that adopted by Kirchhoff. By J. B. N. Hennessey, F.R.A.S. Communicated by Prof. Stokes, Sec. R.S.

Addition to the Paper on "Volcanic Energy: an attempt to develop its true Origin and Cosmical Relations." By Robert Mallet, A.M., C.D., F.R.S., M.R.I.A.

Description of the Living and Extinct Races of Gigantic Land-Tortoises.—Parts I. & II. Introduction, and the Tortoises of the Galapagos Islands. By Dr. Albert Günther, F.R.S., V.P.Z.S., Keeper of the Zoological Department of the British Museum.

On the Development of the Teeth of the Newt, Frog, Slowworm, and Green Lizard. By Charles S. Tomes, M.A. Communicated by John Tomes, F.R.S.

On Polishing the Specula of Reflecting Telescopes. By W. Lassell, F.R.S., V.P.R.A.S., LL.D.

The Croonian Lecture—Experiments on the Brains of Monkeys (Second Series). By David Ferrier, M.A., M.D., Professor of Forensic Medicine, King's College. Communicated by Dr. Sanderson, V.P.R.S.

On Repulsion resulting from Radiation.—Part II. By William Crookes, F.R.S. &c.

Spectroscopic Observations of the Sun. By J. Norman Lockyer, F.R.S., and G. M. Seabroke, F.R.A.S.

Tables of Temperatures of the Sea at different Depths beneath the Surface, reduced and collated from the various observations made between the years 1749 and 1868, discussed. With Map and Sections. By Joseph Prestwich, M.A., F.R.S., F.G.S.

Period 6

(A) Philosophical Transactions A, vol. 225, 1925

The Lunar Diurnal Magnetic Variation at Greenwich and other Observatories. By S. Chapman, M.A., D.Sc., F.R.S., Chief Professor of Mathematics at the Imperial College of Science.

An Investigation of the Flow of Air Around an Aërofoil of Infinite Span. By I. W. Bryant, B.Sc., A.R.C.Sc., and D. H. Williams, B.Sc., of the Aërodynamics Department, National Physical Laboratory. Communicated by Prof. I. Bairstow, F.R.S.

Gaseous Combustion at Medium Pressures. Part I.—Carbon Monoxide–Air Explosions in a Closed Vessel. Part II.—Methane–Air Explosions in a Closed Vessel. By R. W. Fenning, M.B.E., B.Sc., D.I.C. Communicated by Dr. T. E. Stanton, F.R.S.

(B) Proceedings A, vol. 107, 1925

The Union of Hydrogen and Oxygen in Presence of Silver and Gold. By D. L. Chapman, M.A., F.R.S., Fellow of Jesus College, Oxford; J. E. Ramsbottom, D.Sc., Ph.D., Superintendent Chemical Department, Royal Aircraft establishment, Farnborough; and C. G. Trotman, B.A., Jesus College, Oxford.

The General Law of Electrical Conduction in Dielectrics. By Spencer W. Richardson, M.A., D.Sc., F.Inst.P. Communicated by Sir William Bragg, K.B.E., F.R.S.

(C) Philosophical Transactions B, vol. 214, 1925

On the Segmental Excretory Organs of Certain Fresh-Water Ostracods. By H. Graham Cannon, M.A., D.Sc., F.L.S., Lecturer in Zoology, Imperial College of Science and Technology, London. Communicated by Prof. E. W. MacBride, F.R.S.

Resin Canals in the Canadian Spruce (Picea Canadensis (Mill.) B.S.P.)—An Anatomical Study, especially in Relation to Traumatic Effects and their Bearing on Phylogeny. By Robert Boyd Thomson and Harold Boyd Sifton, University of Toronto. Communicated by D. H. Scott, F.R.S.

The Development of the Calcareous Test of *Echinus miliaris*. By Miss Isabella Gordon, B.Sc. (Kilgour Scholar, Aberdeen University). Communicated by Prof. E. W. MacBride, F.R.S.

(D) **Proceedings *B*, vol. 98, 1925**

The Isolation of a Product of Hydrolysis of the Proteins hitherto undescribed. By S. B. Schryver, D.Sc., Ph.D., Professor of Biochemistry, Imperial College of Science and Technology, H. W. Buston, B.Sc., and D. H. Mukherjee, M.B., B. Sc. Communicated by Prof. V. H. Blackman, F.R.S.

The Nucleolus of Tmesipteris Tannensis, Bernh. By J. S. Yeates, M.Sc., Ph.D., National Research Scholar, Victoria University College, Wellington, N.Z. Communicated by Dr. L. Cockayne, F.R.S.

Period 7

(A) **Philosophical Transactions *A*, vol. 278, 1975**

Seismicity and structure of the Kopet Dagh (Iran, U.S.S.R.). By J. S. Tchalenko.

Field emission and field ionization in liquid ^{4}He. By A. Phillips and P. V. E. McClintock.

An application of normal mode theory to the retrieval of structural parameters and source mechanisms from seismic spectra. By F. Gilbert and A. M. Dziewonski.

(B) **Proceedings *A*, vol. 342, 1975**

Magnetic susceptibility of alkali n-butyrates and isovalerates near their melting points. By J. J. Duruz & A. R. Ubbelohde.

Large amplitude Kelvin–Helmholtz waves on thin liquid sheets. By G. D. Crapper, N. Dombrowski and G. A. D. Pyott.

(C) **Philosophical Transactions *B*, vol. 270, 1975**

A physiological analysis of walking in the American Lobster (Homarus Americanus). By D. L. MacMillan.

Colour receptors, and their synaptic connexions, in the retina of the Cyprinid fish. By J. H. Scholes.

Gating currents in the node of Ranvier: voltage and time dependence. By W. Nonner, E. Rojas and R. Stämpfli.

(D) **Proceedings B, vol. 188, 1975.**

Quantitative studies on marine biodegradation of oil. II. Effect of temperature. By C. F. Gibbs, K. B. Pugh and A. R. Andrews.

Incompatibility and incongruity: two different mechanisms for the non-functioning of intimate partner relationships. By N. G. Hogenboom.

Appendix B:
Ranges of Variation for
Overall MD Analysis

PART I: NUMERICAL RANGES OF VARIATION

Period	Dimension 1	Dimension 2	Dimension 3	Dimension 4	Dimension 5
1675	10.8	4.3	7.5	6.7	6.9
1725	8.6	5.8	11.3	9.7	7.6
1775	11.2	2.6	6.0	5.0	6.6
1825	13.8	3.0	9.9	9.2	4.4
1875	10.5	2.1	6.3	6.6	4.7
1925	11.4	1.9	6.9	2.5	9.6
1975	14.7	1.5	8.0	2.4	5.8

PART 2: VISUALLY DISPLAYED RANGES
OF VARIATION*

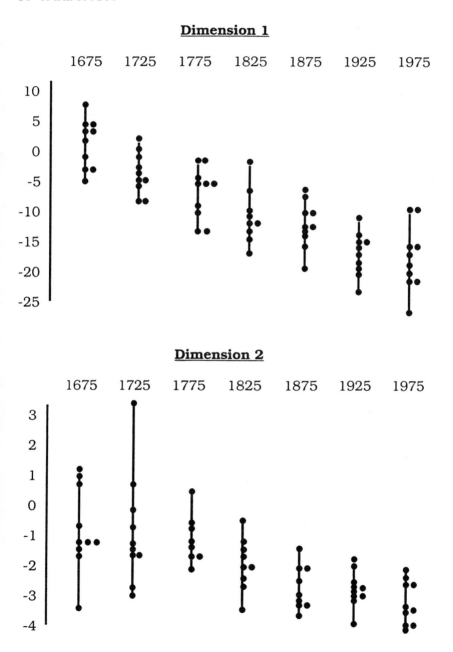

*Points on line or to right of line mark dimension scores for individual texts.

Dimension 3

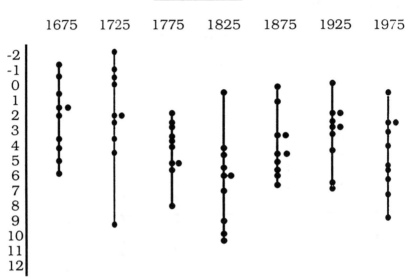

Dimension 4

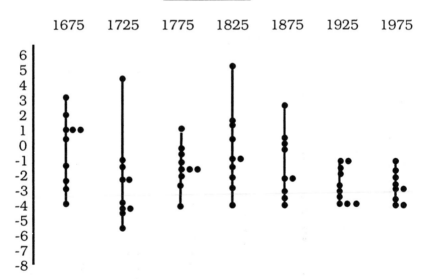

Dimension 5

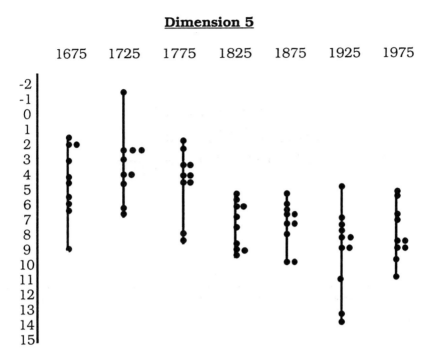

Appendix C:
Standard Deviations for
Overall MD Analysis

Period	Dimension 1	Dimension 2	Dimension 3	Dimension 4	Dimension 5
1675	3.9	1.3	2.5	2.3	2.2
1725	2.9	1.7	3.3	2.8	2.1
1775	4.2	0.8	1.7	1.3	2.2
1825	3.7	0.9	3.0	2.6	1.6
1875	3.2	0.7	2.1	2.2	1.6
1925	3.3	0.5	2.1	0.9	3.0
1975	4.5	0.5	2.4	0.7	1.8

References

Adams, M. J., & Collins, A. (1979). A schema-theoretic view of reading. In R. O. Freedle (Ed.), *New directions in discourse processing* (pp. 1–22). Norwood, NJ: Ablex.

Adams Smith, D. E. (1984). Medical discourse: Aspects of author's comment. *ESP Journal, 3,* 25–36.

Allen, B., Qin, J., & Lancaster, F. W. (1994). Persuasive communities: A longitudinal analysis of references in the *Philosophical Transactions* of the Royal Society, 1665–1990. *Social Studies of Science, 24,* 279–310.

Alter, P. (1986). *The reluctant patron: Science and state in Britain, 1850–1920.* Oxford: Berg.

Anderson, R. (1993). The referees' assessment of Faraday's electromagnetic induction paper of 1831. *Notes and Records of the Royal Society of London, 47,* 243–256.

Andrade, E. N. Da C. (1965). The birth and early days of the Philosophical Transactions. *Notes and Records of the Royal Society of London, 20,* 9–27.

Appadurai, A. (1996). *Modernity at large: Cultural dimensions of globalization.* Minneapolis: University of Minnesota Press.

Ashmore, M., Myers, G., & Potter, J. (1995). Discourse, rhetoric, reflexivity. In S. Jasanoff, G. E. Markle, J. C. Petersen, & T. Pinch (Eds.), *Handbook of science and technology studies* (pp. 321–342). Thousand Oaks, CA: Sage.

Atkinson, D. (1991). Discourse analysis and written discourse conventions. *Annual Review of Applied Linguistics, 11,* 57–76.

Atkinson, D. (1992). The evolution of medical research writing from 1735 to 1985: The case of the *Edinburgh Medical Journal. Applied Linguistics, 13,* 337–374.

Atkinson, D. (1993). *A historical discourse analysis of scientific research writing from 1675 to 1975: The case of the Philosophical Transactions of the Royal Society of London.* Unpublished doctoral dissertation, University of Southern California.

Atkinson, D. (1994, October). *Discourse, society, and history: A call for historically situated discourse analysis.* Paper given at Fall SAMLA/SECOL meeting, Baltimore, MD.

Atkinson, D. (1995, March). *Sociohistorical discourse analysis: A theoretical proposal.* Paper given at the American Association for Applied Linguistics annual meeting. Long Beach, CA.

Atkinson, D. (1996). The Philosophical Transactions of the Royal Society of London, 1675–1975: A sociohistorical discourse analysis. *Language in Society, 25,* 333–371.

Atkinson, D. (in press). Language and science. *Annual Review of Applied Linguistics, 19.*

Atkinson, D., & Biber, D. (1994). Register: A review of empirical research. In D. Biber & E. Finegan (Eds.), *Sociolinguistic perspectives on register* (pp. 351–385). New York: Oxford University Press.

Atkinson, P. (1992). *Understanding ethnographic texts.* Newbury Park, CA: Sage.

Bacon, F. (1620/1900). *Advancement of learning and novum organum.* New York: Collier.

Bakhtin, M. M. (1981). *The dialogic imagination.* Austin, TX: University of Texas Press.

Bakhtin, M. M. (1986). *Speech genres and other late essays.* Austin, TX: University of Texas Press.

Bakhtin, M. M. (1990). From "Marxism and the philosophy of language." In P. Bizzell & B. Herzberg (Eds.), *The Rhetorical tradition: Readings from classical times to the present* (pp. 928–944). Boston: Bedford Books.

Barnes, S. (1937). The editing of early learned journals. *Osiris, 1,* 155–172.

Barthes, R. (1977). The death of the author. In S. Heath (Ed.), *Image music text* (pp. 142–148). Glasgow: Fontana.

Battalio, J. (1996). The interplay between narrative, education, and exposition in an emerging science. *Journal of Technical Writing & Communication, 26,* 177–191.

Battalio, J. (Ed.). (in press). *Essays in the study of scientific discourse: Methods, practice, and pedagogy.* Greenwich, CT: Ablex.

Baugh, A. C., & Cable, T. (1993). *A history of the English language* (4th ed.). Englewood Cliffs, NJ: Prentice-Hall.

Bazerman, C. (1984). Modern evolution of the experimental report in physics: Spectroscopic articles in *Physical Review,* 1893–1980. *Social Studies of Science, 14,* 163–196.

Bazerman, C. (1985). Physicists reading physics. *Written Communication, 2,* 3–23.

Bazerman, C. (1988). *Shaping written knowledge.* Madison, WI: University of Wisconsin Press.

Bazerman, C. (1991). How natural philosophers can cooperate: The literary technology of co-ordinated investigation in Joseph Priestley's *History and present state of electricity* (1767). In C. Bazerman & J. Paradis (Eds.), *Textual dynamics of the professions* (pp. 13–44). Madison: University of Wisconsin Press.

Bazerman, C. (1994). Inclusions, exclusions, and conclusions: Choices on a road to a reading of Priestley's *History and present state of electricity.* In *Constructing experience* (pp. 91–103). Carbondale, IL: Southern Illinois University Press.

Bazerman, C. (in press). *The languages of Edison's light: Rhetorical agency in the material production of technology.* Mahwah, NJ: Lawrence Erlbaum Associates.

Bazerman, C., & Paradis, J. (Eds.). (1991). *Textual dynamics of the professions.* Madison, WI: University of Wisconsin Press.

Ben-David, J. (1960). Scientific productivity and academic organization in nineteenth century medicine. *American Sociological Review, 25,* 828–843.

Bennett, T. (1982). Texts in history. In P. Widdowson (Ed.), *Re-reading English* (pp. 223–236). London: Methuen.

Berkenkotter, C., & Huckin, T. N. (1995). *Genre knowledge in disciplinary communication.* Hillsdale, NJ: Lawrence Erlbaum Associates.

Berman, M. (1975). "Hegemony" and the amateur tradition in British science. *Journal of Social History, 8,* 30–50.

Berman, M. (1978). *Social change and scientific organization: The Royal Institution, 1799–1844.* Ithaca, NY: Cornell University Press.

Besnier, N. (1988). The linguistic relationships of spoken and written Nukulaelae registers. *Language, 64,* 707–736.

Biber, D. (1986). Spoken and written textual dimensions in English: Resolving the contradictory findings. *Language, 62,* 384–414.

Biber, D. (1987). A textual comparison of British and American writing. *American Speech, 62,* 99–119.

Biber, D. (1988). *Variation across speech and writing.* New York: Cambridge University Press.

Biber, D. (1989). A typology of English texts. *Linguistics, 27,* 3–43.

Biber, D. (1991). Oral and literate characteristics of selected primary school reading materials. *Text, 11*, 73–96.

Biber, D. (1992). On the complexity of discourse complexity: A multidimensional analysis. *Discourse Processes, 15*, 133–163.

Biber, D. (1993). Representativeness in corpus design. *Literary and Linguistic Computing, 8*, 1–15.

Biber, D. (1994). An analytical framework for register studies. In D. Biber & E. Finegan (Eds.), *Sociolinguistic perspectives on register* (pp. 31–56). New York: Oxford University Press.

Biber, D. (1995). *Dimensions of register variation: A cross-linguistic comparison.* Cambridge, England: Cambridge University Press.

Biber, D., & Finegan, E. (1988). Adverbial stance types in English. *Discourse Processes, 11*, 1–34.

Biber, D., & Finegan, E. (1989). Drift and the evolution of English style: A history of three genres. *Language, 65*, 487–515.

Biber, D., & Finegan, E. (1992). The linguistic evolution of five written and speech-based English genres from the 17th to the 20th centuries. In M. Rissanen, O. Ihalainen, T. Nevalainen, & I. Taavitsainen (Eds.), *History of Englishes* (pp. 688–704). Amsterdam: deGruyter.

Biber, D., & Finegan, E. (Eds.). (1994a). *Sociolinguistic perspectives on register.* New York: Oxford University Press.

Biber, D., & Finegan, E. (1994b). Intra-textual variation within medical research articles. In N. Oostdijk & P. de Haan (Eds.), *Corpus-based research into language* (pp. 201–222). Amsterdam: Rodopi.

Biber, D., Finegan, E., Atkinson, D., Beck, A., Burges, D., & Burges, J. (1993, May). *A representative corpus of historical English registers (ARCHER): Corpus design and analysis.* Paper presented at the ICAME (International Computerized Archive of Modern English) conference. Zurich, Switzerland.

Biber, D., & Hared, M. (1994). Linguistic correlates of the transition to literacy in Somali: Language adaptation in six press registers. In D. Biber & E. Finegan (Eds.), *Sociolinguistic perspectives on register* (pp. 186–216). New York: Oxford University Press.

Bitzer, L. (1968). The rhetorical situation. *Philosophy and Rhetoric, 1*, 1–15.

Bizzell, P. (1982). Cognition, convention and certainty: What we need to know about writing. *Pre/text, 3*, 211–245.

Bizzell, P. (1992). *Academic discourse and critical consciousness.* Pittsburgh: Pittsburgh University Press.

Bluhm, R. K. (1960). Henry Oldenburg, F.R.S. *Notes and Records of the Royal Society of London, 15*, 183–197.

Bourdieu, P. (1977). *Outline of a theory of practice.* Cambridge, England: Cambridge University Press.

Bowden, D. (1991). *The mythology of voice.* Unpublished doctoral dissertation, University of Southern California.

Brandt, D. (1990). *Literacy as involvement: The acts of writers, readers, and texts.* Carbondale, IL: Southern Illinois University Press.

Braudel, F. (1980). History and the social sciences: The long durée. In *On history.* Chicago: University of Chicago Press.

Broman, T. H. (1991). J. C. Reil and the "journalization" of physiology. In P. Dear (Ed.), *The literary structure of scientific argument* (pp. 13–42). Philadelphia: University of Pennsylvania Press.

Brown, J. S., Collins, A., & Duguid, P. (1989). Situated cognition and the culture of learning. *Educational Researcher, 18*, 32–42.

Brown, R. L., & Herndl, C. G. (1986). An ethnographic study of corporate writing. In B. Couture (Ed.), *Functional approaches to writing: Research perspectives* (pp. 11–28). Norwood, NJ: Ablex.

Brown, P., & Fraser, C. (1979). Speech as a marker of situation. In K. Scherer & H. Giles (Eds.), *Social markers in speech* (pp. 33–62). Cambridge, England: Cambridge University Press.

Butler, C. (1990). Qualifications in science: Modal meanings in scientific texts. In W. Nash (Ed.), *The writing scholar: Studies in academic discourse* (pp. 137–170). Newbury Park, CA: Sage.

Campbell, J. A. (1986). Scientific revolution and the grammar of culture: The case of Darwin's *Origin. Quarterly Journal of Speech, 72,* 351–376.

Campbell, J. A. (1987). Charles Darwin: Rhetorician of science. In J. S. Nelson, A. Megill, & D. N. McCloskey (Eds.), *The rhetoric of the human sciences* (pp. 69–86). Madison, WI: University of Wisconsin Press.

Campbell, J. A. (1990). Scientific discovery and rhetorical invention: Darwin's path to natural selection. In H. W. Simons (Ed.), *The rhetorical turn* (pp. 58–89). Chicago: University of Chicago Press.

Campbell, K. K., & Jamieson, K. H. (1978). Form and genre in rhetorical criticism: An introduction. In K. K. Campbell & K. H. Jamieson (Eds.), *Form and genre: Shaping rhetorical action* (pp. 9–32). Falls Church, VA: Speech Communication Association.

Cantor, G. N. (1983). *Optics after Newton: Theories of light in Britain and Ireland, 1704–1840.* Manchester, UK: Manchester University Press.

Cantor, G. N. (1989). The rhetoric of experiment. In D. Gooding, T. Pinch, & S. Schaffer (Eds.), *The uses of experiment* (pp. 159–180). Cambridge, England: Cambridge University Press.

Carter, H. B. (1988). *Sir Joseph Banks, 1743–1820.* London: British Museum.

Cazden, C. (1992). The myth of the autonomous text. In *Whole language plus: Essays on literacy in the United States and New Zealand* (pp. 139–154). New York: Teachers College Press.

Chafe, W. (1982). Integration and involvement in speaking, writing, and oral literature. In D. Tannen (Ed.), *Spoken and written language: Exploring orality and literacy* (pp. 35–53). Norwood, NJ: Ablex.

Chafe, W. (1985). Linguistic differences produced by differences between speaking and writing. In D. Olson, N. Torrance, & A. Hildyard (Eds.), *Literacy, language and learning* (pp. 105–123). Cambridge, England: Cambridge University Press.

Chaiklin, S., & Lave, J. (Eds.). (1993). *Understanding practice: Perspectives on activity in context.* Cambridge, England: Cambridge University Press.

Charney, D. (1996). Empiricism is not a four-letter word. *College Composition and Communication, 47,* 567–593.

Cherry, R. D. (1988). Ethos versus persona. *Written Communication, 5,* 251–276.

Clanchy, M. T. (1979). *From memory to written record: England, 1066–1307.* Cambridge, MA: Harvard University Press.

Collins, H. M. (1985). *Changing order: Replication and induction in scientific practice.* London: Sage.

Collins, P. (1991). The modals of obligation and necessity in Australian English. In K. Aijmer & B. Altenberg (Eds.), *English corpus linguistics: Studies in honour of Jan Svartvik* (pp. 145–165). London: Longman.

Cooper, M. M. (1989). Why are we talking about discourse communities? In M. M. Cooper & M. Holzman, *Writing as social action* (pp. 202–220). Portsmouth, NH: Heinemann.

Couture, B. (1986). Effective ideation in written text: A functional approach to clarity and exigence. In B. Couture (Ed.), *Functional approaches to writing: Research perspectives* (pp. 69–92). Norwood, NJ: Ablex.

Crawford, E. (1990). The universe of international science, 1880–1939. In T. Frängsmyr (Ed.), *Solomon's house revisited: The organization and institutionalization of science* (pp. 251–269). Canton, MA: Science History Publications.

Crismore, A. (1989). *Talking with readers: Metadiscourse as rhetorical act.* New York: Peter Lang.

Crismore, A., & Farnsworth, R. (1990). Metadiscourse in popular and professional scientific discourse. In W. Nash (Ed.), *The writing scholar: Studies in academic discourse* (pp. 69–92). Newbury Park, CA: Sage.

Crosland, M. P. (1978). Aspects of international scientific collaboration and organization before 1900. In E. G. Forbes (Ed.), *Proceedings of the XVth International Congress of the History of Science* (pp. 114–125). Edinburgh: Edinburgh University Press.

Crosland, M. P. (1982). Explicit qualifications as a criterion for membership of the Royal Society: A historical review. *Notes and Records of the Royal Society of London, 37*, 167–187.

Daston, L. (1991a). Baconian facts, academic civility, and the prehistory of objectivity. *Annals of Scholarship, 8*, 337–364.

Daston, L. (1991b). The ideal and reality of the republic of letters in the Enlightenment. *Science in Context, 4*, 367–386.

Daston, L. (1992). Objectivity and the escape from perspective. *Social Studies of Science, 22*, 597–618.

Daston, L. (1995). The moral economy of science. *Osiris, 10*, 3–24.

Dear, P. (1985). Totius in verba: Rhetoric and authority in the early Royal Society. *Isis, 76*, 144–161.

Dear, P. (Ed.). (1991). *The literary structure of scientific argument: Historical studies.* Philadelphia: University of Pennsylvania Press.

Denzin, N. (1989). *The research act: A theoretical introduction to sociological methods.* Englewood Cliffs, NJ: Prentice-Hall.

Derrida, J. (1977). Signature event context. *Glyph, 1*, 172–197.

DeWalt, B. D., & Pelto, P. J. (1985). Methodology in macro–micro studies. In B. D. DeWalt & P. J. Pelto (Eds.), *Micro and macro levels of analysis in anthropology: Issues in theory and research* (pp. 187–201). Boulder, CO: Westview Press.

Ding, D. (in press). Rationality reborn: Historical roots of the passive voice in scientific discourse. In J. Battalio (Ed.), *Essays in the study of scientific discourse: Methods, practice, and pedagogy.* Greenwich, CT: Ablex.

Dubois, B. L. (1982). The construction of noun phrases in biomedical journal articles. In J. Hoedt (Ed.), *Pragmatics and LSP* (pp. 49–67). Copenhagen: Copenhagen School of Economics.

Dubois, B. L. (1987). "Something on the order of around forty to forty-four": Imprecise numerical expressions in biomedical slide talks. *Language in Society, 16*, 527–541.

Eisner, E. W., & Peshkin, A. (1990). Introduction. In E. W. Eisner & A. Peshkin (Eds.), *Qualitative inquiry in education: The continuing debate* (pp. 1–14). New York: Teachers College Press.

Ervin-Tripp, S. (1972). On sociolinguistic rules: Alternation and co-occurrence. In J. J. Gumperz & D. Hymes (Eds.), *Directions in sociolinguistics* (pp. 213–250). New York: Holt, Rinehart & Winston.

Fahnestock, J. (1986). Accommodating science: The rhetoric life of scientific facts. *Written Communication, 3*, 275–296.

Fahnestock, J., & Secor, M. (1988). The stases in scientific and literary argument. *Written Communication, 5*, 427–443.

Fairclough, N. (1989). *Language as power.* London: Longman.

Fairclough, N. (1992). *Discourse and social change.* Cambridge, England: Polity.

Farr, M. (1993). Essayist literacy and other verbal performances. *Written Communication, 10*, 4–38.

Feldman, T. S. (1990). Late Enlightenment meteorology. In T. Frängsmyr, J. L. Heilbron, & R. E. Rider (Eds.), *The quantifying spirit in the 18th century* (pp. 143–177). Berkeley: University of California Press.

Ferguson, C. (1983). Sports announcer talk: Syntactic aspects of register variation. *Language in Society, 12*, 153–172.

Ferguson, C. (1994). Dialect, register, and genre: Working assumptions about conventionalization. In D. Biber & E. Finegan (Eds.), *Sociolinguistic perspectives on register* (pp. 15–30). New York: Oxford University Press.

Finegan, E., & Atkinson, D. (1993, May). *Issues in sample collection for a historical corpus of English.* Paper presented at ICAME (International Computerized Archive of Modern English) Conference. Zurich, Switzerland.

Fleck, L. (1979). *Genesis and development of a scientific fact.* Chicago: University of Chicago Press.

Fleischmann, S. (1990). *Tense and narrativity: From medieval performance to modern fiction.* Austin: University of Texas Press.

Foucault, M. (1972). The discourse on language. In *The archaeology of knowledge* (pp. 215–237; A. M. Sheridan Smith, Trans.). New York: Pantheon Books.

Foucault, M. (1977). What is an author? In D. Bouchard (Ed.), *Language, counter-memory, practice* (pp. 113–138). Ithaca, NY: Cornell University Press.

Francis, W. N., & Kucera, H. (1979). *Manual of information to accompany a Standard Corpus of Present-Day Edited American English, for use with digital computers.* Providence, RI: Department of Linguistics, Brown University.

Francis, W. N., & Kucera, H. (1982). *Frequency analysis of English usage: Lexicon and grammar.* Boston: Houghton Mifflin.

Freed, R. C., & Broadhead, G. J. (1987). Discourse communities, sacred texts and institutional norms. *College Composition and Communication, 38,* 154–165.

Galindo, R. (1995). Amish newsletters in *The Budget:* A genre study of written communication. *Language in Society, 23,* 77–103.

Galton, F. (1874/1970). *English men of science.* London: Cass.

Garfield, E. (1976). Significant journals of science. *Nature, 264,* 609–615.

Garfield, E. (1977a). Citations-to divided by items-published gives journal impact factor; ISI lists the top 50 high-impact journals of science. In *Essays of an information scientist* (Vol. 1, pp 270–277). Philadelphia: ISI Press.

Garfield, E. (1977b). Journal citations studies X. Geology and geophysics. In *Essays of an information scientist* (Vol. 2, pp. 102–106). Philadelphia: ISI Press.

Garfield, E. (1983). Journal citation studies 38. Earth sciences journals: What they cite and what cites them. In *Essays of an information scientist* (Vol. 5, pp. 791–797). Philadelphia: ISI Press

Gee, J. P. (1990). *Social linguistics and literacies: Ideology in discourses.* London: Falmer Press.

Gee, J. P. (1992). *The social mind.* London: Bergin & Garvey Press.

Geisler, C., Kaufer, D., & Steinberg, E. (1985). The unattended anaphoric "this": When should writers use it? *Written Communication, 2,* 129–155.

Geison, G. L. (1972). Social and institutional factors in the stagnancy of English physiology 1840–1870. *Bulletin of the History of Medicine, 46,* 30–58.

Geison, G. L. (1978). *Michael Foster and the Cambridge school of physiology.* Princeton: Princeton University Press.

George, P. (1952). The scientific movement and the development of chemistry in England, as seen in the papers published in the *Philosophical Transactions* from 1664/5 until 1750. *Annals of Science, 8,* 302–322.

Giddens, A. (1979). *Central problems in social theory: Action, structure, and contradiction in social analysis.* Berkeley: University of California Press.

Giddens, A. (1984). *The Constitution of Society.* Cambridge, England: Polity.

Gilbert, G. N., & Mulkay, M. (1984). *Opening Pandora's box: A sociological analysis of scientific discourse.* Cambridge, England: Cambridge University Press.

Gleason, M. L. (1991). *The Royal Society of London: Years of reform, 1827–1847.* New York: Garland Publishing.

Goffman, E. (1974/1986). *Frame analysis: An essay on the organization of experience.* Boston: Northeastern University Press.

Golinski, J. (1987). Robert Boyle: Scepticism and authority in seventeenth-century chemical discourse. In A. E. Benjamin, G. N. Cantor, & J. R. R. Christie (Eds.), *The figural and the literal: Problems of language in the history of science and philosophy, 1630–1800* (pp. 58–82). Manchester, UK: Manchester University Press.

Golinski, J. V. (1989). A noble spectacle: Phosphorous and the public cultures of science in the early Royal Society. *Isis, 80,* 11–39.

Golinski, J. V. (1990). Language, discourse, and science. In R. C. Olby, G. N. Cantor, J. R. R. Christie, & M. J. S. Hodge (Eds.), *Companion to the history of science* (pp.110–123). London: Routledge.

Golinski, J. V. (1992). *Science as public culture: Chemistry and enlightenment in Britain, 1760–1820.* Cambridge, England: Cambridge University Press.

Goodwin, C. (1994). Professional vision. *American Anthropologist, 96,* 606–633.

Gorsuch, R. L. (1983). *Factor analysis.* Hillsdale, NJ: Lawrence Erlbaum Associates.

Gosden, H. (1993). Discourse functions of subject in scientific research articles. *Applied Linguistics, 14,* 56–75.

Grabe, W., & Kaplan, R. B. (1997). On the writing of science and the science of writing: Hedging in scientific text and elsewhere. In R. Markkanen & H. Schröder (Eds.), *Hedging in discourse* (pp. 151–167). Berlin: deGruyter.

Granville, A. B. (1830/1969). *Science without a head, or the Royal Society dissected.* Farnsborough, UK: Gregg International Publishers.

Gross, A. (1988). On the shoulders of giants: Seventeenth-century optics as an argument field. *Quarterly Journal of Speech, 74,* 1–17.

Gross, A. (1990). *The rhetoric of science.* Cambridge, MA: Harvard University Press.

Gross, A. G., & Keith, W. M. (Eds.). (1997). *Rhetorical hermeneutics: Invention and interpretation in the Age of Science.* Albany, NY: State University of New York Press.

Hacking, I. (1983). *Representing and intervening.* Cambridge, England: Cambridge University Press.

Hall, A. R., & Hall, M. B. (Eds.). (1965–1986). *The correspondence of Henry Oldenburg* (Vols. 1–9). Madison, WI: University of Wisconsin Press. Vols. 10–11. Chicago: Mansell. Vols. 12–13. London: Taylor & Francis.

Hall, M. B. (1965). Oldenburg and the art of scientific communication. *British Journal for the History of Science, 2,* 277–290.

Hall, M. B. (1975). The Royal Society's role in the diffusion of information in the seventeenth century. *Notes and Records of the Royal Society of London, 29,* 173–192.

Hall, M. B. (1984a). *All scientists now: The Royal Society in the nineteenth century.* Cambridge, England: Cambridge University Press.

Hall, M. B. (1984b). The Royal Society in Thomas Henry Huxley's time. *Notes and Records of the Royal Society of London, 38,* 153–158.

Hall, M. B. (1991). *Promoting experimental learning: Experiment and the Royal Society, 1660–1727.* Cambridge, England: Cambridge University Press.

Halliday, M. A. K. (1985). *Introduction to functional grammar.* London: Edward Arnold.

Halliday, M. A. K. (1988). On the language of physical science. In M. Ghadessy (Ed.), *Registers of written English* (pp. 162–178). London: Pinter Publishers.

Halliday, M. A. K., & Martin, J. R. (1993). *Writing science: Literacy and discursive power.* Pittsburgh: University of Pittsburgh Press.

Hannaway, O. (1975). *The chemists and the word: The didactic origins of chemistry.* Baltimore: Johns Hopkins University Press.

Haraway, D. (1997). *Modestwitness@second_millennium.female Man©meets_oncomouse™: Feminism and technoscience.* New York: Routledge.

Harmon, J. E. (1989). The structure of scientific and engineering papers: A historical perspective. *IEEE Transactions on Professional Communication, 32,* 132–138.

Harré, R. (1990). Some narrative conventions of scientific discourse. In C. Nash (Ed.), *Narrative in culture: The uses of storytelling in the sciences, philosophy, and literature* (pp. 81–101). London: Routledge.

Harris, J. (1989). The idea of community in the study of writing. *College Composition and Communication, 40,* 11–22.

Harris, R. A. (1991). Rhetoric of science. *College English, 53,* 282–307.

Harris, R. A. (Ed.). (1997). *Landmark essays on rhetoric of science: Case studies.* Mahwah, NJ: Hermagoras Press.

Harwood, J. T. (1989). Rhetoric and graphics in *Micrographia*. In M. Hunter & S. Schaffer (Eds.), *Robert Hooke: New studies* (pp. 119–147). Woodbridge, UK: Boydell Press.

Heath, S. B. (1983). *Ways with words: Language, life and work in communities and classrooms*. Cambridge, England: Cambridge University Press.

Heilbron, J. L. (1979). *Electricity in the 17th and 18th centuries: A study of early modern physics*. Berkeley: University of California Press.

Heilbron, J. L. (1983). *Physics at the Royal Society during Newton's presidency*. Los Angeles: William Andrews Clark Memorial Library.

Heilbron, J. L. (1993). A mathematicians' mutiny with morals. In P. Horwich (Ed.), *World changes: Thomas Kuhn and the nature of science* (pp. 81–129). Cambridge, MA: MIT Press.

Heyck, T. W. (1982). *The transformation of intellectual life in Victorian England*. New York: St. Martin's Press.

Holland, D., & Quinn, N. (Eds.). (1987). *Cultural models in language and thought*. New York: Cambridge University Press.

Holmes, F. L. (1987). Scientific writing and scientific discovery. *Isis, 78*, 220–235.

Holmes, F. L. (1991), Argument and narrative in scientific writing. In P. Dear (Ed.), *The literary structure of scientific argumentation: Historical studies* (pp. 164–181). Philadelphia: University of Pennsylvania Press.

Horowitz, R. (1987). Rhetorical structure in discourse processing. In R. Horowitz & S. J. Samuels (Eds.), *Comprehending oral and spoken language* (pp. 117–160). San Diego: Academic Press.

Houghton, W. E. (1942). The English virtuoso in the seventeenth century. *Journal of the History of Ideas, 3*, 51–71, 190–219.

Huckin, T., Curtin, E. H., & Graham, D. (1986). Prescriptive linguistics and plain English: The case of "Whiz-deletions." *Visible Language, 20*, 174–187.

Hunston, S. (1993). Evaluation and ideology in scientific writing. In M. Ghadessy (Ed.), *Register analysis: Theory and practice* (pp. 57–73). London: Pinter.

Hunter, M. (1981). *Science and society in Restoration England*. Cambridge, England: Cambridge University Press.

Hunter, M. (1982/1994). *The Royal Society and its fellows 1660–1700*. Chalfont St. Giles, UK: British Society for the History of Science.

Hunter, M. (1989). *Establishing the new science: The experience of the early Royal Society*. Woodbridge, UK: The Boydell Press.

Hunter, M. (1990). First steps in institutionalization: The role of the Royal Society of London. In T. Frängsmyr (Ed.), *Solomon's house revisited: The organization and institutionalization of science* (pp. 13–30). Canton, MA: Science History Publications.

Hunter, M. (1995). *Science and the shape of orthodoxy: Intellectual change in late seventeenth-century Britain*. Woodbridge, UK: The Boydell Press.

Hutchins, E. (1993). Learning to navigate. In S. Chaiklin & J. Lave (Eds.), *Understanding practice* (pp. 35–63). Cambridge, England: Cambridge University Press.

Hutchins, E. (1995). *Cognition in the wild*. Cambridge, MA: Harvard University Press.

Huxley, T. H. (1866/1968). On the advisableness of improving natural knowledge. In *Methods and results: Essays* (pp. 18–41). New York: Greenwood Press.

Hyland, K. (1996). Talking to the academy: Forms of hedging in scientific research articles. *Written Communication, 13*, 251–281.

Hymes, D. H. (1972). On communicative competence. In J. B. Pride & J. Holmes (Eds.), *Sociolinguistics: Selected readings* (pp. 269–293). Harmondsworth, UK: Penguin.

Hymes, D. (1996). *Ethnography, linguistics, narrative, inequality: Toward an understanding of voice*. London: Taylor & Francis.

Iliffe, R. (1992). "In the warehouse": Privacy, property and priority in the early Royal Society. *History of Science, 30*, 29–68.

Jamieson, K. H. (1974). Generic constraints and the rhetorical situation. *Philosophy and Rhetoric, 7*, 162–170.

Jarratt, S. (1994, February 18). *Sappho and Socrates: Rhetoric and pedagogy.* Plenary address delivered at Feminism and Composition/RLL Conference, Los Angeles, CA.

Jenkins, S., & Hinds, J. (1987). Business letter writing: English, French, Japanese. *TESOL Quarterly, 21,* 327–349.

Johansson, S., Leech, G. N., & Goodluck, H. (1978). *Manual of information to accompany the Lancaster–Oslo–Bergen Corpus of British English, for use with digital computers.* Oslo: Department of English, University of Oslo.

Johns, A. (1991). History, science, and the history of the book: The making of natural philosophy in early modern England. *Publishing History, 30,* 5–30.

Johns, A. (in press). Miscellaneous methods: Authors, societies and journals in Early Modern England. *British Journal for the History of Science, 31.*

Kamberelis, G. (1995). Genre as institutionally informed social practice. *Journal of Contemporary Legal Issues, 6,* 115–171.

Kaplan, R. B. (1987). Cultural thought patterns revisited. In U. Connor & R. B. Kaplan (Eds.), *Writing across languages: Analysis of L2 text* (pp. 9–21). Reading, MA: Addison-Wesley Publishing Co.

Kaplan, R. B., & Grabe, W. (1991). The fiction in science writing. In H. Schröder (Ed.), *Subject-oriented texts: Languages for Special Purposes and text theory* (pp. 199–217). Berlin: deGruyter.

Katzen, M. F. (1980). The changing appearance of research journals in science and technology: An analysis and case study. In A. J. Meadows (Ed.), *Development of Science Publishing in Europe* (pp. 177–214). Amsterdam: Elsevier.

Killingsworth, M. J. (1992). Discourse communities: Local and global. *Rhetoric Review, 11,* 110–122.

Killingsworth, M. J., & Gilbertson, M. K. (1992). *Signs, genres, & communities in technical communication.* Amityville, NY: Baywood Publishing Co.

Kim, Y.-J., & Biber, D. (1994). A corpus-based analysis of register variation in Korean. In D. Biber & E. Finegan (Eds.), *Sociolinguistic perspectives on register* (pp. 155–185). New York: Oxford University Press.

Kirsch, G. (1992). Methodological pluralism: Epistemological issues. In G. Kirsch & P. A. Sullivan (Eds.), *Methods and methodology in composition research* (pp. 247–269). Carbondale, IL: Southern Illinois University Press.

Klein, L. D. (1986). Berkeley, Shaftesbury, and the meaning of politeness. In O. M. Brack, Jr. (Ed.), *Studies in eighteenth-century culture* (pp. 57–68). Madison, WI: University of Wisconsin Press.

Klein, L. D. (1994). "Politeness" as linguistic ideology in late seventeenth- and eighteenth-century England. In D. Stein & I. Tieken-Boon van Ostade (Eds.), *Towards a standard English, 1600–1800* (pp. 31–50). Berlin: deGruyter.

Knorr-Cetina K. D. (1981). *The manufacture of knowledge: An essay on the constructivist and contextual nature of science.* Oxford: Pergamon.

Kress, G. (1989). *Linguistic processes in sociocultural practice* (2nd ed.). London: Oxford University Press.

Kress, G. (1991). Critical discourse analysis. *Annual Review of Applied Linguistics, 11,* 84–99.

Krige, J. (1990). Scientists as policymakers: British physicists' "advice" to their government on membership of Cern (1951–1952). In T. Frängsmyr (Ed.), *Solomon's house revisited: The organization and institutionalization of science* (pp. 270–291). Canton, MA: Science History Publications.

Kronick, D. A. (1976). *A history of scientific & technical periodicals* (2nd ed.). Metuchen, NJ: Scarecrow Press.

Kronick, D. A. (1978). Authorship and authority in the scientific periodicals of the seventeenth and eighteenth centuries. *Library Quarterly, 48,* 255–275.

Kronick, D. A. (1988). Anonymity and identity: Editorial policy in the early scientific journal. *Library Quarterly, 58,* 221–237.

Kuhn, T. S. (1970). *The structure of scientific revolutions* (2nd ed.). Chicago: University of Chicago Press.

Labov, W. (1971). Methodology. In W. O. Dingwall (Ed.), *A survey of linguistic science* (pp. 413–491). College Park, MD: Linguistics Program, University of Maryland.

Labov, W. (1972). *Language in the inner city.* Philadelphia: University of Pennsylvania Press.

Latour, B. (1987). *Science in action.* Cambridge, MA: Harvard University Press.

Latour, B., & Woolgar, S. (1986). *Laboratory life: The construction of scientific facts.* Princeton, NJ: Princeton University Press.

Lauer, J. (1984). Composition studies: Dappled discipline. *Rhetoric Review, 3,* 20–29.

Lauer, J., & Asher, J. W. (1988). *Composition research: Empirical designs.* New York: Oxford University Press.

Lave, J., & Wenger, E. (1991). *Situated learning: Legitimate peripheral participation.* Cambridge, England: Cambridge University Press.

Lawrence, C. (1985). Incommunicable knowledge: Science, technology and the clinical art in Britain 1850–1914. *Journal of Contemporary History, 20,* 503–520.

Lazaraton, A. (1995). Qualitative research in applied linguistics: A progress report. *TESOL Quarterly, 29,* 455–472.

Lewis, D. (1969). *Convention: A philosophical study.* Cambridge, MA: Harvard University Press.

Locke, D. (1992). *Science as writing.* New Haven, CT: Yale University Press.

Lund, R. D. (1985). "More strange than true": Sir Hans Sloane, King's Transactioneer, and the deformation of English prose. In O. M. Brack, Jr. (Ed.), *Studies in eighteenth-century culture,* vol. 14 (pp. 213–230). Madison, WI: University of Wisconsin Press.

Lyne, J., & Howe, H. F. (1986). "Punctuated equilibria": Rhetorical dynamics of a scientific controversy. *Quarterly Journal of Speech, 72,* 132–147.

Lyons, H. (1944). *The Royal Society 1660–1940: A history of its administration under its charters.* Cambridge, England: Cambridge University Press.

MacDonald, S. P. (1994). *Professional academic writing in the humanities and social sciences.* Carbondale, IL: Southern Illinois University Press.

Mackay, D. (1985). *In the wake of Cook: Exploration, science & empire, 1780–1801.* New York: St. Martin's Press.

MacLeod, R. M. (1971). The Royal Society and the Government Grant: Notes on the administration of scientific research, 1849–1914. *Historical Journal, 14,* 323–358.

MacLeod, R. M. (1983). Whigs and savants: Reflections on the reform movement in the Royal Society, 1830–48. In I. Inkster & J. B. Morrell (Eds.), *Metropolis and province: Science in British culture, 1780–1850* (pp. 55–90). London: Hutchinson.

Martin, J. R. (1985). Process and text: Two aspects of human semiosis. In J. D. Benson & W. S. Greaves (Eds.), *Systemic perspectives on discourse,* vol. 1 (pp. 47–74). Norwood, NJ: Ablex.

Martin, J. R. (Ed.). (in press). *Reading science.* London: Routledge.

Master, P. (1991). Active verbs with inanimate subjects in scientific prose. *English for Specific Purposes, 10,* 15–33.

McClellan, J. E. (1985). *Science reorganized: Scientific societies in the eighteenth century.* New York: Columbia University Press.

McIntosh, C. (1986). *Common and courtly language: The stylistics of social class in 18th-century English literature.* Philadelphia: University of Pennsylvania Press.

McKie, D. (1948). The scientific periodical from 1665 to 1798. *Philosophical Magazine, 39,* Commemorative No., 122–132.

Meadows, A. J. (1974). *Communication in science.* London: Butterworths.

Medawar, P. (1964, August 1). Is the scientific paper fraudulent? *Saturday Review,* 42–43.

Meyer, B. J. F. (1985). Prose analysis: Purposes, procedures, and problems. In B. K. Britton & J. B. Black (Eds.), *Understanding expository text: A theoretical and practical handbook for analyzing explanatory text* (pp. 11–64). Hillsdale, NJ: Lawrence Erlbaum Associates.

Miller, C. R. (1984). Genre as social action. *Quarterly Journal of Speech, 70,* 151–167.

Miller, C. R. (1993). Rhetoric and community: The problem of the one and the many. In T. Enos & S. C. Brown (Eds.), *Defining the new rhetorics* (pp. 78–94). Newbury Park, CA: Sage.

Miller, D. P. (1983). Between hostile camps: Sir Humphry Davy's presidency of the Royal Society of London. *British Journal for the History of Science, 16*, 1–47.

Miller, D. P. (1986). The revival of the physical sciences in Britain, 1815–1840. *Osiris,* 2nd series, *2*, 107–134.

Miller, D. P. (1989). "Into the valley of darkness": Reflections on the Royal Society in the eighteenth century. *History of Science, 27*, 155–166.

Mishler, E. G. (1990). Validation in inquiry-guided research: The role of exemplars in narrative studies. *Harvard Educational Review, 60*, 415–442.

Montgomery, S. L. (1996). *The scientific voice.* New York: Guilford.

Moore, K. (1995). *A guide to the archives and manuscripts of the Royal Society.* London: The Royal Society.

Morrell, J., & Thackray, A. (1981). *Gentlemen of science: Early years of the British Association for the Advancement of Science.* Oxford, England: Clarendon.

Morrell, J. B. (1990). Professionalisation. In R. C. Olby, G. N. Cantor, J. R. R. Christie, & M. J. S. Hodge (Eds.), *Companion to the history of modern science* (pp. 980–989). London: Routledge.

Moseley, R. (1978). The origins and early years of the National Physical Laboratory: A chapter in the pre-history of British science policy. *Minerva, 16*, 222–250.

Moseley, R. (1980). Government science and the Royal Society: The control of the National Physical Laboratory in the inter-war years. *Notes and Records of the Royal Society of London, 35*, 167–193.

Myers, G. (1985). Texts as knowledge claims: The social construction of two biology articles. *Social Studies of Science, 15*, 593–630.

Myers, G. (1989). The pragmatics of politeness in scientific articles. *Applied Linguistics, 10*, 1–35.

Myers, G. (1990). *Writing biology: Texts in the social construction of scientific knowledge.* Madison, WI: University of Wisconsin Press.

Myers, G. (1992). "In this paper we report . . .": Speech acts and scientific facts. *Journal of Pragmatics, 16*, 295–313.

Myers, G. (1996). Out of the laboratory and down to the bay: Writing in science and technology studies. *Written Communication, 13*, 5–43.

Nunan, D. (1992). *Research methods in language learning.* Cambridge, England: Cambridge University Press.

Nye, M. J. (1989). On gentlemen, science, and the state. In T. Frägsmyr (Ed.), *Solomon's house revisited: The organization and institutionalization of science* (pp. 322–330). Canton, MA: Science History Publications.

Ochs, E. (1979). Planned and unplanned discourse. In T. Givon (Ed.), *Discourse and syntax* (pp. 51–80). New York: Academic Press.

Ochs, E. (1990). Indexicality and socialization. In G. Herdt, R. Shweder, & J. W. Stiegler (Eds.), *Cultural psychology* (pp. 287–308). Chicago: University of Chicago Press.

Ochs, E. (1992.) Indexing gender. In A. Duranti & C. Goodwin (Eds.), *Rethinking context: Language as an interactive phenomenon* (pp. 335–358). Cambridge, England: Cambridge University Press.

Ochs, E. (1996). Linguistic resources for socializing humanity. In J. J. Gumperz & S. C. Levinson (Eds.), *Rethinking linguistic relativity* (pp. 407–437). Cambridge, England: Cambridge University Press.

Ochs, E., Gonzales, P., & Jacoby, S. (1996). "When I come down I'm in the domain state": Grammar and graphic representation in the interpretative activity of physicists. In E. Ochs, E. A. Schegloff, & S. A. Thompson (Eds.), *Interaction and grammar* (pp. 328–369). Cambridge, England: Cambridge University Press.

Olson, D. R. (1977). From utterance to text: The bias of language in speech and writing. *Harvard Educational Review, 47*, 257–281.

Ong, W. J. (1982). *Orality and literacy: The technologizing of the word.* London: Routledge.

Paradis, J. (1987). Montaigne, Boyle, and the essay of experience. In G. Levine (Ed.), *One culture: Essays in science and literature* (pp. 51–91). Madison, WI: University of Wisconsin Press.

Paul, D., & Charney, D. (1995). Introducing chaos into science and engineering: Effects of rhetorical strategies on scientific readers. *Written Communication, 12,* 396–438.

Pennycook, A. (1994). Incommensurable discourses. *Applied Linguistics, 15,* 115–138.

Pennycook, A. (1996). Borrowing others' words: Text, ownership, memory, and plagiarism. *TESOL Quarterly, 30,* 201–230.

Perkin, H. (1969). *The origins of modern English society 1780–1880.* London: Routledge & Kegan Paul.

Phelps, L. W. (1985). Dialectics of coherence: Toward an integrative theory. *College English, 47,* 13–29.

Phelps, L. W. (1988). *Composition as a human science.* New York: Oxford University Press.

Phillipson, R. (1992). *Linguistic imperialism.* Oxford: Oxford University Press.

Porter, J. E. (1986). Intertextuality and the discourse community. *Rhetoric Review, 5,* 34–47.

Porter, R. (1977). *The making of geology: Earth science in Britain 1660–1815.* Cambridge, England: Cambridge University Press.

Porter, R. (1978). Gentlemen and geology: The emergence of a scientific career 1660–1920. *Historical Journal, 21,* 809–836.

Porter, T. (1992). Objectivity as standardization: The rhetoric of impersonality in measurement, statistics, and cost-benefit analysis. *Annals of Scholarship, 1992,* 19–60.

Porter, T. M. (1995). *Trust in numbers: The pursuit of objectivity in science and public life.* Princeton: Princeton University Press.

Potter, G. R. (1943). The significance to the history of English natural science of John Hill's "Review of the works of the Royal Society." *University of California Publications in English, 14,* 157–180.

Prelli, L. J. (1989). *A rhetoric of science: Inventing scientific discourse.* Columbia, SC: University of South Carolina Press.

Price, D. J. De S. (1986). *Little science, big science . . . and beyond.* New York: Columbia University Press.

Pumfrey, S. (1995). Who did the work? Experimental philosophers and public demonstrators in Augustan England. *British Journal for the History of Science, 28,* 131–156.

Purver, M. (1967). *The Royal Society: Concept and creation.* London: Routledge.

Quirk, R., Greenbaum, S., Leech, G., & Svartik, J. (1985). *A comprehensive grammar of the English language.* London: Longman.

Rafoth, B. (1988). Discourse community: Where writers, readers and texts come together. In B. Rafoth & D. Rubin (Eds.), *The social construction of written communication* (pp. 131–146). Norwood, NJ: Ablex.

Rafoth, B. (1990). The concept of discourse community: Descriptive and explanatory adequacy. In G. Kirsh & D. Roen (Eds.), *A sense of audience in written communication* (pp. 140–152). Newbury Park, CA: Sage.

Rodman, L. (1994). The active voice in scientific articles: Frequency and discourse functions. *Journal of Technical Writing and Communication, 24,* 309–331.

Rogoff, B. (1990). *Apprenticeship in thinking: Cognitive development in social context.* New York: Oxford University Press.

Rowlinson, J. S., & Robinson, N. H. (1992). *The record of the Royal Society of London: Supplement to the fourth edition for the years 1940–1989.* London: The Royal Society.

Royal Society. (1940). *Record of the Royal Society of London.* (4th ed.). London: The Royal Society.

Royal Society. (1995). *Women, science and the Royal Society.* Catalog of an exhibition to commemorate the 50th anniversary of the election of the first women to Fellowship of the Royal Society.

Royal Society. (n.d.). *Review of the year: September 1995 to August 1996*. London: The Royal Society.

Rudwick, M. J. S. (1963). The foundation of the Geological Society of London. *British Journal of the History of Science, 1*, 325–355.

Rudwick, M. J. S. (1985). *The great Devonian controversy*. Chicago: University of Chicago Press.

Rymer, J. (1988). Scientific composing processes: How eminent scientists write. In D. A. Jolliffe (Ed.), *Advances in writing research*, vol. 2 (pp. 211–250). Norwood, NJ: Ablex.

Salager, F. (1984). Compound nominal phrases in scientific–technical literature: Proportion and rationale. In A. K. Pugh & J. M. Ulijn (Eds.), *Reading for professional purposes* (pp. 136–145). London: Heinemann.

Sarewitz, D. (1997). Social change and science policy. *Issues in Science and Technology, 13*, 29–32.

Sclove, R. L. (1995). *Democracy and technology*. New York: Guilford.

Scollon, R., & Scollon, S. L. (1981). *Narrative, literacy, and face in interethnic communication*. Norwood, NJ: Ablex.

Scollon, R., & Scollon, S. W. (1995). *Intercultural communication*. Oxford, England: Blackwell.

Shapin, S. (1984). Pump and circumstance: Robert Boyle's literary technology. *Social Studies of Science, 14*, 481–520.

Shapin, S. (1987). O Henry. (Essay review of *The Correspondence of Henry Oldenburg*). *Isis, 78*, 417–424.

Shapin, S. (1988). The house of experiment in seventeenth-century England. *Isis, 79*, 373–404.

Shapin, S. (1989). Who was Robert Hooke? In M. Hunter & S. Schaffer (Eds.), *Robert Hooke: New studies* (pp. 253–285). Woodbridge, Suffolk: Boydell Press.

Shapin, S. (1991). "A scholar and a gentleman": The problematic identity of the scientific practitioner in early modern England. *History of Science, 29*, 279–327.

Shapin, S. (1994). *A social history of truth: Civility and science in seventeenth-centry England*. Chicago: University of Chicago Press.

Shapin, S., & Schaffer, S. (1985). *Leviathan and the air-pump: Hobbes, Boyle and the experimental life*. Princeton, NJ: Princeton University Press.

Shapiro, B. (1983). *Probability and certainty in seventeenth-century England*. Princeton, NJ: Princeton University Press.

Smith, D., & Nicholson, M. (1989). The 'Glasgow School' of Paton, Findlay and Cathcart: Conservative thought in chemical physiology, nutrition and public health. *Social Studies of Science, 19*, 195–238.

Sorrenson, R. (1996). Towards a history of the Royal Society in the eighteenth century. *Notes and Records of the Royal Society of London, 50*, 29–46.

Sprat, T. (1667/1959). *The history of the Royal Society of London, for the improving of natural knowledge*. London: Routledge & Kegan Paul.

Stichweh, R. (1992). The sociology of scientific disciplines: On the genesis and stability of the disciplinary structure of modern science. *Science in Context, 5*, 3–15.

Stimson, D. (1968). *Scientists and amateurs: A history of the Royal Society*. New York: Greenwood.

Street, B. V. (1984). *Literacy in theory and practice*. Cambridge, England: Cambridge University Press.

Stubbs, M. (1996). *Text and corpus analysis*. Oxford, England: Blackwell.

Svartvik, J., & Quirk, R. (Eds.). (1980). *A corpus of English conversation*. Lund: CWK Gleerup.

Swales, J. (1981). *Aspects of article introductions*. Birmingham, UK: The University of Aston, Language Studies Unit.

Swales, J. M. (1990). *Genre analysis: English in academic and research settings*. Cambridge, England: Cambridge University Press.

Swales, J. M. (1993). Genre and engagement. *Revue Belge de Philosophie et d'Histoire, 71*, 687–698.

Swijtink, Z. (1987). The objectification of observation: Measurement and statistical methods in the 19th century. In L. Krüger, L. Daston, & M. Heidelberger (Eds.), *The probabalistic revolution*, Vol. 1 (pp. 261–285). Cambridge, MA: MIT Press.

Tannen, D. (1987). Repetition in conversation as spontaneous formulaicity. *Text, 7*, 215–243.

Tannen, D. (1990). Discourse analysis: The excitement of diversity. *Text, 10*, 109–111.

Tarone, E., Dwyer, S., Gillette, S., & Icke, V. (1981). On the use of the passive in two astrophysics journal papers. *ESP Journal, 1*, 123–140.

Taylor, C. A. (1996). *Defining science: A rhetoric of demarcation.* Madison, WI: University of Wisconsin Press.

Thompson, D. K. (1993). Arguing for experimental "facts" in science: A study of research article results sections in biochemistry. *Written Communication, 10*, 106–128.

Thompson, S. (1987). The passive in English: A discourse perspective. In R. Channon & L. Shockey (Eds.), *In honor of Ilse Lehiste* (pp. 497–511). Dordrecht, Holland: Foris Publications.

Thomson, T. (1812). *History of the Royal Society from its institution to the end of the eighteenth century.* London: The Royal Society.

Thornton, J. L., & Tully, R. I. J. (1971). *Scientific books, libraries and collectors.* London: Library Association.

Trimbur, J. (1990). Essayist literacy and the rhetoric of deproduction. *Rhetoric Review, 9*, 72–86.

Valle, E. (1993). *The talkative community: Rhetorical, textual and pragmatic features in Royal Society texts, 1711–1870.* Licentiate thesis, University of Turku, Turku, Finland.

Valle, E. (1997). A scientific community and its texts: A historical discourse study. In B.-L. Gunnarsson, P. Linell, & B. Nordberg (Eds.), *The construction of professional discourse* (pp. 76–98). London: Longman.

van Naerssen, M., & Kaplan, R. B. (1987). Language and science. *Annual Review of Applied Linguistics, 7*, 86–104.

Vande Kopple, W. J. (1994). Some characteristics and functions of grammatical subjects in scientific discourse. *Written Communication, 11*, 534–564.

Vickers, B. (1985). The Royal Society and English prose style: A reassessment. In B. Vickers & N. S. Struever. *Rhetoric and the pursuit of truth: Language change in the seventeenth and eighteenth centuries* (pp. 1–76). Los Angeles: William Andrews Clark Memorial Library.

Vickers, B. (Ed.). (1987). *English science, Bacon to Newton.* Cambridge, England: Cambridge University Press.

Walker, R. D., & Hurt, C. D. (1990). *Scientific and technical literature.* Chicago: American Library Association.

Watson, G. (1987). Make me reflexive—but not yet: Strategies for managing essential reflexivity in ethnographic discourse. *Journal of Anthropological Research, 43*, 29–41.

Weiner, E. J., & Labov, W. (1983). Constraints on the agentless passive. *Journal of Linguistics, 19*, 29–58.

Weld, C. R. (1848). *A history of the Royal Society, with memoirs of the presidents,* 2 vols. London: John W. Parker.

Welkowitz, J., Ewen, R. B., & Cohen, J. (1982). *Introductory statistics for the behavioral sciences* (3rd ed.). New York: Academic Press.

Wells, R. (1960). Nominal and verbal style. In T. Sebeok (Ed.), *Style in language* (pp. 213–220). Cambridge, MA: MIT Press.

Winterowd, W. R. (1989). *The culture and politics of literacy.* New York: Oxford University Press.

Wood, P. B. (1980). Methodology and apologetics: Thomas Sprat's *History of the Royal Society. British Journal for the History of Science, 13*, 1–26.

Yates, J., & Orlikowski, W. J. (1992). Genres of organizational communication: A structurational approach to studying communication and media. *Academy of Management Review, 17*, 299–326.

Yeo, R. (1981). Scientific method and the image of science 1831–1891. In R. MacLeod & P. Collins (Eds.), *The Parliament of science* (pp. 65–88). Northwood, IL: Science Reviews.

Yeo, R. (1985). An idol of the market-place: Baconianism in nineteenth century Britain. *History of Science, 23*, 251–298.

Zuckerman, H., & Merton, R. (1971). Patterns of evaluation in science: Institutionalization, structure and functions of the referee system. *Minerva, 9*, 66–100.

Author Index

197

Subject Index